DOWN TO EARTH

Brian Lavery

This work includes some character names that have become part of Australia's history. Tumultuous festivals did erupt in the places described. This world did need a re-make.

However, this book is a work of fiction. It is a product of the author's imagination. Similarities to real people, places, or events are entirely coincidental.

DOWN TO EARTH

ISBN: 978-06488466-6-6

Published by Brian Lavery

Queensland Australia

downtoearth-thebook@blavery.com

2 3 4 5 6 7 8

Spoiler

It's not really a history book.

It's an earthly love story.
One that starts on another planet,
and arrives here thinking to fix this one.

Chapters

Revolution

I walked up the steps of the ageing Parliament House, brilliant white in the Canberra winter sunshine. Parapets, bays and balconies, neoclassical, clean. But this grand seat of Government was listed for replacement.

Only Leon was here yet, wearing his farm boots and beret.

We waited. Today was quiet, as Parliament wasn't sitting. There were guards, but guards in 1976 just looked. In the large lobby hung framed portraits of every Australian Prime Minister since Federation.

The others straggled in, including three from Leon's commune. Plenty of jeans and colours, but not a tie among us.

Cairns's parliamentary assistant, Junie Morosi, arrived to gather us and then lead us through the maze to Caucus Room 2.

And so twelve people seated themselves at a formal meeting table covered with dead microphones and live jugs of water. MP Jim Cairns with cool passion laid out his subversive dream of a people's revolution.

— Intermission —

*Do you remember that Member of
Parliament who led the Moratorium marches
against war? Who gave the hungry press a
feast of scandals, and helped bring down the
Government? Remember those naked
festivals with all the Minister's hippie mates?*

*Well, this old hippie was there, and those
mates were his mates, all living their stories.
But it was so long ago—the version here
probably isn't what happened. He insists it is.*

Brian – Melbourne

1970

The stack of this week's Melbourne University rag *Farrago* sat untidily high at the entrance to the Student Union. I picked out a copy and headed down to the Cafeteria instead. No-one I knew was around this evening. Settling to a spaghetti bolognese, the default cheap meal, I ate, waited and idly read, all three together.

"*Why You Must Act*". More undergraduate posture-play politics? What was it this time? No, this headline was Jim Cairns, no less. "*The Morals of the Moratorium*". Campus life was a time to expand who I was, to explore new fields.

I was learning to look at strangers who might smile or talk. After I came home a few years ago, that terrified me, and it had to change. Several years older—and always trying to catch up.

My younger sister was already on campus, so I was effortlessly slotted into a pre-made social scene. It worked.

After last night with Rose, my body still buzzed. Rose, my skinny-limbed anxious friend, with the long reddish dark hair and the green eyes. It was Catholic girl Rose who had broken me in, tightened the bridle on this jerking and terrified brumby until I learned to hear the whispers, accept the handling, and agree to an unexpected new rapport.

Same woman claimed she never farts. Makes no sense, I told her.

I had finished the bowlful when Rose arrived. "Hi, sweetie. All done?"

"Oh, Brian, I'm so tired. Yes, I'm done for today. That was Biology Prac, and it's always heavy going."

That's two of us. "Go get something to eat, and I'll drive you home. Tonight is spag bol special night."

Pasta bolognese! It reminded me of the monastery meals in Lent. No, that couldn't be right; we ate no meat at all in Lent. Hmm, a cosy past life, but a life of negatives, impaired vision. Non-negotiables that make the puzzle unsolvable. I had needed so hard to belong there.

I was desperate now to explore, prise life open. To relearn the social arts. Test beliefs. Defy the superego. Question. The book of life was getting a rewrite, because the first edition was full of untruths.

"You're done too?" Rose was trying to ask, looking at me, puzzled.

"Oh, yes, I punched up the last of those Fortran cards for this week."

Rose went, and returned with her spaghetti bowl, and with two skinny fingers through two cups of tea.

"Now, what's the tired bit?" I asked. "You're not sleeping again?"

"I'm not. I'm so uncomfortable at home I go most of the night all uptight, and not sleeping, and then the tiredness makes me so anxious and irritable. I don't know what to do."

"Your Mum?"

"Of course it's my bloody mother. I fight with her all the time. But it's not a clean finished argument, ever. It's just sniping and criticising. I can't do anything right. I'm dragging them down into disgrace, she says."

"You mean I am?"

"I'm big enough to make my own decisions, but Mum will never think that. She and Father have a whole pattern ahead they need me to stick to. I failed some of last year, and they think it's your fault because you take up my time. They wanted me to study medicine. I'll never do medicine, I'm not that bright. I know that, so I am doing what I chose for myself. They feel humiliated."

Rose and I had considered marrying. It would be satisfying to have someone to go home with every night. Parent issues would be solved in one go, both sides. Money and study would be easier. But we were not talking about that anymore. She was younger, and it was all too hard. Hard? Different hards. She would spill her conflicted thoughts. I would say little, and she saw it as some serenity and strength.

Gerri breezed into the Caf, and we dropped our discussion. Some issues were mine and Rose's.

"Hey Brian. Hi Rose. Seen the broadsheet?"

"Hello Gerri, you mean this one?" I pointed to the *Farrago* supplement, still unread.

"Yes. Tomorrow's Moratorium rally. Are you joining us? After yesterday's Kent State massacre, the Vietnam War is even more wrong."

Little Gerri was in jeans and a white top that curved tightly around her. I flicked my eyes away. She saw.

———

I didn't take the Mini to the city. I caught the train from Footscray, and the trains were packed. The newspaper posters outside Flinders Street Station read panic. "*Police Helmets Against Peace*". "*SitDown ShutDown*". I headed to the Treasury Gardens and lost myself in the rump of a huge crowd. It was still early. I wasn't joining anyone. I had decided only this morning I would come.

I hadn't been demonstrating before. Placards were important. "*Aussie Boys Aren't Yankee Toys*". "*Stop Viet War Now*". "*We Want Out*". Most banners bore an affiliation, to a union or lobby group. I was just me.

Gerri I couldn't find anywhere.

At three the speaker ahead crackled into life. Parliamentarian Jim Cairns addressed the crowd. "We are here in peace. Let us keep it a day of harmony. Our aim is to bring about the immediate withdrawal of the Australian Forces in Vietnam. The war is wrong, it's immoral. We are the people, and they will hear us.

"We will march together down Bourke Street, and there we'll pause. We will sit there for fifteen minutes. Australia will hear us. We will parade back up Collins Street, and again we will sit in the city. All this with calm and deliberation.

"Follow the directions of the marshals and walk calmly. Let's return here after we have sent our message in the streets of the city."

We walked, Jim Cairns at the front, and the mass poured out into Bourke Street. There were no trams, no traffic, almost no other pedestrian movement. The police had secured that portion of the city. Melbourne was at a standstill. Melbourne was watching with total anxiety.

We occupied half the length of Bourke Street when we sat. A lone helicopter rattled overhead, and the voice of Jim Cairns boomed out again from the back of the support truck.

"Australia, we are the people. The war is wrong. Bring our soldiers home."

This was history. I'd never seen history happening before, and no-one had been shot yet.

The masses shuffled around to Collins Street and Cairns repeated the people's statement. It was well after five when the last of the marchers merged back into Treasury Gardens.

"They have called us crazy radicals. They have labelled me 'Ho-Chi-Jim'. They have called you deluded and dangerous. My friends, we have stared them down. Was our march today risky? Yes, today had potential for great and senseless violence. We have occupied the city to speak our message of peace. We are a hundred thousand strong here

                    Down to Earth

today. Nobody thought we could do this. This is a big day for freedom and for our country."

———

A Few Years Earlier

I laid out the religious habit on the bed of my cell, folded the items neatly. None of my Brothers knew, only the Brother Superior. That was the way it was done. The others were all in Chapel now.

Two days ago I had been escorted on a short shopping expedition to buy a shirt, a cardigan and some civilian trousers. That's what I now wore. I carried nothing else than a prayer book and a difficult diary.

Along the crunchy white stoned driveway, I walked out through the front gate. The border transfer. I dropped one book by the gate.

My parents were waiting in a car. No-one spoke, beyond a quiet "Hello".

———

I made the back garden my cloister, and paced that. Suggestions arrived that getting a shop assistant job might be useful. It would help in talking with other people.

After a couple of months, I stirred myself to get a clerk's position in the city assisting a government design team of microwave tower engineers.

Currency changed from pounds to dollars.

One of the typists introduced me to yoghurt, and I hated it.

A dance school was nearby, so I enrolled for a class; after the six weeks I did not renew.

My bosses said they liked my work, and I admired the graphic plots and the equations they played with.

Rose – Canberra

1971 Autumn

Brian and I move to Canberra soon after he graduates, taking good honours. Canberra has good and stable employment for engineers, and it is still enticing interstate immigrants with rental relief. We rent first a rendered home in old Narrabundah, but move ourselves shortly after into a newer brick veneer house in Curtin.

Canberra isn't Melbourne—it has no history. It's a new start. Both of us. No minders. No reminders. No black bits, so we can paint our own colours.

I gave up my laboratory job at St Vincent's Hospital, and up here I have now found something matching at the Medical Research School at the Australian National University.

Could I make a new academic start here? Melbourne University threw me out. If I apply again to study at ANU, will all that be still counted against me?

Brian – Canberra

ithout her knowledge, I lodged an appeal to the Science Faculty. Granted an appearance, I appealed for her on the grounds of past parental discords, depression and financial stresses, all factors that, approximately, we hoped no longer applied. They accepted my petition, and allowed Rose to study, conditional on a clean future record.

As I expected, she was both furious and grateful. I took it with head bowed and with hands protecting my ears. I loved her.

We determined to secure our position in our adopted city. Canberra has no ownership of housing land—it is all assigned on ninety-nine-year lease. This was the only capital in the country where the bureaucrats who drew up the town plans had control over the developers.

So how much did a land lease cost? About the same as freehold land would cost. They used to sell the leases, releasing them in monthly lots, but under new arrangements all new land was now being auctioned. Costs for a block were rising dramatically, now routinely well into four figures, and it was a frightening burden for an aspiring house-owner to take on.

We were not financially ready yet to pay out for land and a builder, and we were watching in alarm as the prices rose faster than we could match. Auctions required cash, and banks demanded a substantial cash deposit for a house mortgage.

"Brian, I've been looking at the rural section. Do you think we could handle living out of town?"

"Out in the country? We've barely arrived here, and you're thinking of leaving? What have you found?"

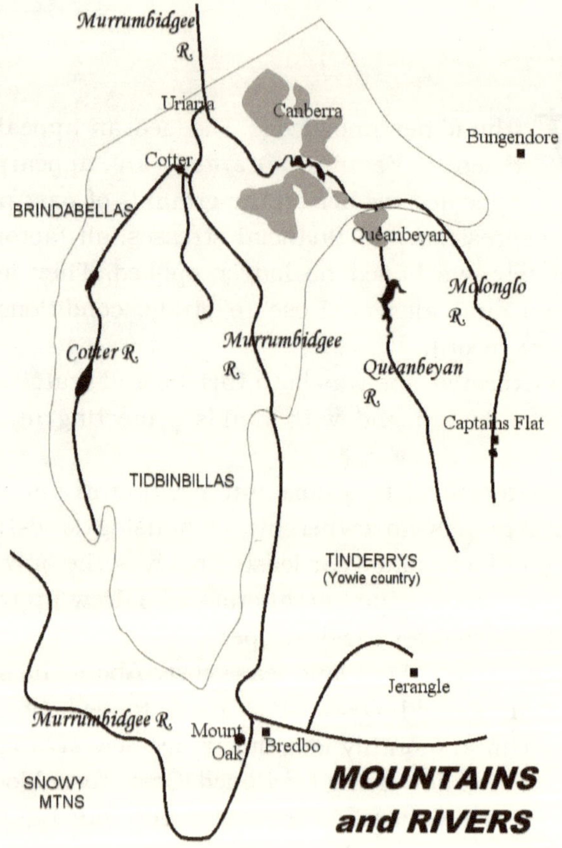

"Well," she said, "there are houses in Bungendore for ten and twelve thousand. We went through Bungendore when we went down to the coast some months ago. Can you remember how far from here Bungendore was?"

It was forty kilometres to Bungendore, out across the border, through Queanbeyan, and along the Kings Highway, still on the tablelands. Past Bungendore, the highway

Down to Earth

continued another hundred steep kilometres down to Canberra's seaside playground of Batemans Bay and beyond.

Bungendore was a sleepy country town, first settled in the 1840s, and complete with those memories that old country townships have, old post office, court, churches, wide dusty streets and several pubs. The railway station was on the line from Goulburn that went down through Queanbeyan, Bredbo and Cooma. Gold had been discovered nearby, and gold money leaves its echoes in towns. Bungendore had even once been a candidate for Australia's capital, a contest won by Canberra.

It was a weatherboard house we looked at, a shack on a quarter acre. The street was unsealed—they all were—and was three blocks back from the highway and the minimal town centre. The asking price was twelve thousand dollars. We couldn't raise that. But the search had started.

I called to the auctions office in the city each month to get the list of Canberra house blocks for auction, and we drove to Macgregor and Latham to look over the pegged sites. Then in the auction room we cringed at the aggressive bidding that pushed prices higher each time.

Rose's colleague Rachael invited us one weekend for lunch at the Captains Flat cottage where she lived. Rachael and boyfriend Wal were in the last house in "the Flat", past streets of fibro-asbestos houses, many unoccupied. Many blocks were vacant as those buildings had been transported away as holiday shacks elsewhere.

Their place was in a gully on the left at the town outskirts on the Jerangle Road south. Trees and shrubs grew across the house, covering it almost completely. Captains Flat was a derelict mining village, but this house was a pioneer cottage pre-dating the mine days. As we waited for friends of Wal who were to join us, we walked and inspected the little old gem. This was rural with a quaint brutal character.

"So where does your property reach to?" Rose asked. I loved her.

"To the base of that cliff. The plans show we go to that forlorn old hedge." Some distance beyond that was the Molonglo River.

"Nobody else is along here. Perhaps you could get hold of the rest of the strip to the water?" I suggested.

"We don't care. There's no-one there. We did put the question to Council a while ago, and they said they'd prefer not to know. If we moved our fence-line ourselves, and there isn't a fence anyway, then they were unconcerned. But what's the point, we can walk to the river, and we don't want to do anything special with the extra land. It's just a bit of Aussie dirt."

"What's upstream behind the cliff?" asked Rose.

"The Molonglo has a dam up there. The mining company built it, and we have unlimited clean piped water. The whole Flat has."

We wandered inside. Two rooms, one older than the other, and attached outhouses. They were renovating the ceiling in one room using refurbished flooring boards.

"We love it here, and we can afford it. It cost us fifteen hundred dollars outright last year."

I wondered if the commuting costs were under what they saved. Probably. But the tiny house owned an atmosphere that money could never duplicate—exquisite feral.

Wal's friends arrived, Miri and Joan. They lived on an old farmhouse halfway between here and Queanbeyan. The six of us settled in to enjoy some Flat hospitality.

An Early Summer

"It's Time!" thundered Whitlam, the wannabe Prime Minister.

　　　　　　　　　　　　　　Down to Earth

Rose's father had been a working man, always voting Labor. Rose had never voted anything else, but Labor had been out of office for more than twenty years. The old conservative Government was losing its stranglehold on the average voter, and the Labor camp were convinced a turn at power could be theirs this time.

Labor had new policies on Aboriginals, on women, on incoming migration. It was the new issues that were raising the public excitement, not the perennial economy, which was prospering comfortably. The young and those in newer social movements were thinking Labor by default.

Labor wanted to wrap up the last vestiges of Australia's involvement in the Vietnam War. Shadow Minister Jim Cairns lost no opportunity to remind all that it had always been Labor who had stood against the war, and the conscription of young Australians that sustained it.

In the election build-up, Rose started going in two evenings a week to Parliament House to join the pre-election work team. She wanted to do her part in a campaign she believed was important. She would make friends, too.

She would come home tired and excited, after talking, stapling, stamping, preparing lists of addresses, debating options, listening to try-outs of policy wordings, and phoning colleagues and faithful all across the country. She found it all heady stuff. This was the nerve centre of a critical struggle, a turning point for the nation.

It was the same year a new women's movement was unfolding, the Women's Electoral Lobby, WEL. Many of the women on the Labor campaign team quickly identified with the new force. Rose would head out to a Labor event and return from WEL.

Dave – Captains Flat

Mid-Summer

His Mum was still furious. Dave had brought the bus home unannounced two weeks ago, and had parked it at the side of the family house in Weston, a new area of Canberra. Where else could it go? Where do you store a full-sized Sydney passenger vehicle?

The single-decker nine-ton bus was a 1953 Leyland Tiger, from the Commonwealth Engineering workshops in Sydney. It still wore its blue fleet colours, and still had its cloth destination rolls in those little windows front and rear. 'Elizabeth Bay' and '155'. It would be a party trick to crank the handles and set a new destination. There was a small peephole from inside, but it took a good outside look to confirm the sign had accurately rolled to the placename you wanted.

It had read 'Broadway' when Dave picked up his new toy on the Central Coast. He had received little instruction on how to control the beast. The trip home—highway, mid-city and hills—was an exercise in learning fast, avoiding knocking anyone else, and owning some road bravado.

His route on that first day was across the Harbour Bridge and right through Sydney, and several folk waiting at traffic light corners had sought to board. He had to wave away the would-be commuters.

Over the fortnight, Dave had replaced the 24-volt battery bank, as the old ones were no longer starting the big motor easily. He wanted the vehicle ready for Sunbury.

He had lifted the engine covers, which were a monstrous saddle inside the bus and beside the driver. The ten litres of motor was one straight-six diesel steel monster with minimal fittings. Too primitive to look at, basic but huge. When it started, it idled along with its slow metallic deep thunder throb, an unmistakable threat of untamed crude power if asked.

He liked his gadgets, but this was too awe-inspiring and too ancient. He was scared to touch, adjust or tighten anything, at least yet. He had checked it had oil, and replaced the covers.

Johnny, the seller, had owned it only five months. He wanted cash. From Johnny, only a few more items of guidance were forthcoming. The large screwed panel in the wooden floor at the centre of the bus was over the gearbox—that gearbox was huge, should never be touched, and was going to be "big trouble" if it ever had problems. Don't rev the motor too fast, and the red line on the tachometer indicator was, well, it was the red line. "One last caution, when you start the motor, let it idle for several minutes until the air pressure for the brakes comes up past this line."

What had he bought?

The bus seats were gone, but fitting out as a house-bus was barely started. Behind the driver, Johnny had built a raised platform that served as storage and as a generous bed, good for two people, and more if a need arose.

Johnny had fitted a black plastic water tank to the bus roof. Water piping led to a shower fitting inside behind the rear door. In the floor was a drain tray, and a drain-hole dropped the shower water to the ground. It was a crude job.

Dave was under no illusion. It would be a lot of work to turn this stillborn house-bus creature into a beautiful child of the 1970s. But he was the man. Carpentry and fitting out was not going to be a problem.

After Sunbury.

———

Around the back doorwell, Dave had lashed sleeping gear and food and some chairs. He wore his black trousers and black shirt. He started the motor, and his Mum stood at the house steps, hands on hips, frowning.

Clambering back out over the engine bay, he walked around the bus and looked at the compressed gas tank underneath. Dirt and compressor oil clung to the fittings. That might need some attention before long. But not today. The pressure gauge was there alongside the tank, oily like the other parts. It took some while for the pressure to rise, but Dave had once before been through the fright of slow under-performing brakes. That was on a test run, and he hadn't heeded Johnny's warning, hadn't taken the care to get the air ready.

The motor was noisy, but he could still hear his Mum's thoughts as she glared at him. Mum had seen her own man walk away years ago. Her first son Barry she was still proud of, but she had lost him to the Vietnam War. In Dave, though, she saw only sorrow and trouble, and it made him resentful. He held a graduate clerk job on the Art Gallery team, even though they hadn't completed the new Gallery building yet. She should be satisfied.

The bus thundered out of Weston and made its way up the Hindmarsh Hill. The red line of the tachometer matched fifty miles an hour on the speedometer. So was it a danger to the motor to be going faster? He needed to talk to a diesel person.

It was easy enough to hold the bus at "eighty" (in the new measurement) on level road—and downhill too, braking each time it raced away. But this vehicle was able to do the same speed uphill. The diesel worked harder and grew throatier, but the speed stayed.

It made some sense, he thought. It would cope with Sydney metropolitan streets with a full passenger load. The city had no need for anything beyond fifty miles an hour, but it did have some steep short hills.

The highway down to Victoria will be another story. Coming from Sydney a month ago, the semi-trailers sped downhill, and slowed to a tortoise pace on the uphills. They had hated the Leyland.

The change-over to the new metric system he wasn't finding easy. His mind ran in a hybrid mode. Eighty. Fifty.

Yards. Metres. Miles.

He drove down along Uriarra Road through Queanbeyan.

The Wilson pre-select gearbox had a pedal for the fluid clutch, and a pneumatic hissing short lever at his left for gear select. Standing at Kings Highway to turn left past the RSL, he realised he could engage first gear, still be stationary, and pre-select second gear.

So, while struggling then with the heavy cornering, he needn't make any more gear-change operations until he needed third gear.

He'd get this old machine to the Sunbury Rock Festival yet.

It was Johnny O'Keefe in particular he wanted to hear in Sunbury. O'Keefe's rock'n'roll had always been Aussie stuff, local, not the imported rock music. The man was a legend, a showman, a larrikin, Australia's "Wild One". Many claimed he was long ago burned out, a mess, but Dave needed to hear O'Keefe for himself.

Of course, Max Merritt and Billy Thorpe and the Aztecs would drag him to Sunbury anyway. It was all good. And fancy, television's Paul Hogan as the compere?

Dave had stacked some beer in the back. Possibly he could score his first grass?

The bodhran drum was aboard, too. He had fashioned it a month ago, using a plywood barrel he spotted while dumping at the Mugga Lane tip. He had cut a short cylinder from the barrel and stretched a skin across the ring. His playing was still clumsy.

Whether he brought it out at Sunbury depended on what he found there. Will they provide only a rough rock commercial formula, or would there be a place for amateur players, private jamming? He wasn't hopeful. If there was a chance, out it would come.

Down along the Captains Flat Road, he headed downhill. Here it was narrow and straight, and double-lined. On the left side was an embankment, but a treacherous drain gully was beside that bank. The bus wanted to race away and was quickly past its red line speed. Worse, an oncoming car was approaching. The surface was bumpy and broken, so the worn steering mechanicals of the (now) 'Elizabeth Bay' blue passenger vehicle were making it difficult to stay cleanly in the correct lane on this rough country road.

He braked to slow the lumbering giant. The right side air brakes acted. The machine lurched to the right, across the line. A second later, the left side brakes operated, and the bus, now well over its line, was at least stable to control. The oncoming driver flashed his headlights as Dave hauled his bus to its correct place on the road.

That was one adventure he wasn't telling Miriam.

Past the bottom of the hill, he slowed and now turned his bus on to the dirt track. He was opening the gate when he saw the sign alongside. It was a subdivision application notice. They were going to cut up the old Sandford farm property.

Miriam was a tenant in the original corrugated iron house—it hadn't been occupied as a farming house for several years. So, the Sandford owners had been biding their time. Miriam and her friend Joan had been here for two

Down to Earth

years, and they commuted together daily to college in Canberra.

Often lately Dave had been here to visit Miri, and their relationship was feral cosy, intimate enough to be planning this trip away to the big gig in Sunbury.

Independent bitch at times, but Dave knew he would win at the end. The house-bus was part of the game. They should be into Sunbury by tomorrow night. Anything can happen when you are both at fairyland.

They'll be hopping and bopping to Elton John's 'Crocodile Rock'.

Iris – Rainbow

Autumn

Iris had not intended coming. But her student newspaper *Tharunka* had been full of the plans, the hopes and hype for months. The event promised a spectacle, an immersion, a challenge. Life, she decided only early yesterday, deserved that dare right now.

The road north from Lismore was so narrow that oncoming vehicles must put a wheel on the grass edges to pass. But most traffic was northwards: kombi vans, shabby cars of some old vintages, small painted buses, some with trailers, all with full seats. The old 8-track cartridge played Bob Marley again, and her friend Carol hummed aloud. It was Carol who had really wanted to come.

Iris's professor father, who had doted on her in her childhood, had insisted she study at Sydney's Kensington campus, and she had resented that. But Dad's plan did have some perverse logic, she was finally conceding. She would have done her studies in Canberra, would doubtless have still lived at home, and would be the same risk-averse mouse she'd always been.

In Sydney, she spent a year in college, then moved out with two girlfriends. None of them had natural kitchen or house skills, and the simmering disputes were inevitable, until only Iris and Carol battled on, settling on a workable regime. Friends now? In a way.

They had slept fitfully last night in the Ford Anglia at a roadside gully. The exposure and danger in sleeping along the highway had terrified them.

Finally: *Nimbin.*

The garish newer sign read "Second Aquarius Festival of the Arts, 1973". Would she ever dare tell Dad?

———

"Iris, huge soap bubbles are floating past us outside," Carol hissed. "They're coming from a naked man across in the long grass. With ear-rings. Him. Iris, wake up." Carol shook her. "I don't know how you can still sleep."

"Oh, it was so noisy for hours, that drumbeat. And those strange smells all night." Carol had prepared some cordial.

"Thanks." Iris swallowed. "Carol, sh-should we go home?"

"We do not go home! We bloody well step out and see what we came for."

"Didn't we see more last night than we knew what to do with?" Iris closed her eyes. She couldn't call on Dad this time. Probably never again. She sat up again and peered out. This is what she came for; Carol was right. Carol was always right.

And the naked man was still there.

The campground was a huge valley astride the Mulgum Creek. People had slept on the ground, with rugs and canvas. They crowded into thousands of tiny tents. They were in vehicles of every condition, in domes and tepees. Bodies were emerging into the clearing mist of morning. The smoke of little fires was everywhere. Music of pipes or flute wafted across.

The dress colours, for those who had dress, were a riot. It wasn't a fashion Iris recalled from anywhere. Capes, skirts, ponchos, scarves, tights, hats, headbands, saris all worn in wrong and strange ways. Seeing so many strangers enjoying themselves, greeting, laughing, cavorting, smiling, hugging, she was terrified. But what had she expected? A tea party?

"Iris, come on, get out. Let's walk up the hill to town. Find a milk bar. Get your pack. We'll take it step at a time. We're going to enjoy this."

———

On their second day, they learned how to secure an afternoon beachhead outside the Central Cafe—a small table on the footpath.

Alongside was a vivid photo display from the Sunbury Music Festival a few months earlier. Iris loved her music, but to go to Sunbury had been too unthinkable an adventure that short while ago. Huge sound stage, massive speakers, people climbing atop. Tents and buses and igloos. Coloured hair, long hair, bald head. Guitar close-ups, crowds of people, dancing people, sleeping people, waving people. Those photos told of a wild Sunbury.

But the overwhelming eyeful that was Nimbin today was making competition.

On a stool in the main road, a busker sat naked but for a cowman's hat and a guitar. Through the summer heat Iris caught phrases from the Hair anthem.

Carol came back out. "The best I could find was some mango and soy milk. At least it's cold."

Iris had never tried soy. The festival posters were boasting how Nimbin was dairy country, but the dairying was a failed industry. That was why the organisers chose here. It was a ghost town, run down, and the carnival would bring fun and new energies. There was certainly an overflow of new energy this week, psychedelic power. The street-long mural on all the shopfront tops was freshly painted, but the

Down to Earth

shopfronts below the new artworks were crumbling and rotting.

Carol pointed. "And what's that?"

"Ah, that one I know. I saw him last night. It's B-Benny Zable. He always wears that nuclear gas mask as a protest, I heard. His troupe is doing HG Wells' *The Time Machine* in the community hall."

An old woman approached, dramatic long brushed white hair shining in the sun. She had two arms loaded with armbands of all colours. Her breasts were bare, and they too fell a long way down. Her tumbling skirt was as jumble-coloured as the bands. "Hello, sisters. Can I sit here with you? It's so hot out there, and I need a drink and something."

Iris hesitated. She wasn't sure what "something" might have meant, wasn't asking. "Sure. We're exhausted, too. Go in for what you want, and we'll hold the seat. We're not moving. No, on second thoughts, what do you want? I'll go in. We need another drink too."

Iris returned loaded up. "Carol, this cafe is fascinating. They have the strangest food. They don't sell coffee. A cafe without coffee? They gave me Nature's Cuppa and said it was healthier."

"Huh, same line as they gave me."

Iris addressed the visitor. "Here's your drink. I'm Iris." She sat against the wall, not attempting to reclaim her seat.

"Thanks, Iris. I'm Star. I read cards at the fairs, but for this festival I decided on a new lark. So I celebrate festival unions."

"Sorry?" asked Carol.

"I do twenty-four-hour carnival trothals."

"Trothals?"

"Yes, trothals. If you want to sleep with someone tonight, you could just do it. But if you want to make it official, that's what I do. I make it official, for twenty-four hours."

Iris was blushing.

"Nearly married?" said Carol, "Legal sex for one night? That's absurd."

"But why?" This was not the logic that should be coming from someone's grandmother. "Ancient Plato thought festival trothals were a grand idea."

"It's immoral. It's a pretence, an excuse. It's not right."

"Oh, dear, and they all tell me they love me for it. I get two dollars each time, too." Star's eye had a twinkle.

"Can't you see it's evil?"

"No, it's not wrong. It's a magical and healthy experience we can enjoy."

"But it's a sin. Sex can hurt people. Everyone knows that."

"Sister, everyone is mistaken. People believed the earth was flat, and they were wrong then."

"Well, I'm having a problem. How do you bless their night? Can you call it 'bless'?"

"Yes, I anoint them. We have a public ceremony here at my stand. They both place one foot in my basin, and I pour water on their feet. Then I give them each one band. Today's colour is red. They put their matching bands on their washed feet and stand officially together. Finally, I give them two condoms."

Iris remembered seeing people wearing ankle bands. Perhaps most of those had been walking in couples. A thrill shivered through her. How could they be so brazen as to declare what they would be getting up to tonight? Or maybe earlier. Two women with anklets walked past holding hands. Iris pointed and tried to speak, but a splutter came out. "I need to think about it all," she said. She paused. "It's not how I grew up."

"But I have to go. Gotta do trothals." The woman looked at Iris. "We'll meet again."

"Bye." Iris frowned and regained her seat. The long-haired Godiva smiled and turned away.

"Bye, Star," called Carol. But she looked back to Iris. "It's so wrong."

"I don't think I'm into ankle bands." Iris paused. "She makes you think, though." She reached back, let down her slept-in hair, and shook her head.

Carol glared at her. "We should have stayed home," she said.

A shout came across the road.

"Someone knows you, Iris."

It was Gavin, from this year's biology class. "Hey, I didn't know you were coming here. This's great."

"Hello, Gav. I wasn't coming. Blame Carol, my house-mate."

"Gee, Carol. Thanks." He grinned.

Iris winced. "Gavin is our practical man. He can gut 'em and slice 'em when the rest of us go green."

"Iris, I can't chat now, I'm trying to find the hall for Paul Joseph, the Aquarius Songman, and I'm late. But quickly, where are you staying?"

"There's the Nimbin Hall, over up there a bit. And we are camping down right of the river, past the double-decker green bus. It's a red and brown pup tent flying a yellow ribbon."

"Trying to stand out?"

"We worried about never finding home. Eight thousand of us are here, remember. Bye."

Some strollers had a slow glazed look. The universe is eternal, and we are that universe. God is the cosmos and we are all god and we are the cosmos. We must open our eyes and we must be together. All the governments and all the wealth are as nothing if only we love.

Another shuffling, bearded old fart. An Old Testament movie clip. But then, his message was barely Bible doctrine. Iris decided it was no sane creed at all; it wasn't coherent enough to be anything. He was no threat either. It was just c-crap.

Carol wanted to spend tomorrow at some workshops. "They have batik and screen printing. Or something safe like choral practice." Iris wanted to look again at the offerings; she would choose her own.

———

"Iris, I've been so worried. Why didn't you leave a message?" It was the seventh morning of the festival. The sun was well up.

"It's tricky. I stayed in the big dome with Gavin. Sorry, I didn't plan it."

"With Gavin? You met him again?" Carol scuffled inside the awkward tent, finished dressing, and crawled out.

"Yes, several times over the l-last few days." She hung her head. "Have we any real coffee down here. I've had no breakfast."

"You dark one! This is my Iris?"

"Carol, hold me. I didn't sleep with him. Well, yes I did sleep with him. But I didn't *sleep* with him. We didn't do anything, that's all. Come on, there were a lot of people crowding in there. Carol, I'm terrified. What do I do?"

Carol, frosty, found coffee and made cups for them both. They tracked down Gavin, and thenceforth, a bit awkwardly, they were a festival trio. But not with anklets.

But the demon was not male. The seducer was the "try me", the sampler tab of LSD offered at the campfire gathering on the eighth night. Just the tiniest piece of blotter, and it promised to bring a truly spiritual experience, meeting the universe. Iris had agonised, recalling the version of spiritual her Dad had cherished and passed lovingly to her for all her years.

Gavin was to meet them soon, but on impulse, she chewed the paper before he arrived. It tasted nothing. She spat out the wad, disappointed and relieved. Carol hadn't noticed; she would have been not amused.

Down to Earth

It was a long night. Her two friends dutifully sat with her until dawn, until Iris's world merged once again with theirs, the usual one of coherent noises, recognisable people, rain-drizzle and smoke, of hunger and panic. "Thank you," was her main refrain, "and I'm so sorry. But you have n-no idea what I've seen."

"I don't want to see." Carol stood up. "We should go home today." She started to pack her possessions, implicitly expecting her companion to follow. Gavin walked aside a hundred yards, sat on the grass, and put his head in his hands. Iris, still foggy from her ordeal, looked from Gavin to her housemate.

"Are you coming?"

Iris turned slowly and went to stand beside Gavin. Carol untied the tent's marker ribbon and continued packing. Leaving her empty tent for Iris, she drove her Anglia out of camp.

———

On the last day, Gavin and Iris filed into the Nimbin Hall for a community meeting. Could the festival experience and lifestyle become an ongoing life? As many as wanted could live in the area, keeping the philosophies and ideals they had explored for the past ten days. Back to the land. Free. In peace. Self-sufficient. Non-consumer. Supporting one another through life's crises, applying spiritual values to all of life. An ongoing rainbow of possibilities.

They walked in doubtful. "Utopian dreams," said Gavin, "Athens resurrected."

But many did dream that utopia. Did they have enough passion, clout and hard-headedness to make it happen? Substantial tracts of local forest or old grazing land were obtainable, and if they bought a property communally, each resident would need to contribute only a few hundred dollars. The *May Manifesto* from the meeting would be printed and available in a few hours.

A crazy idea flicked into Iris's soul, hovered a moment, then went the way of anklets and cosmic c-crap.

But she barely slept that night. There was a long drive with Gavin ahead. Back home to what? He was warm beside her. "Gav?" she whispered as dawn was breaking.

"Hmm?" The dome was full of sleeping bodies.

"Do you think we could get together two hundred dollars?"

Brian – Canberra

A Winter

Arty, wearing gloves and jacket, was waiting for me outside his front door. His faithful labrador was sitting in the frost beside him. He patted the dog affectionately and let her back into the house, picked up his light pack, and hopped into the car.

It was still dark, and the Morris 1100 windows were troublesome on crisp mornings like this. I had scraped off the ice before leaving home. I kept a cloth within reach.

"Morning. Get enough sleep?"

"Hi, Brian. Some. I might still have a nap on the way though. Are you driving first?"

"I'm fine. I can drive right through. You drive tonight."

I drove south out to the Monaro Highway. Arty arranged a cushion beside his head and closed his eyes.

I had a dog once, a black labrador too. I was fourteen. Dog arrived one day, half-grown and eager, and they said it was mine. They said I needed him. Cats we had a succession of—they appeared litter after litter, and we always allowed one in as a house pet. But dogs? I was lightly mauled by one when I was younger.

I had tied dog on a rope at the side of the house, and changed its water when reminded. After two months, my Uncle Jim came to visit. Piano player and theatre actor, Jim now lived alone. We didn't get the concept of *closet* then. He told me he would take dog to his house from now on. Uncle

Jim named dog "Timmy", and Timmy was his devoted companion for many years.

The Monaro Highway was in a long valley between the Tidbinbillas on the right and the Tinderrys eastward. The Murrumbidgee River was heading north all along here, hugging the foothills. The lightly-used railway line crossed the road again and again, at S-bend corners that were not altogether safe. This valley was dry country, a rain shadow area of the greater Snowy Mountains.

Arty slept past Michelago. Past Bredbo. I didn't know how, as I was listening to an 8-track cartridge of Pink Floyd, *The Dark Side of the Moon*. Rose would have played a Bob Marley.

He woke when I stopped at a crossing to wait for a train, and he shuffled himself back to life. "Sorry, I needed that."

He stretched.

"You led Rose on a merry chase last week, I heard," he said.

"Oh, she told you about the bridge?"

"Sure did. She panicked."

We had camped out last week, winter notwithstanding, and in the morning I had been sitting under the new bridge construction in the town, thinking.

"Rose was concerned you were missing so long."

"Come on, it wouldn't have been more than an hour."

"So what was so intriguing?"

"I was inspecting the rocking mount point for the bridge's weight. There was no post or mount that was rigid into the ground at all, very clever exercise in strut theory." Rose had been unimpressed with the strut theory. She had stood there shaking her head.

We were approaching Cooma. The town was buzzing with rugged-up people. I filled the tank at the Ampol and went in to pay.

"What's the road condition?"

    Down to Earth

"We got the report in a few minutes ago. Overnight we had a fair amount of new snow they've not cleared yet, but there's also some ice remaining in some parts. You'll need chains up near the top. How far are you going?"

I hired a set of chains. I had used chains before, and that was several years ago in Victoria. I owned those chains then, but they went with the Mini.

We always budgeted an hour in Cooma. Customers crowded the tourist cafes, making slow service at this early hour. On the outskirts of town, two competing ski hire outlets advertised bargain prices. They wouldn't be bargain; this was peak season.

When you live only a few hours from the ski fields, or those limited ski fields that Australia can boast, it was practical, just, to drive there and back in one long day. Arty and I had become regulars at that. About once a month during the last couple of seasons, we headed off in the dark and returned in the dark. Sometimes, as now, it was only us two. Rose had come on two of the trips, and other friends on occasion.

We were all amateurs, and went for the fun, not for the skill. On some trips, we would get no further than the beginner runs for the day. Later into each season, when our levels had improved, we would venture up the higher slopes and dare ourselves down.

Arty and I had both last year been naive enough to buy second-hand skis from the newspaper in Canberra. We hadn't bought well-suited length or style, and we had abandoned those skis to garage exile, and returned to the routine of hiring outside Cooma. We selected skis each and strapped them atop the car. Up the road now until we had to stop to put chains on.

I needed to raise the issue, the subject that was not spoken. Arty wasn't going to, clearly. Didn't know how to?

"Rose has been enjoying the music nights."

Silence.

"Your collection is rather broad, and you have such a passion about it. Rose says you always know what the lyrics are about, the messages and the hidden meanings."

"The records have cost me a lot over the years," said Arty. "My family was musical, and I've inherited that. With the cassettes now, being a music buff has unlimited potential."

"We have some music at home," I said, "but it's a bit boring probably to an enthusiast. We buy a few LPs when we can afford to, but that's not often. I had been thinking we might upgrade the old player we use to something new. The modern stereos have a clarity and depth our old machine can't match."

Better than the repaired record player I had in my room as a lad. I had owned one 78 record then, 'Shanandoah', and it played all day until I was ordered to stop.

In the past few weeks, Rose had been staying various evenings with Arty to listen to the music. She would return home excited, having been transported to realms of rhythm and melody that were new and seductive.

Seductive, but of course.

She had to be aware where it was leading. I had no doubt Arty knew that too. He was wary with me the past couple of weeks.

"Arthur, let me talk plainly. We are friends. I enjoy your friendship. But I don't want to hide or play games."

"OK." I took that as an admission.

"I know Rose enjoys your music. I know also that Rose is enjoying your company. It's all exciting and it's all unknown and challenging for her. I'm not blind."

Silence for a moment.

"I love Rose. I don't want to lose her." There was more, but possibly Arty didn't know: Rose was five weeks pregnant.

"But I don't always assess life the same way as many people might. Both of us have always tried to confront life and to dare to discover new ways, ways that work for us. We have our ups and our downs, but we muddle our way along. At different times each of us has our moments of growth. Rose is enjoying the adventure with you.

"I want to say to you as a friend, that I don't have a problem with that. I don't have any issue with the music sessions. I don't have a challenge if both of you want to make more of it than the music."

Had they already?

"I didn't know how to talk about it with you. I'm sorry."

"No, don't be unhappy. We are all here living our life out. Most people's rules for life don't make consistent sense. I don't believe in them. I don't want ownership rules over Rose or you. Don't be apologetic. Just be open with me."

"Thanks. Have you said any of this to Rose? Or will you?"

"No, I won't. I think she'd be furious if she knew I'd raised it with you. She's trying to work through it for herself, find some clarity and some decisions for herself."

"So, you're short-circuiting that?"

"I suppose so. But I needed to put the subject into the open."

"So where's the jealousy?"

"Jealousy is one of those complicated emotions that I think is a task in life. A maturing too many are blindly afraid of." Perhaps I didn't have much of the jealousy thing anyway.

"Your rules are different," he said.

"Well, we need a fresh view."

We drove on in silence up the mountain.

"OK," Arty said, "everyone is pulling to the side here. It looks like chain time."

Leonard Cohen had been there, in his 'Paper Thin Hotel', stood there with his ear against the wall.

My Nanna had me to stay for a week on some school holidays, a privilege my other cousins weren't often given.

I'd poke around the quiet house with its strange smells, inspect every little statue, trinket or relic that filled all the shelves, or read a book or some of Nanna's magazines that never appeared at our place. Musty cases and books in the garage were a treasure trove, and I even unearthed a water-stained school report from my mother's schooldays.

Uncle Jim still lived at Nanna's then. Sometimes I'd spend hours tinking away on Jim's piano, trying to under-stand how music worked, chords that sounded good or awful, soft and loud, pedals, keys, strings and hammers. Eventually Nanna would suggest I leave the piano and do something else.

I would be sent the three blocks to the shops as an errand. Mostly I would come home with the right items, but I forgot some at times, and I'd be sent back.

One beautiful day I sat on Nanna's back step. The radio had reported the Americans had exploded a new atomic bomb, so much bigger than any before, on an island out in the sea but much closer to Australia. I sat looking at the grass, not cut for a while.

One blade was twitching and trembling. I looked for a mouse or a worm that might be moving the base of that blade. Nothing. I looked to see if an insect were crawling on the reverse of the green shoot. Nothing. No connecting spider web. It was truly a mystery. I watched it.

Nanna came out the door heading for the chook-house to check the results of the hen clucking a while ago, and she almost fell over me. "Brian, are you still here? What's so interesting?"

I explained my puzzle.

"Brian, honey, what about the wind? Maybe there is a little breeze?"

———

                                             Down to Earth

Spring

Gerri and husband Paul drove up for the football Grand Final, a rematch of last year's final teams. The television channels didn't broadcast the finals series live in Victoria, as that might steal some crowd from the MCG itself. So every year some fanatic and enterprising fans visited interstate friends to view the television broadcast on that last Saturday. Gerri visited us in Canberra.

Funny that, why was the Melbourne Cricket Ground the home place of football?

The four of us still met often these days. Three of us had knocked about as best buddies for some of our undergraduate years. Then Gerri met and married Paul, and that made little difference, as we became a foursome of friends. Paul was an electrician, not a Uni type, but we cared little about that.

We had many occasions of going together to the pictures, of heading out of town on a camping weekend, of dining and spending the evenings together. We spent plenty of time mulling on the meanings and hassles in life.

When Rose and I left Melbourne to live in Canberra, it disrupted the gang. But not completely: we still managed to meet midway for weekends at the Hume Weir or at Bright. Or we made the full trip to stay with the others.

Gerri was Japanese. She looked Japanese. But she had grown up in Melbourne with her mother and her English stepfather. I had heard the story several times over the years, but the details always got foggy in my head. It was an adventure of occupied postwar Japan where all the society patterns were in tangled upheaval. Now all the speech and mannerisms and instincts coming from the little Japanese frame were pure Aussie.

Gerri pattered out early on Saturday morning. Last night's six hundred kilometres of driving was still in evidence.

"Brian, I'm so weary." She wrapped her arms around my back, buried her face into my shoulder.

"Then why are you up?"

"I heard someone, and I came out hoping it was you. Brian, I might be pregnant." She clung on harder.

"You might be? Why only might be?"

"Because it's too early to be sure."

"Hey, that's so exciting if you are. It's big news. Joining Rose, eh? You do want to be pregnant?"

"I'm not sure. I think so. Hold me."

I waited for her to continue.

"It's just that ..." Pause. "I think it's what we need. It's been a bit rough lately. Paul, I mean."

I held her longer, then led her to the couch and sat beside her. A tear rolled down her cheek.

"I don't know what I want anymore. I'm feeling lost."

"Lost like when you were agonising over leaving the nun's habit in your first year at university?" Adrift like the perpetual refugee I sometimes see in her eyes?

"Brian, Paul is getting edgy. He says he doesn't know how to handle me. I'm not helping. I don't have the same feelings for him as I used to. It's not there, and I can't make it come back."

"Then you get pregnant?" That was a dumb comment.

"I don't know if I am. I'm a bit late, so far. I don't know whether I want to be. In one way, it would settle things, because I would need to be Paul's woman and start a family with him. Accept him. Accept everything, like I should."

We four sat indoors all afternoon, and we swore and abused the players and umpire alike. That's how footy should be, with beers and football and TV.

Real TV.

Not like the TV set I built by hand in high school. Bent all the metal. Bought or made every piece. Wound all the coils. Soldered it all. I had learned the theory behind every section, every component. It used a five-inch green screen radar tube from Walthams Wartime Disposals. At least we got to have a TV, because my parents couldn't afford a bought one. And we got a TV the whole street wanted to come in to see.

We all snuggled on the one sofa. By final siren time, Richmond had beaten Carlton 16 goals 20 to 12 goals 14, and Gerri was not pregnant.

———

Next Spring

Bailey Arcade was opposite the old Canberra monumental Sydney Building in Civic, the city centre. It was the only proper arcade here, unlike Melbourne, which has a surfeit, or even Sydney. I walked through, and found a florist, a tobacconist, shoe shop, dry cleaner. What I wanted wasn't here.

I checked my note again. Ah, first floor. A poky staircase took me up. Here was another world, but were they offices or shopfronts? The corridor was narrow and crooked. I passed rooms of the Wilderness Society and two dingy travel agents. Then I found my target.

The Canberra Learning Exchange was publicly funded, but its business was scarcely Government oriented. It looked run down, window long unloved with an old curtain drawn half across, carpet worn. Inside the door was clutter. I couldn't see anyone.

Two of the walls had books for sale, but those were a bit tired too, well-fingered, still waiting for a buyer to walk off with them. Some publications were the gentle help-the-newcomer sort, notes on Government nursery free trees for homebuyers, mud-maps of services in the city, composting guides.

Most books, however, were activist titles. Anarchism, strike etiquette, libertarian treatises, ideological and Marxist tomes. Some stood in piles on the floor. The walls around the shelves sported several posters of Guevara, closed fists, and dark black and white protest photos. Even so, Canberra didn't have the frightening real anarchist bookshops of Sydney or Melbourne. One Mary Martins didn't count. Canberra was a genteel, toy capital. Its anarchist bookshop was a toy as well.

I wasn't expecting a bookshop. I was looking for a particular noticeboard. A listing of jobs and activities, creative and offbeat jobs, anything different. The Learning Exchange was where Leon had recommended. Damn Leon, I should have guessed.

I walked past the corner bookshelf, and the room opened out. An office desk faced away, cluttered again. The noticeboard I sought covered the other side wall.

But a large low table-tennis table occupied the main room area. It was littered with yet more books and papers, and the lone staff member was leafing through each book, pencilling a price inside the front cover of each. The marked books were being placed into a side pile.

"Oh, hello. Sorry I didn't hear you come in. How can I help you?"

Maggie was a part-time teacher at the Steiner school, but had long been a volunteer on Tuesday mornings at the Learning Exchange. The "LEX", she said, opened only on two mornings, with volunteers.

She was easy to talk with. The sense of being in an alien place faded away.

The philosophy behind Steiner was people and their potential, and Maggie was devoted to it. Develop the capacities in our children, whatever capacity that may be. Each

                                   Down to Earth

young person should be allowed to explore and flourish. Much of education teaches our kids on the requirements and skills to fit to the existing society, and that is a schooling that has its priorities backwards.

"I'm sorry. I've been rattling on too long. You did ask, mind you. What brings you here?"

"The noticeboard."

Maggie led across to the notice wall. "We have some impressive items on there. It beats the classified adverts."

"I wanted to check the notices on work. A friend suggested to me I might find it broadening. He said there were so many ways people were advertising their time or their labour."

"Much of what's on here is people doing cooperative things. A lot is not paid. Look, here's an invitation to join a proposed bulk food ordering cooperative. Here is a Yoga class—that's a paid class. Or creative writing—an established group has vacancies, meeting on a Sunday morning. Who was suggesting us?"

"Leon. Leon Charles. He's a mate across town."

"Leon? Of course, I know Leon. He helped us get the bookshop established earlier this year. Leon was on the Learning Exchange committee for a while. He's a teacher, too, at Canberra High, but I know he's moving to the School Without Walls. So what did Leon send you here for?"

"We had been talking about jobs we do to make money, and jobs we do because we want to. I had been working with the Department of Works, but I left a week back, and I haven't worked out another way to earn a living yet, unless I take a Defence job that's on offer."

"Doing the job we love. That sounds like Leon."

"You know, listening to Leon is hard sometimes. He treats so many things theoretically, in an intellectual way. Indigestible. It's difficult not to feel put down, a bit inferior. I feel lectured."

"I should confess," she said. "I went out with him for a short while about two years ago. Sure, he can scare some people off. His intellect is like a weapon, to me too. I wanted the man, his soul, but I had problems getting past Leon's thinking."

So Maggie understood secular "souls", too. That total of our dreamings, our loves, our creativity and knowing.

We had left the noticeboard for the moment. The kettle had been boiling as I'd entered. I accepted a lemon tea.

"I want to like Leon," I said. "I keep trying to believe his ideas are correct. Difficult, but right." I sat on a stool at the big central table.

Maggie smiled.

"He's researched libertarianism widely. His words keep calling for personal freedom and responsibility. There's even a book he wants to publish sometime.

"But enough of Leon. You came here on a mission."

"Leon thinks ..." Leon again? "Leon thinks I could earn some money repairing cars. I don't have any trade certificate to be fixing cars, but I have rebuilt my own cars several times. If my vehicle needs work, even serious work, I just pull it down and fix it. When it gets heavy going, my wife Rose helps out. I think Rose could take a head off and grind valves by herself now."

"So?"

"I don't feel correctly qualified to advertise working on car service."

"And Leon says, just do it?"

"Precisely. 'Brian, you have expertise. You enjoy doing repairs and service. Take responsibility for yourself. Dare to use what you are. Use your skills. Simply advertise your services and work out what happens. Make it work.'"

"The anarchist."

"I am trying to get my head around it. All my experience and conditioning tell me I have no right to do that. I'm not trained. I might make a fool of myself. I might lose

                                        Down to Earth

money. I might make an appalling botch of someone's car through ignorance. I might confront jobs I don't know how to do.

"Today I came here to see if anyone posted something comparable on your noticeboard. Were there really others operating like this? If it's not in the newspaper, is there still someone doing this among the subculture, in the informal networks?"

She ducked. "Sorry. Study our notices and make your own decisions."

———

Two weeks later was the paste-up day for the Learning Exchange Newsletter. Maggie had asked me.

The LEX published six each year, six thousand copies each time, and it circulated free through the libraries, schools, health food outlets and some newsagents in Canberra.

And so I was inducted into the 1970s version of newsletter layout, as practised by volunteer and amateur organisations.

Material was mostly type-written ahead of time.

We could handle a couple of photos, black and white, but not directly. Instead, Maggie had taken those to the local printing shop earlier, and they had come back in a dotted version, like pictures in a newspaper.

All copy we cropped with scissors, and we aligned it all by hand on double foolscap pages, using set square and ruler. Clipped temporarily under each sheet was a lined margins page. With everything tacked by glue, we drew some separator lines into the layout, applied liquid white to fix errors, and placed page numbers from an adhesive transfer sheet.

Magic nonreflective sticky tape went over all paper edges to stop those edge lines from showing later. The newsletter was done.

We had pasted an article on the campaign for a nude beach for Canberra. A pool on the Murrumbidgee south of town was being proposed, with a sand beach and a little privacy. A public meeting was scheduled.

One page we devoted to describing the various funds and grants available from Government sources, what the conditions were, where to apply.

There were six of us today. I had convinced Rose to join us. Judy from Leon's anarchist clique was here, and Maggie and two more. Our Jo played in the corner, where we had put a playpen.

"Judy, this is yours?" Judy had started a food cooperative for bulk and organic foods, and Rose was considering we should join. The co-op sent an order every eight weeks to Russells Healthfoods in Sydney, as Canberra had no equivalent bulk store, and Russells freighted the order by train. Judy held a party for divvying up each time the consignment arrived. The article was a promotion for joining her co-op, but it was also a fact sheet describing how to set up and manage a cooperative.

Leon had a plan for inner urban renewal.

There were several pages of private advertisements, like the ads on the notice board. And columns of *I want, I need, I give, I exchange.*

Some paid adverts went in, and these helped subsidise the costs: The Nearly New Shop, Gus's coffee shop in Civic, Pedal Power cycles, The Hermit theosophical bookshop.

LEX had one light-duty copier, definitely not for big runs like the newsletter, so the masters went to the printing shop. They, magicians that they were, reduced each double foolscap to a single size before doing the bulk printing. The collation and stapling were a task for two days' time, another team.

"What a most amazing process! Look what we finish with?" I said.

Rose came over to me. "Brian, sit down. Listen to me. The amazing process is not this today. The wonder is what we think, what we write and share. It's what people then read, and it's the changes in our lives, our new excitements, fresh options to explore. We are all the awesome process, not these few pieces of scrappy paper on the table."

——

Summer

The place proposed as free beach was Kambah Pool. Kambah was a new development estate getting roads, water, electrics, and the first few houses south under the Woden Valley suburbs. It should grow into a huge dormitory city, Tuggeranong Valley.

The pool was on the Murrumbidgee, and had been a swim hole for years. The "free" tag was new, or at least legally it was new. Folk had sunbaked and swum naked there for some time—but not many, because it had been unmarked and hard to find.

We left Jo for the afternoon at a friend's and drove out the Monaro Highway way past town limits, halfway to Bredbo. A new small sign on the right pointed to a dirt track heading across to the river. After kilometres of dusty rolling pasture-lands, we could see the river coming up by the trees that always grow on watercourses, here sheoaks and box. We parked among the trees and tried to find the river, but it took another half kilometre of walking to arrive at the first swimming spot. A new sign read, "This is a clothed area. Free beach 500 m. north." Metres. Yards. The schoolkids were starting to learn the new metric system.

No-one was here today. It was hot, early summer hot. Our resolve to see had melted, and see is all we were planning. Being naked wasn't going to happen. We swam for ten minutes, sat and ate the fruit we had brought, and retraced our steps.

So, those morals we absorb as youngsters still resist change. We could pretend, just do it, be like everyone else.

Starting to hang around the Uni here, I considered doing a second degree. I had allowed myself to join a research group, a specimen team for some students preparing their thesis. It paid a few dollars for the Saturday morning.

"We need you to be completely honest in answering these questions. Be assured it is all anonymous."

OK. My heart pounded as I answered pages of probing questions. My eyes shot fire. Truth they wanted.

We shared a light lunch after the tests, while the study team assembled the results. They gathered us again to reveal what they had been testing for, because they hadn't told us that beforehand.

They were going to present their "findings", a hasty pop version for us, not the considered report they would later submit to their superiors.

I spotted the report footnotes. "11 subjects." But there had been twelve of us.

It won't happen again.

Autumn

Rose had come home from work yesterday with a small bag of blackberries. One of her colleagues at the Medical Research School had picked a bucketful and was sharing them around. They had been growing wild out past Cotter in several places by the roadside. Growing wild?

"A trip to the Cotter?"

                                        Down to Earth

The Brindabella Ranges run north-south to the west of Canberra. They extend down to meet the Snowy Mountains and the Australian Alps. Australia's ski areas are in the Snowys, but even the lower Brindabellas are snow-topped most winters, and the glimpses of snow in the west give Canberra part of its wintertime charm.

The complex pattern of the Brindabella Ranges, the Tinderrys out coastward, and especially the even greater enfoldings in the Snowy high country proper, together create a river and creek map that looks crazy. But without the ranges then the rivers would not be there at all. The rivers feed from the high country, and much of the water is snow melt.

Canberra is a junction area where several of those waterways finally merge.

The winner was the Murrumbidgee, with two major river junctions west and north-west of Canberra. The 'Bidgee, rightly called one of the country's "mighty" rivers, springs from high in the Snowys, and rather falsely starts to the south. It backtracks via Bredbo before it can come north past Canberra. It still has more than a thousand kilometers to go before it will pass back down through Wagga Wagga, across the irrigation lands and the Hay Plains, and join the Murray near the State corners of New South Wales, Victoria and South Australia.

The Molonglo should have been the baby of the big four rivers around Canberra. It starts in the Tinderry Ranges to the far south-east, services the nearly derelict old copper and gold town of Captains Flat, and winds past Queanbeyan. At Queanbeyan, it meets its Tinderrys twin the Queanbeyan River, and steals its inheritance. The Molonglo creeps over the border into the bottom of Canberra, and supplies a fine water-ski scene. Then at the heart of town, it fills the lake that is the modern feature of landscaped Canberra. The Molonglo picks up its last job as a water resource for the sewerage farm shortly before it finds the Murrumbidgee at Uriarra, a few kilometres north of "Cotter".

The Cotter River itself is the least tortured of the rivers. It comes more directly from the south and turns eastwards near its end, looking for its mates. It starts at five thousand feet not far from the Murrumbidgee headwaters, but it arrives here the direct route. The river is dammed three times along its way, and that supplies Canberra with generous water. The bottom dam, the oldest and the tiniest of them, is the Cotter Dam itself. So now we arrive at a valley of great beauty and some magic, "The Cotter".

Or, to us locals, simply "Cotter".

Cotter means Cotter River, or perhaps it means Cotter Dam. But "The Cotter" is a whole area, Canberra's playground nature park, some seventeen kilometres due west from the city centre. Of the several river playgrounds, The Cotter is the largest and unabashedly the favourite.

———

We loaded the little old Morris with an extension ladder and some folded cardboard boxes, tied to the roof rails that once were the ski racks. We didn't see a lot of Arty these days, no skiing, no skis. But the racks still did assorted domestic chores like today.

Gerri, Rose and I were all dressed in overalls, old tops, hat and garden gloves, and we were sallying forth, young Jo too, to do blackberry battle. Well, we brought all those coverings with us, but to don later, because it was a warm Canberra day. It might even rain, storm rain?

Rose drove out past the edges of town on the Cotter Road, where the extensive pine forest plantations started.

"Gerri, I don't believe I ever told you how I drove through the bottom of the rainbow?" I said.

No.

"I was driving from Cotter back home one day. It was on this road about here."

                    Down to Earth

"Some rain was about, pocket showers, but the sun was still shining. I could see a rainbow up ahead of me, and it was the smallest rainbow I ever saw. I worked out it was shining in the leading face of the falling rain. It was as if the rainbow projected into a screen across the road in front. The magical part was when I caught up with the wall of rain, and I drove clean through the end of the projected rainbow."

"Should I believe that?" asked Gerri. "Where is the booty?"

"He's still looking." Rose laughed.

'Heaven's Gift to Me' was playing softly on the radio, "*You are so beautiful to me.*" Joe Cocker again.

We were heading out past the Mount Stromlo Observatory with its dome trying to hide in the pines. Canberra was proud of Stromlo, and to work there was a medal on your chest. Unplanned, Rose turned right up the Stromlo Road to give Gerri a tourist's look.

It was steep, and twisted, and we needed to climb about five hundred feet in the three kilometres. The water treatment plant for all Canberra was partway up the Stromlo Road. I knew it well, as I had installed some control functions there. Someone smarter than me had calculated that this waterworks needed to be perched on the slopes of Mount Stromlo.

I couldn't offer to take my party in. I no longer worked there, and tourist activity wasn't encouraged. Well, someone might throw LSD straight into those open mixing tanks.

We stopped at the top and had a quick look around from near the dome telescope that makes Stromlo famous. Even through the pines, we enjoyed commanding views to the south towards the Snowy Mountains, and west to the Brindabellas. The breeze was a bit crisper than it had been in town.

Down from Stromlo, we continued to the Cotter. Canberra is two thousand feet above sea, on the Southern Tablelands. The Cotter valley is four hundred feet lower than

Canberra, and we were now descending that four hundred. It was rolling terrain, mixed pasture-land and trees. To the right of the road ran two water pipes, each about thirty inches across. So that supplies water for a whole city? One pipeline vanished, striking back to Bendora Dam far up the river over further hills. One stayed with us going down the Cotter.

"What's that?" asked Gerri. *Camp Cottermouth*. The sign was on our left.

Rose replied, "Cottermouth is for kids. A Scouts' camp. They have residential groups out here, and do training and outdoor activities. The Cotter and the Murrumbidgee are close, so that offers a variety of adventure trips. The place has enviable views. It's near the city yet it's not in the city, so it is a good place to run workshops. I spent a weekend here on one last year, while Brian looked after Jo. The bunkhouse was acceptable, the food was generous. We had a successful group."

She turned right into Casuarina Sands, and we were in a car park under trees, the Murrumbidgee beside us. We stepped out and walked to the water. "This is our beach," said Rose. "The Murrumbidgee, clean flowing water, swimming areas, some sand, and some rocks in the water. On a warm sunny day, this beach fills with families. They come to swim, to picnic, to barbecue, to sit and watch under the Casuarina sheoaks. Come on, take off your shoes and paddle with me."

Then we drove on. On the left was the old pump building.

"I suppose you know what's in there, too?" said Gerri, to me.

"I do. I have never done any work there, but I have had a look around, engineer to engineer. The pump-house has two ageing electric driven water pumps. The old fellow doesn't need to start them often, because the Cotter Dam is too low and isn't used for our water any longer. He greases

                                    Down to Earth

and cleans up in the old-fashioned way, carrying his rags, looking after his darlings. He told me they'll replace them in the future, with a complete new pump station probably. It's not a future he's looking forward to."

We stopped and waited at a traffic light. The bridge over the Murrumbidgee was single lane, and was on a blind corner.

On a saddle was the intersection with Uriarra Road, which would follow the Murrumbidgee north to the Uriarra Crossing recreation area and the Molonglo River junction. Uriarra, the name kept popping up. "Urayarra", uray arra, the old tribal feasts on the swarms of seasonal Bogong Moth, cooked in the stones and nourishing.

It was Cotter park we headed to now, and our road fell steeply again, and we descended to the Cotter proper.

There were large grassed picnic areas to the left, and over the bridge and rightwards was a broad avenue of magnificent deciduous trees. The Dam was up there, but Rose drove straight through and upwards. *Paddys River Road, Tidbinbilla.*

Up through the twists, some of the embankments were losing rocks. We climbed into forest land, a patchwork of eucalypt and pine. On the left was a very old slab hut.

Countless gravel tracks led off into the forests, but our advised target was on the main road six or eight kilometres further. There we found the blackberry briars massed from the track off into a large gully. Yes, we could see the little black devils in their thousands.

I unroped our load and assigned each of us a folded cardboard carton for a shield against the thorns. The opened ladder I threw out onto the top of the briars.

———

Generous pots of stewed blackberries had made for plenty of berry pie.

Fed, tired, Gerri and I lay now naked on the lounge.

"It's so good to have you back, Sheriko," I said. It wasn't often I used her real name. Most people didn't know it. "It's been a long time."

Rose had gone to bed early, after the blackberry day out. I stayed up talking with Gerri. We were always chatting.

It was talking that got everything started in Melbourne some years ago. Gerri had met Paul and wedded impatiently, and they lived across town because that was where Paul's work was. Still as undergraduates, Rose and I had married and moved to a small flat in Brunswick near the campus. The four of us nevertheless remained inseparable.

We considered many new ideas those times. I suppose it was I who was pushing the discussions along more than the others; sexuality and relating was a quickly opening new territory. But it was Gerri who had called our bluff.

"We've talked open marriage, community living and new versions of intimacy and radical sexual ideas many times over with ourselves and our friends. We have been reading Watts and Rimmer and even *OZ* magazine for ages, and now O'Neill. I think it's about time we started doing some things," Gerri had said back then. We were at their house.

She was right. The other three of us had sat there stunned.

"How about for tonight we swap partners. I don't believe any of us has real moral scruples about where we have been heading. We're too timid to follow our convictions."

I'd looked across at Rose. "OK," I said, "I'll make a move."

After some hesitant negotiation, the other two had decided they too were willing to spend their night together. This was consistent enough with whatever we'd been working towards. It had been several years post "flower power" then, and we all had been married for only a few months. We may not have been brave and out front, we weren't the Sydney Push, but we were still pioneering a new ethic.

We were barely more than kids. To create our communal household was beyond our skills. We didn't know how to be communicative and clear enough to negotiate our way through to the lifestyle we imagined. There were no models. Rose and I moved to Canberra for work reasons, but we were still all changed for the rest of our lives.

Rose and Paul never quite made it work for them. Yet they accepted that Gerri and I had continued to sleep together on some occasions we met up. It wasn't any wild love affair; our long-distance relationship became simply part of our landscape.

That was all until a year back. I had decided to put on hold the sleeping with Gerri. I became suspicious that Rose hadn't been OK with me and Gerri for the several years. Did she tell me that? No, she denied it. I was becoming not convinced, something wasn't as transparent as it should be, and I'd made my own decision.

Tonight, Gerri had been uneasy Rose mightn't be comfortable if we had sex once again. We'd all moved on, I said. Rose had had her own liaison with Arty some time back to get her head and heart around.

I felt any statute of limitations had expired regarding the Albury debacle. We'd met there for a weekend early last year. The agreement, a simple one negotiated at the moment, was for Gerri and me to have our own space for an hour, and then we would return and spend the night with our partners.

But we two stayed in bed, slept, and didn't come back until morning. The mood was cool that day: it wasn't the sex; it was the broken agreement, the long night, that had been the sin.

Gerri's skin was always so different from Rose's, soft yet taut, like a well Dubbined leather, that was ever a delight to me. The little candles we'd placed on the floor were now flickering and threatening to die, so I rose and turned on a table lamp to take their place. On the carpet beside Gerri I sat and faced the light.

"I've enjoyed our bond down the years," I said softly. "I have this feeling that in some form we'll always have it."

"We have so much in common, you and I," she said. "Your monastery years and my time with the Nuns, they are hard to explain to someone else. We had experiences that don't have any parallel for most folks. The last few years we've shared some intense moments, very precious ones."

"I suppose we'll both keep changing over time," I said, "but I'm sure that connection will still be there."

I turned back to her. She looked at me. "Brian, I don't know the answer to that. That's too far to see." Her eyes clouded.

I showered and slept with Rose. We had nothing to hide, and Rose was unperturbed next morning.

I no longer worried about Rose's bouts of suicidal gloom. Those days were gone, I hoped. I'd never fully talked with Gerri about that area; it was too dark, too deep. That stemmed right back to our student years. It's bewildering what inner turmoil we can shield from even our friends and our lovers. Behind every front door at every house in the street is an unexpected and unshared saga of the human existence.

Rose had been through plenty of the tough in our first few years. I liked to believe I made a difference.

For now, life was onwards. Jo was two now, and Rose had become adapted to that enough, the childbearing and motherhood. She didn't find it easy. She was resuming a few of her studies. We were working that out somehow.

I hoped.

———

As Christmas or Easter money, Dad had often used the back yard to raise twenty or so chickens from day-olds bought at Victoria Market. A few of the pullets we might keep to become layers, but we fattened all the roosters, and

Down to Earth

dressed and sold them. It was quite difficult to buy a chicken at the butcher's then, and supermarkets did not yet exist.

I was the head chopper—the left hand held them upside down with neck on the block, the right hand wielded the axe in one clean cut. Mum plucked the feathers and cleaned the birds for selling. We had a reputation as the chook people, and twenty sold meant an extra twenty guineas for the family.

I was the drowner for the regular unwanted kitten litters, too. Sugar bag tied at the top, washing trough full of water, a few underwater struggles. It wasn't hard.

We were all out one day, and we returned to find our current pet kitten had been killed under a falling car wheel. Dad had left the wheel leaning on the wall. A pool of cold blood had spread on the concrete floor, and it was me who found it. I sobbed inconsolably; I can suppose any child would have. I had not known I'd been so fond of the thing.

Rose – Commune: Canberra

Winter

It's a clear, cool Friday in June. I've left Jo at home with Brian. By a little after four o'clock, we are heading south from Canberra for Jerangle, deep in the Tinderry Ranges.

Damn, I've landed myself in the wrong car.

Sam and I are in our tutor Stuart's Austin 1800, with his surprise partner Mike. Four more of my study mates are in Georgia's Falcon wagon following. We have all brought sleeping packs and food meant for sharing, so the cars are quite loaded.

Two cars more are to come early tomorrow, and they have their detailed sketch map. Stuart says his shack is hard to find on its mountain track.

I try to steal a glance at Georgia in the car behind. She's not looking. Two hours, at least.

Two routes can reach Jerangle, one driving straight down the valley of the Monaro Highway to the little town of Bredbo, and turning in left to the Tinderrys; the other going through Captains Flat and south from there through the hills most of the way. The easiest and fastest is the highway route, but this weekend is for adventure, not boredom.

Within an hour we are passing through Captains Flat. That prick Stuart is enjoying a role of guide. Captains Flat is Australia's forgotten big mine, he starts. This was under the sea 400 million years ago, and continental plates were colliding here, one sliding beneath the other, and producing furious heat and acid lavas that bubbled out and solidified at the ocean floor. It was heavy with sulphides and many metals, and it became covered with sea sediments for aeons, and was then thrust into mountain ranges. We have a very old history around here.

For a young lecturer, Stuart is irritatingly proprietorial. "Blondie", he calls me. I was born dark red, but bottles do wonders.

But when was it mined? Sam asks. It sure looks quiet now, as we drive through. Appallingly run down, even derelict.

There were settlers around here from the 1830s. They discovered a little gold in the 1860s, but it was the '80s when they opened a reef of metals for mining. The ridge we have just climbed over, still out there on our right, was the main ore body. We drove over a lot of gold.

Can we go back and look for more?

Ah, it was the gold they wanted back then, too, but the gold was mixed with so much copper and silver and lead that it was fearfully hard to extract. Many companies tried for the gold and went bust before they concentrated on the copper and silver content, and then made a fortune. So much sulphur came from the smelting that no forest remained for many miles around here. It was a wild, brutal mining town in the late 1800s, and then by 1900 the mines crashed and the Flat was almost a ghost place. So it was over in a flash.

We are coming to the end of this boom and ghost town. That's Rachael's cottage hidden down there.

However, in the 1940s and 1950s, the mines opened again, the town thrived, and they made a dam on the Molonglo. Several thousand lived here, building many fibro houses. Then the ore ran out, and it all crashed once again about fifteen years ago. It's still dead. The one part still active is the mine tailings that leach nasty chemicals into the Molonglo and worry the heck out of prissy Canberra further along the river.

I speak up. I've never heard a convincing answer. So why is it called "Captains Flat"?

Mike replies. We haven't heard from him past the introductions. Mike doesn't have the jovial and boisterous teacher character of Stuart. Several old lakebeds in this region are called flats. If Lake George had no water—and sometimes it does have little—it might have been George Flat or similar. Perhaps the level area of the township we were passing through was the flat. But the Captain part of the name, we don't quite know about that either. Most think Captain was the name of a famous old white bull that was on a property here in the early days.

We are on gravel road by now, winding and forested. The daylight isn't going to last much longer. This is starting to feel it is creepy country, still holding a secret or two. How is Georgia's crowd travelling? They have missed Stuart's myths of Captains Flat. That man might be bearable. For a moment I miss Brian.

Dark is falling when we stop at the Strike-a-Light Pub and store in Jerangle to collect some last supplies for the weekend, and his mail. Jerangle has little else bar a small school. No-one else steps out into the crisp air.

Our convoy of two turns sharply right up the Sandy Flat Road and winds along through some cleared land and some dense bushland, climbing ever higher. Four thousand feet. He hasn't even been asked. Twice the height of Canberra. I hope you brought warm bedding. He takes a sidetrack where a shack is visible ahead in the trees.

This is winter, and this is high ground. I'd been warned, but now perhaps I haven't brought enough. Enough for how many?

                          Down to Earth

However, we'll soon have the fire going. We can be snug all night.

Hmm.

The woodpile has been stacked ready, so lighting the slow combustion heater is my quick task. Then as the smoke clears and the shack warms slowly, our Stuart orchestrates an impromptu meal. We pool our food contributions and make the obvious decision on the first night's menu—a large stew pot and bread rolls. There are enough pots and utensils ready.

It is clear that Stuart ("here in the ranges I'm Stu") has played this game before and is enjoying it. Edgy bastard again.

Under the battery-powered light of the two lamps, Mike plays an old ukulele, and I watch the eye-sparks that shoot between Stu and Mike all evening, Georgia feeding on their energy like an unwanted leach.

No-one rises early. Too much music, a little much beer. And it started savagely cold out there. Bodies lay spread on sofa, chair, floor, up in the shack's loft, anywhere available. All visitors slept single. Would tonight be different? Does she even know?

The middle of the day is a walk through the mountain bush, and then a search for firewood, which we pile ready for later. Georgia throws a smile while we stack. My nipples answer. When Georgie?

It is Saturday night that the ghosts really rattle. Nell and Hugo, from further along the Sandy Flat Road, are joining us for dinner. Stu introduces them. My newest neighbours. They're setting up a mountain nursery, and hope to have saleable seedlings ready by late spring.

Stu and Mike have contributed a large beef roast, and the wood-fired oven is being tested to capacity feeding our group of now past a dozen. I chat with Nell while dinner cooks. If you are new neighbours, where are you from? Why move to here? It's so isolated.

And a bit creepy.

Well, Hu and I love the hills, and we adore the forests. Both of us come from families on the land further south, and we cry when we see the destruction and damage condoned as progress. How can we make a difference? We want to be in the high country.

But it's so cold here for much of the year, says Sam.

Yes, but are you cold now?

No, not right now, but ...

No, and we can arrange ourselves to keep warm most of the time, just as Mike and Stu do.

But you keep warm by burning wood and polluting the atmosphere?

I know, I know. We're doing as much as we can manage for now. We would prefer to move to Queensland to be warmer, and to do our nursery and preservation work there.

And ...?

And Queensland politics is still "Joh" politics. It's too redneck for me at least. I think Hugo would go. We might move one day, but for the moment, we're building our plant business here in the high country, finding and preserving the plant species in danger of becoming extinct. We fell too much of our forest as timber, and we replace it with pine forests for yet more timber, but of only one type. Native species are being lost, and we want to fight that.

So I suppose you don't support the Eden wood-chipping either?

Good heavens, no, calls Nell, wide-eyed. We have both been in newspaper photos holding protest placards down at Eden. Blondie, it's a crime what's happening. We're selling our birthright.

Damn. That's the only name she knows me by. People read things in a name.

But—mulled wine, warm fire, full bellies, singing—we are a mellow group when the Hu and Stu team begin working us. I can see it so plainly now.

We have to get home not too late tonight, leads out Hugo, addressing no-one and everyone.

And Stu knows his line. You still have the traps set?

Yes, although we haven't seen any damage in the last month. Just one print in the mud that could be something. Don't know.

The conversation lapses. Mike plucks a few desultory bars on the uke, thinking through his fingers, trying a tune but letting it fade. We sit enjoying the cosy warmth inside from the winter crispness. The breeze has slowed outside; the turbine generator has gone silent.

Georgia stirs. What are you wanting to trap? Is anything out here in the winter? She looks around for support, and I catch her attention for a moment. She won't hold it.

Aah, no-one's sure what we're looking for.

Hu's explanation is explaining nothing.

Well, I think we are sure, Stu is saying quietly. But no-one wants to say it out loud.

Sam joins. What is it you can't say aloud? This is a bit silly.

Stuart draws in a deep slow breath. It's a long story, and it has a long murky history. It's a Tinderry hill country legend from the blackfella and settler days, and the blacks died out many years back. I grew up in the Tinderrys, but Hu here is still learning some of our secrets, and he's nervous. Us old people, we know what we know, and we don't get too fussed by it all. Sorry, we should forget it.

The pan of Gluhwein is getting hot on top of the heater, and Stu steps over, adds another bottle of red, and throws in a stick of cinnamon. He tastes it, smiles and gestures. Who wants another mug?

Stu, why should anyone be nervous? What are you hiding? I think my puzzlement is leaking.

He pauses a moment, and then continues. The Tinderry Ranges are steep, and many places are inaccessible. There's been no-one ever into the difficult spots in these ranges. The cliffs are rocky, the trees are tall, the under-growth is impenetrable. You saw some wild bush this afternoon.

We had.

The Aboriginal people were always nervous in these mountains. Their mythology had stories of a large man who lived in the forest, far taller and heavier than any of them-selves, and covered in reddish hair. He was rarely seen, and many black people had never seen him at all. But they all believed he existed, and they were afraid of him.

He would eat the same kangaroos as the blacks hunted. He wasn't simply bad luck or a fright to see, he was also known to sometimes stalk and capture humans. Women and children were especially at risk. Their bodies would be found deep in a gully later, partly eaten.

Georgia baulks. No, you're pulling our legs.

Georgia. Shivers of confusion through me, a blush I hope no-one notices. It is like at tutorials on campus, and she knows. She knows. But we never mention it. Some matters are too tricky, too lost deep down, to know how to confront. Why don't we talk?

Georgia, we don't talk about it ... *Oh, this is someone else's argument* ... because people don't want to accept it. That's OK, because we too would prefer it all went away. If no-one knows the story, and no-one hears from this hairy animal, then we can all forget it. It was a silly myth the Aboriginals had, for their own reasons. We don't want to be known as the stupid whites who took the myth of the blacks, believed it and perpetuated it, when it was all wrong in the first place.

So stop telling the story.

                                        Down to Earth

I don't tell the story. Well, normally I don't. Tonight it just popped out. Blame the wine. But you see, there is one problem.

What? Georgia looks scornful. White women having large red-haired babies?

No, don't scoff. We have some mysterious happenings here in the ranges—things that don't have a sensible explanation.

What things?

Footprints, for one. Sometimes we find human prints that are too big to be human. Occasionally someone sees a tall figure escaping into the darker gullies, clearly avoiding contact.

Have you seen this animal?

Me? Perhaps. I did see something skulking in the bush, and it was something too large to be a normal human. But it fled too quickly. I keep asking myself, playing it again, recalling what I did see. Hu has had several footprints around his property. He set a trap last year.

What, he'd trap it? Like a huge rabbit trap? Would you kill it, Hugo?

No, I'm not trying to kill it. I want to catch it alive. I want to capture the beast and hold it alive.

So you don't have any captives yet?

Nearly.

Nearly?

Something triggered the trap last summer on a dark night. We didn't catch any animal, but there were tufts of red fur stuck in the sides of the snare. I don't have any doubt a heavy upright animal is out there in these ranges.

... and Stuart retires to the loft with Georgia. She catches my eye just as she disappears. What the fuck does that look mean?

Mike goes on. I'm not the only one knows there are strange beasts here. But as Stu says, we don't normally talk about it. Other folk embarrass us over how we think. But we know we're right.

Well, I don't believe it.

I get up abruptly to refill my mug.

———

Spring

Canberra boasts a generous number of shared households. We are a small city, so it has a higher portion of fringe dwellings than a "real" capital. And it's no surprise the ACT has many collective semi-rural houses. We all accept it is hippie heaven. But we have only the one genuine commune, the Other Canberra libertarians on the Pialligo orchard.

They bought the apple farm as a running commercial enterprise. That whole road is nurseries and orchards, and it's only a few kilometres from the centre of town.

So I wouldn't be far away.

As all good communes should, the Pialligo mob hold their periodic meetings to share personal issues, solve disagreements, and settle practical affairs, household and business. Well, that's the theory. In real life, it gets erratic and bumpy.

I am the visitor, so I sit to one side.

So have we finished with the issue of whether we can try yet for our first clean year without pesticide?

No, and we've had this out a dozen times. We can't be running the apples with no insect control. It doesn't matter a hoot if we call ourselves "organic" or anything else. It's against the law to sell apples grown without a correct regime against codling moth and other pests. In fact, it's law that we must use pesticide even if we exist nearby another commercial orchard but sell nothing ourselves.

I think the law's wrong. We have to lobby and get it changed.

Yes, well maybe. For now, we have to comply. As I said, we have considered this before. Talking about it in this room does not solve anything.

I think we ignore the law.

No, I can't agree. We may need to change the system, but we can't simply flout it. We may want our principles, but we need this farm to make us substantial money. Collectively we have a serious mortgage to service. If we can't trade, or we go to jail or pay lots of fines, we're stuffed.

We call ourselves "The Other Canberra", says Leon, but I can't see how we're other to anything. We're just the same.

I'll order the stuff this week, says Jill quietly. Let's move on.

Leon shuffles. OK. I have one more item. We all know Rose has spent an occasional night over here with me recently.

I watch Jill stiffen. She's been Leon's partner for the past year.

Well, Rose and I would like to announce that she will stay with me for the next month or two. Her daughter Jo will be here too.

I haven't spoken, and I'm not speaking now. Well, yes, Leon and I had been discussing I would move in for a while. But it wasn't supposed to come out like this. *Oh, shit. I'm so sorry Jill. I guess it's settled then. I'll need to sort it out with Brian, too.*

Why is love hard?

Leon – Canberra

Leon and the others waited in the lobby. They were a motley lot, and a spectacle as Parliament House had never seen. Sherry from the Cooperative School in O'Connor. A fellow that Jim Cairns had asked up from Melbourne, a care worker from some New Age centre there. Community Radio 2XX hotshot Evonne. Nev Yeomans, who ran the Paddington markets. A couple of others Leon didn't know, and three from Leon's "Other Canberra" commune. And Brian. Jeans and colours, but no tie or formality.

Three days ago, an aide of Jim Cairns, and Leon had forgotten her name, had called him as the (unwilling) leader of the Other Canberra group. Jim had an idea of a "liberation" gathering of some kind, and was looking for a sympathetic local group who might lend logistical support. Over the few days, that had escalated to today's meeting. The phone calls this week were the only times Leon had spoken with Cairns. He had never met the man.

Assistant Junie Morosi, no stranger to controversy, arrived to usher the ten visitors into Caucus Room 2, and MP Jim Cairns spelled out his proposal.

"I believe we live in an acquisitive, alienated, industrial society that now poses a threat to our survival. We don't create our own identities, others make them. I am concerned with the search for the true nature of the human person."

Boilerplate polemic, thought Leon, but OK.

"By now, you are all aware I have been thinking about a festival gathering of many people interested in alternatives to the normal way of living in our Western culture. We are all repressed, we are all crushed by the conventions we live under.

"I know there are in Australia a great many people who are in their own ways trying to contest that repression. It's time we gathered all these people together, so we can learn to overthrow the old society, become liberated and live as free humans in the way we deserve. We need a new society."

We have our own Jean-Paul Sartre?

"I want to lead a revolution, a transformation from below. I have worked for many years as a politician in this country to bring a new order from above. I dream of freedom from war, of sexual sovereignty, of control of our own lives. We do not have that control now, but we should. I find this is impossible to achieve using the channels of politics and government. Politics and government seem always to reinforce the personal repression in our lives."

Right words, so far.

"The police raids in Cedar Bay this morning are how our culture crushes any freedoms.

"Many of you are at the forefront of your own revolution. Each in your own area, you are in a struggle for new ways, for personal autonomy. Collectively, among the many alternative lifestyle groups in Australia, you have a wealth of experience and hope that I want to reach out to. So it's time to look for personal liberation from a new quarter.

"I want all the counterculture groups to meet, under one arching umbrella. Together we will celebrate our commonality in a national conference, a festival. That's never been done in this country. We can find a unity in what we want, and we can become the seed of the new revolution, revolution from below."

Hmm?

"Last week I met with a group in Sydney and canvassed my thoughts on a gathering. It was at the Paddington counselling and drop-in centre. They also run the Saturday markets in the village square. I have asked Neville Yeomans from Paddington to join us here now."

Jim glanced towards Junie. "We knew of the Paddington centre, because they're very visible among the alternative scene in Sydney. They sponsor activities that cover a wide group of people, the poor, the inner-city folk, the gay community, the urban alternates, the artists, the activists. All those people come through their doors. Paddington seemed a good place to first raise my plans."

Neville took up. "Jim met with us in Paddington last week. He laid out his proposal to us. The festival idea excites us. We have seen events akin to this in Australia before, but not so big and ambitious. I'm not sure Jim was aware enough of our heritage of earlier happenings, like Watsons Bay in '68 and the two Aquarius.

"But when we began to imagine a location for Jim's gathering, we felt it should be somewhere between the biggest population centres. That points to either near the Murray or near Canberra."

"In Paddington," said Jim, "we have access to many different groups and movements. So I should continue to have planning meetings there. But I have decided to hold the new national conference-festival near Canberra. This meeting today is to enlist Canberra support for finding and preparing a suitable place."

Leon had been frowning. "Jim, do you think considering a venue for a big event might be premature? We've yet to consider what this experience is to be, what it is to mean. We've barely heard of the festival. What is its purpose, and is it feasible at all? Do we have some aim we agree on, and if we do, is this festival even a fitting way to be achieving our needs? Only after all that should we be seeking just where it should be."

                                        Down to Earth

"Leon, you are my friend. I invited you here as a friend. You and your colleagues are here because I learned we share many attitudes to the nature of man and human freedoms. I am inviting you to take part in a grand festival with me."

Leon did not reply.

"My name is Patrick," said the Victorian. "I am coordinator of the Well-Being Centre in Fitzroy. I am here to represent Melbourne as best I can at this early stage. It's a tall ask, because only a small few in Victoria so far have any idea of Jim's festival proposal. The plan sounds marvellous, I have to say, and I think we should keep an open mind. We should be encouraging the vision Jim is proposing." The others were nodding.

— Intermission —

*That's how it began. No-one else remembers
back to then. Indeed several are dead, so his
narrative so far can stay uncontested.*

*But then, who might care? The adventure, the
vision, the disputed accounts, the differings,
were still to come. Still many pages on.*

Brian – ConFest: Cotter

Summer

Eight days before the event, I drove out to the Cotter.

At the several general planning meetings among the Canberra folk, the conference-festival proposition had exploded into enthusiasm and high expectation. Cotter River had emerged as favourite site, but it had taken Jim some extended negotiations to win the approvals to use public space like this.

We had adopted the moniker "Down to Earth" that someone had noticed being used by a similar Canadian group. Rose and I both joined in the meetings. We knew Jim had gatherings in the other States as well. Something big was happening, and we intended to be swept along with it.

The only voice of hesitation we knew was Leon's.

I'd been to another of the discussions at Jim's parliamentary office. A rather feral group we were, inside Parliament House. Jim had unchecked mailing capacity from his office, and his message and invitation went from there to hundreds of people across the country.

It was clear there would be considerable setup work needed at Cotter before the start day of the "ConFest", as we called it. Word had filtered out from Jim that the National Capital Development Commission (the Canberra equivalent of both State and Local Government) was giving us site access ten days early. They were also providing increased toilet huts around the whole area, and would do a municipal collection service on those.

So here I was now, reporting to the Cotter. I guessed I was volunteering.

Across the open space past the Cotter Bridge were piles of galvanised steel tubes, arranged into rough stacks, and stacks again of folded coloured vinyl fabric. Several figures were moving among the heaps, looking, checking, talking, and pointing to different grassed spots nearby.

These people were not Canberra suits; the flared multi-coloured trousers, the ponytails, the headbands, the thonging and bracelets were not Canberra wear, at least not in this quantity. Whatever trucks had delivered all this material had gone, and the team left was planning the construction. "Three geodesic domes."

"Geodesic?"

"It's a sphere made out of simple triangles," she said. Sweet. A bit smug, I thought, explaining once again to the dumb bloke. "We'll assemble the steel rods tomorrow, and you'll see every shape is a triangle, which has great strength.

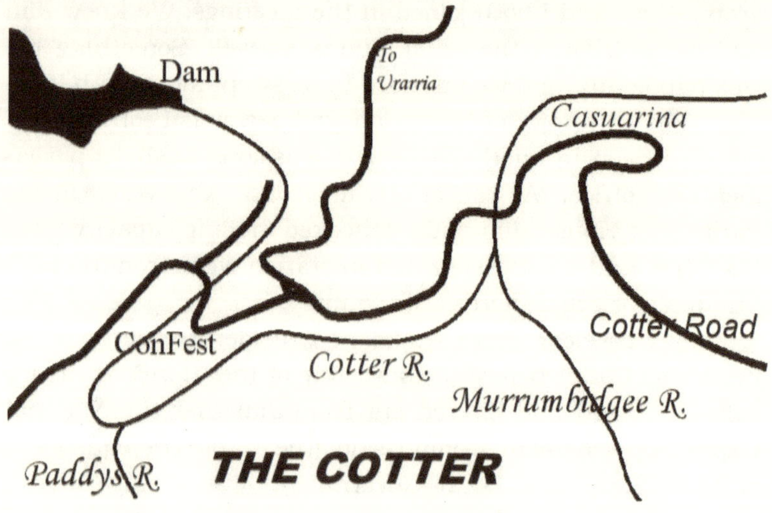

Down to Earth

Each rod is a tube with flattened ends and a hole through the flats."

"The vinyl goes over?"

"No, the vinyl is under the frame, hooked out to the triangle points."

"OK, I guess I'll see it all tomorrow. Will you need any more hands? I'm Brian."

"Thanks. My name is Flora. We can certainly do with hands to hold the structure while it's unfinished. You see, the stability is locked into place only when we put the last bolt in. We have three domes to put up in the morning, in a three-way layout over there," and she pointed to the side.

The adventure was afoot.

A large shambles of a marquee tent had been erected nearby, and this was the working "office". Jim's assistant Junie and her husband David had settled themselves at a trestle table at the rear, and they were fussing over a pile of boxes and bags. I was to learn it was their space alone. What went in the boxes behind there was not public property.

Another trestle was across the open wall of the marquee, and a half-dozen assorted old folding chairs were about. Jim Cairns sat with three people I didn't know, and they had spread a large plan of the Cotter area. They were debating where to locate various facilities, what areas should be camping, meeting space, kitchens, where fencing lines should go.

The strangers had done planning like this before. I had thought this ConFest was a unique and possibly inaugural event.

Three small personal tents were nearby and a few cars. But no other people were around. I would return tomorrow with a tent and some basic supplies in case I stayed the night. Rose was working each day, but I had the freedom to be out here.

By next morning, there were about twenty people at the Cotter. All were sitting in a tight circle on the grass holding hands, and all had eyes closed, singing an "Aum" sound together. I had just missed it.

The dome erections took most of the day, and I took the weight of steel rods, rescued spanners and helped hand out bolts, always being the dumb lackey. The topmost pieces were trickiest, and we jiggled and tugged on the flexing structure until we placed the final bolt. The spherical framework now was rigid and workable.

When all three were up, and one was smaller and differently designed than the others, Flora decided to move two out a little. Twenty bodies together (and by now we had enough) were able to lift the frame and finetune the positioning.

The precise alignment of the three domes held a spiritual importance to the team, and until Flora was satisfied the job wasn't over.

The domes were to be the focus of all the important activities at the festival. A large flat grass gathering area was nearby, but the domes themselves were to be the principal workshop and meeting places.

The vinyl covers were to be hoisted tomorrow. That would be a much quicker job, she said. The dome team from Nimbin wanted to start before today was done on construction of a clay firing kiln down near the river. The clay was ready, the moulding shape was ready, the bricks were waiting, but without the kiln itself there would be no start to the medallion making, and there were many thousands of those to make and fire.

Jim Cairns walked around the domes looking happy. He, Junie and David left to return into Canberra.

Today, magically, a kitchen had appeared back up the Cotter towards the dam, among the proud avenue of poplars and close to the river. It was well away from the domes and what was shaping as the spiritual energy centre for the big event. Who had brought all the kitchen equipment? The main fire was wood-fuelled, with a huge steel grill over it, and a bench had an array of utensils and large pots. All were old from long and functional service. This was the "workers' kitchen", and rice and dhal were cooking to feed everyone on the site.

"Dhal?" A lentil-based stew, Indian style, cheap, easy, nutritious and full of flavour. I needed to learn the hippie ways. This was becoming a functional little community. It felt good. I'd stay. I wandered off to put up my old tent.

My friend Dave arrived as we were eating, and wasted no time. That man knew most of these folk. I should hang around with Dave more. Many of these people were local Canberra folk, from circles I didn't know.

The first drum came out after our meal and after the cleanup. A small campfire was alight, and we were sitting around it chatting. There was no band, no melody. There was only the slow tapping of a bongo, rhythm morphing into new rhythm, from rattling to eerie to background and back to a strong beating pulse. To some of it we tapped a foot or nodded our heads, and some of it we ignored as we talked.

A drummer with a larger instrument walked in from the half-dark and sat next to the first, and the two traded knowing glances. The bigger drum brought a bigger sound, and the two drums played a chasing game known to themselves. Our talk stopped, and we stayed listening to the tribal and undulating throb. Two women, just their waists towelled in sarongs, rose to dance on the grass by the firelight. Full moon was rising even down in this Cotter valley.

———

It was now two overnights before the start date, and the mood at Cotter was changing. Full moon had passed, and the nights started dark.

It had been a small community this week, tasks to do, problems to solve, water piping to lay, radios to source, fencing to put up. We were a village in our own right, a commune with a vision we were creating on the run. A pattern for a small and temporary city of people was being created.

Well, we presumed there would be a small city of people. We hoped they would come. How could we know? Would there be a thousand? Or three? We had only hearsay reporting from the fledgling groups interstate who were aligning under the Down to Earth theme. A few hundred from there, a thousand from elsewhere, "lots" from further. The figures were fluff, flights of hope and fancy.

The early incoming groups had by now set up their patch, their meditation spaces, their kitchens, their displays. The orange Hare Krishna people were part through building a large kitchen and eating space, as were Ananda Marga.

The *Nimbin News* team had a primitive information and news centre working. A massage space was marked, and tables were being laid out. I had never seen any proper massage before, and this was a massed array of purpose furniture.

The main areas had been set aside in the past couple of days. A map showing the theme sectors was on display at the coordinators' tent—a spiritual village, the kids care village, a craft workshops village, a healing one. They were all termed village. Was there a discipline of festivals, a manual?

But still the question hung—how many would be coming? If twenty thousand came, how blindingly wonderful! Then how would our "city" cope? If few came, our days of setup had been a game. An experience I could never forget, but ultimately a phantom.

We had a bond between us this week that had a magic I had never known. All our work and our decisions we put out in front of our community. The Morning Sharing sessions, the hugs, the shared shoulder rubs, Jim's talks on the new society, the chanting, the endless debate of all issues until we found a consensus. The work parties. The washing in the Cotter because there were no showering facilities. The kitchens, the drums.

It was a team that had built to about fifty of us, and we had learned to trust each other, to immerse ourselves in the euphoria of what was unfolding. It was the birth of a new era, a dawning of an age.

Until today.

From this afternoon the arrivals had become more frequent. The gate control wasn't in place up the hill yet, and the new groups were quickly assessing the layout of what existed, and splicing themselves in. Strangers were overrunning the intimacy we had been building. I felt an assault.

I walked back into my old shabby tent and found a notebook, and took it along the Murrumbidgee bank to where no-one could intrude on my thoughts. Light was starting to fade, but the air was still warm enough to be a comfort. Sitting on a rock in the stream, I let the clear water rush past me with its relentless hiss and splash.

It was time to surrender what I'd found. The week gone has no purpose other than to be a servant of the week to come. The past few days have completed their own inner meaning. Let them go, remember them with love and awe.

This festival, this conjoining, is for the thousands who are coming, not for the fifty who had loved it so far.

I scribbled quickly before I could no longer see the page, then I tore it out and struggled back to camp. Others found my thoughts next morning taped to a tree near the kitchen, and no-one knew who had penned them.

—

In the animated Star Trek series a couple of years ago, the characters in one episode took recreation in the "rec room", an arena of virtual reality, and they could experience adventures to a deceptively "real" degree. It bothered me. If they were born and lived there, could they ever know everything was a deception?

We see the colour blue, and feel the beauty of sky and sea. We think we understand "blue", but it is perhaps nothing more than nerve cells getting vibrated by waves of one frequency. Maybe nerve cells are only quantum vibrations themselves? Could it be we comprehend nothing?

We think we understand deeply human moods, but are they explainable more by pre-op medications and adolescent chemicals?

Is everything an illusion, even our own existence? Is nothing guaranteed to be real? Can we truly know anything?

—

                                        Down to Earth

Rose and I shared the new tent for the night. I had slipped back to town yesterday, and we had chosen it together. It was European, small but heavy-duty, double-skinned, floor included. This was a different design from what either of us had grown up with. We could stand in it, but otherwise it had a snug and protective feel. It would withstand any storm.

I had been in our old damaged upright camp tent the last week alone, but now it was time to share space. How comfortable could we be together? Together was becoming a difficult concept. Well, we would each try our best. Be civil. Be encouraging. Forget the hurting bits. Just hope.

We had slept holding hands for an hour or two. It was enough, and it was OK.

Today, the first real ConFest day, our daughter Jo would join us. Jo was staying overnight with a friend, who would be arriving later.

"I've been up early before you woke," Rose said. "They've issued a program sheet. I don't know where they're printing it, but it must have been here on-site."

"Oh great," I replied. I could hear a throbbing noise in the distance. The drumming music that had gone on well into the dark of night was starting again. It was barely past sunrise. "So let's see it."

"There's to be a ConFest full gathering at nine, called the 'Morning Sharing'. Outside the coordination tent."

I interrupted: "Morning Sharing is what we have been doing each day the past week."

Rose carried on. "Then at ten thirty, Jim Cairns is holding his own general gathering down near the domes. It's the 'Spirit of ConFest'."

"All good if you have a watch! I haven't worn one for several years," I said. "Wow, look at all these events programmed for today. The massage tent will be in service from midday. A body painting workshop at five. 'Meditation for Beginners'. A grassroots activism discussion. 'Drumming the African Way'. It's going to be a busy day."

"And hot. Do we have any sun cream?"

"Yes, I brought the jar from home. It's in here."

"Look, on the back is a map," said Rose. "Let's see. Front gate at the top of the hill. River. Camping areas. Main amphitheatre. Volunteer tent, coordination table, first aid. Hare Krishna kitchen. Over here are tents for Ananda Marga and Findhorn."

"Who are Findhorn?"

"I know them. Leon and the others at Pialligo referred to them a lot while I was staying there. They're a spiritual community in Britain that have been growing for the last ten years or so."

"Hmm, more religious stuff?"

"No, not really. They don't have any formal religious beliefs. It's a large communal group interested in spiritual and ecological themes of all sorts. They live in the Scottish village of Findhorn. They hold many conferences and events and workshops there that attract people from all over the world. In a generic sense, they believe they are learning how to apply spiritual values into practical human life. Learning to use channelling and meditation as forces in their lives. They run their own shops, printery, conference centre, and a self-sufficient garden that is famous. It all sounds like a big permanent ConFest!"

"So I suppose you'll want to contact them and find out more?"

"Well actually," said Rose, "Leon has invited the Find-horn visitors to Pialligo after the ConFest. I might go out there at the same time, next week. I would need the tent, because it'll be a bit crowded in the old house."

"Yeah, it's our tent. OK."

We went our ways to explore the brave new world. We would look out for each other at the big talk.

                                              Down to Earth

I headed up to the gate to check how the communications radios were functioning. We were running low on batteries.

I needed to give up on keeping the rechargeable batteries supplied. There was no good place to plug them into for charging other than the coordination tent, and that was a scene of chaos and of ever-changing staff. Someone kicked out the charger overnight, and several batteries went missing, thrown out when flat, presumably. The radios themselves would go off-air, and we couldn't call them in for service.

Any communication service at all was a daring novelty.

But tech was my trade and my hobby, and I had volunteered three days ago to track down a few legitimate handheld walkie-talkies so the top gate control could call the coordination post. They'd arrived urgently from Sydney, and we tried them out yesterday. The little fleet of three radio handsets was only just up to even the tiny task we were hoping for it.

Telecom had supplied one wired telephone into the coordination tent, and one coin-phone on a pole. Jim's clout was behind that coup. So last night I managed to get a message out to Jo's babysitter in Canberra, pleading for a big supply of plain batteries. Then we could cure the battery shortage by this afternoon.

I had participated in the Wireless Institute's ham radio field-day a few months ago, where they played at operating an emergency radio network for a disaster, in case the official crisis squads failed. The sort of movie scenario where a "ham" is the lone life-saving link out of a cyclone devastated town. I was a link for that field day.

I wasn't sure how we arranged cash expenses yet, but an uneasy sense remained that problems arising, many costing real dollars, had to be solved quickly by whoever was closest. But who was there to ask? Jim and Junie? They were drowning in detail, when they could be found at all.

This was going to be a financial nightmare. Some "authority" in the coordination tent? There was no authority. No, there simply was no-one to ask.

We have to trust in the responsibility of each other. No authority should be needed. We are all mutually responsible. We trust in the process.

All it really was, was bedlam.

———

I was early for the Cairns talk. I found Rose, and we sat on the grass waiting. She put her head in my lap and I stroked her long hair, and she lay there for a while. There were no words. Dave, Miri and three-year-old Sunday sat to join us on the ground.

Clapping and some cheers greeted Jim as he walked to the front of the crowd. It wasn't the whole camp, but still there must have been more than a thousand people come to hear the great man speak. This was the moment he had his gathering of the assembled counterculture.

"My friends, this is a splendid occasion. This is the start of a grand change in our country. I've asked you to come together to explore with me how we can find greater freedom in our lives, how we can be ourselves, authentic, and how we can be the foundation of a new society."

Jim was yelling. Above the background noises of the ConFest morning, being heard at the rear of his crowd was a problem.

"It is obvious we all see something exciting happening at Cotter. There's a spirit here we have never seen in the streets of society outside. We can hear it in the music, we can smell it in the freshness of the air. We can taste it in the foods we eat and drink. We can see it shining in the eyes of everyone here. The friendliness, the sharing, the joy, the diversity we have here at Cotter today.

"You came here from various walks of life, from different phases in your life, with diverse histories of your past and diverse hopes for your future.

"But you come here with something in common, and I know that, because you are all telling me that. You are all seeking a better life, a clearer peace with yourself, a higher freedom in how you live and how your soul breathes. You have a vision of a positive society to live in. We perceive it in different lights, yet it's the same dream, that yearning that lives in every heart."

At the outskirts of the crowd, newcomers came, listened a while, then either sat or wandered away.

"Our culture oppresses us, represses us. We're afraid to be who we really are. Our culture is wrong. It needs to change. It is we here this week who can be the seed of that new society. The spirit we have here at Cotter can be the enthusiasm we use to leaven our society. Down to Earth, and that is all of us, can be the basis of a completely new community."

Rose lay down again across me, and looked at my eyes.

"This ConFest doesn't end next week. It's only a start. Our liveliness will grow and flourish after we leave here. Let's celebrate our free spirit here now. Have fun. Play. Learn. Let us find our common goals. Let's find the ways to change our own lives and the lives of all those in our community. We can be the example to the repressive society that is the norm today.

"I will be here for the whole ConFest. Please come up to me and talk with me anytime. Tomorrow, we'll meet again here, and we will talk on alternative ways our culture can work, ways that offer more freedom and love."

So this looked to be a series of Cairns talks, not just today. Would the press be here for every day, because two photographers were here now.

As we left, a cheering parade was moving past. Peter "Pedals" vanLin, one of the Nimbin identities, and involved in both the *Nimbin News* and the Nimbin cycling group, had arrived at Cotter after riding from Nimbin, a thousand kilometres. The procession was an escort of welcome.

I hadn't ridden a bike now for years. Most of my high school I cycled daily six miles each way through the Footscray and Dynon Road traffic. I didn't have to join the crowds on the bus.

We walked back to our tent to find a bite to eat. We should try something at the food market sometime, but that would cost money. Near us was a thin young woman, naked, performing a slow sequence of contorted poses and arches. "Is that a Yoga or her exercises?" I whispered to Rose.

We both watched a while in awe, awe at her flexibility, and we wondered at her gameness. "I'd call it exhibitionism," Rose whispered back eventually, as the performer's pubic hair was the topmost point of her arch.

We rummaged in our supplies and managed to make a jam sandwich, and tea on our gas camp stove. Add a banana each, and that was to be lunch for today. Then our neighbours, a couple younger than us, saw our tea, and begged for a cup of water for themselves.

"Oh, sure, I can soon make more. Do you have a cup?"

It was the hot water they wanted. Bev and Ali. They had cups and lemongrass for tea. Their food was nuts and dried fruit. Dried food was good to take away because it needed no cooling and it didn't go off. We ate an unfair portion of their nuts. Why couldn't we have been as creative?

———

By the second day, waking to the tentative throbs of distant drumming was becoming a familiar pattern.

After some cereal, Jo headed off with Rose to check out the body painting.

I walked to the domes and information area, and a new multi-headed signpost stood there today. There were arrows to the Healing Village and every other village, to the market-

                                        Down to Earth

place, to the communal kitchen (which had grown from and replaced the workers' kitchen when the ConFest started).

Outside each dome, and they were not far apart anyway, was a noticeboard divided into hours of the day. Chalked on each board were the booked activities. I studied the first one. After the Morning Sharing shortly at nine, another Jim Cairns presentation was on 'The Theory of the Alternative'. So today's Cairns talk was to be inside the dome, not outside massed on the open grass like yesterday's.

Not another Sharing. Too much hippie stuff.

A friend from town strolled past, so I made that into an opportunity to head across and yarn at the food market over a watermelon juice for an hour or so.

"Did you get to Jim Cairns's big meeting yesterday?" I asked.

"Wouldn't have missed it. I like his grand vision for what we can do. He wants us all to help form a new emerging society. We could be a society where the law of love will be the law of humanity. It's stirring stuff. You should've heard the cheering."

"Yes, I know. I was there too. He speaks so compellingly."

"Well, we've been here long enough watching the world dance by. Come with me and check out the Reich workshop."

"Jim was talking about Wilhelm Reich yesterday at his evening talk," I said. "So who is this bloke?"

"He died in a US prison a few years ago. A psychoanalyst or psychologist from Europe, one of Freud's and Carl Jung's lot. All our hang-ups and personal problems come from lack of expressing our deepest passions, he said, and particularly sex. We defend our emotions behind a body armour. We all should instead become orgasmic and emotionally released."

"Whoa, heavy stuff."

"Oh yes. He started off into Marxism as well ..."

"Like Cairns himself? I heard Jim had a business office in Moscow at one time."

"Sure, but for Reich it was the 1920s and 30s. A free society needed a sexual revolution, he reckoned, and good Marxism needed that same sexual revolution. The Russian Revolution early on abolished the family and declared total sexual liberty. Then the Bolsheviks clamped back down and became as darkly prudish as the Freudians always were. The Marxists and the Freudians both tossed Reich out. But he persisted: we need to cure sexual repression."

"You sound like Jim Cairns last night," I said.

"Of course. Jim believes in Reich. I think his relationship with Junie has introduced him to it. I've heard her talking. It's the way of unlocking our repressions."

"Well, I'm all thin bravado hiding the inhibited, neurotic man."

"Let's go. Eva Reich is Wilhelm Reich's daughter, and she's trying to keep alive her father's work."

Eva Reich spoke with a difficult European accent, though her message was strong and clear. But this wasn't to be a talk-fest today. It was a public demonstration of the Reichian therapy with a willing volunteer. It was a real therapy session.

"Can you believe this? That bloke's just lying on that padded table in front of everyone," I whispered. There were fifty or sixty people assembled to watch. "How can he stop being self-conscious and stifled?"

Then the music started. I don't know where the power came from. It started soft, but it was a heavy beat, complex and rich, and it slowly became louder.

Eva was talking with her patient, encouraging him to breathe deeply and to keep his eyes closed. She wanted him to move his limbs to the music, shaking and thumping his arms in time, and his legs.

Soon he was a wildly writhing, thrashing body, being encouraged all the while to keep breathing strongly—deep

                                        Down to Earth

breaths, fast deep breaths. The beat was loud. The breathing continued. Five minutes, ten minutes.

Then started a low moan from the table, an unearthly growl. It grew and swelled, and it erupted into the most hell-awful prolonged scream, and a convulsion that should have been a violent epileptic fit anywhere else.

"Keep breathing," called Eva. "Breathe."

For the next forty minutes, I witnessed a scene foreign, fierce and shocking. Here was a grown man, willingly placing himself into a state where he was venting pain and anger and feeling that had no limit, no stopping. Without words he screamed, with very effective words he cursed, he trembled and shook, he cried with bottomless despair.

It all subsided into a quiet meditation, and even broke into a maniacal laughter, before quietening into what looked like sleep. Eva had stopped calling to breathe more. She waited softly beside her client, until he awoke from his reverie. She served him a drink of orange, and chatted quietly with him. Perhaps it was ninety minutes from the start.

Both Eva and her client spoke with us after the therapy session. This had been a standard enough Reichian therapy event. The tools were hyperventilation, overpowering music, and body rhythm.

No, he hadn't been out of control or out of consciousness. A small portion of his awareness had still watched over him, despite that he'd felt able to go into his violent trance and confront his buried traumas. Did he know what was the meaning or story of his pain? No, not this time. That's how it is sometimes. The body remembers, but the conscious memory might remain lost. It doesn't matter. In some cases he does get insight into where his emotional blocks had come from, the primal conflicts and pains that had remained until now buried in his emotions and in his body.

Never had I seen a spectacle like this. I knew how to think all day, but the understanding came harder than the thinking, and the world of feelings was a pit of horrors.

Rose and I went to the domes to sit in on another major gathering in the afternoon. Peter Cock was to speak at length about the experiences of launching the Moora Moora community in the hills beyond Melbourne.

We had failed in the communal living. Our dreams of several years ago with Gerri and Paul had led us into adventures of our own, but it wasn't what we had envisaged.

Cock was a sociologist, and a war protester and anti-consumer enthusiast. With his wife and a group of kindred souls, they gathered into what they termed an "intentional community", first in genteel suburban Melbourne (where roomy houses could be had) and then in the mountains beyond Lilydale.

"Communes in Australia are not a new phenomenon," said Cock. "We have a rich communal history. A rural community of communalist Christians lived in Victoria in the 1850s waiting on the Second Coming, and they survived strongly for twenty-five years."

"Thousands of people live in communes today," he continued. "The range of motivations and lifestyles is wide. Many are spiritually based, and even Findhorn, who are with us here at Cotter from Scotland, have a big spiritual basis." Cock gestured to Eileen Caddy, Findhorn founder, sitting listening. "Dharmananda community from near Nimbin has a Buddhist foundation, and I understand Dudley Leighton from there will join us here tomorrow for the general forum on communal lifestyles.

"Other communes are driven more by a rejection of the consumerist and capitalist lifestyle and the nuclear family isolation. Their need is to create a compound family community where they minimise their destructive footprint on our mother earth and maximise their intimacies and their caring for one another.

"Some groups share intimately everything in their household, from communal-only cooking and eating, down to toothpaste and cars, while others may set up hamlets of separated family units who come together to share some of their life. Some communities are comfortable while some struggle at subsistence level, and that conflict can be hard to carry for a longer time.

"Our utopia shares some beliefs about personal and sexual relationships with the Kerista Commune of San Francisco, and sharing of wealth and effort, but hopefully more humanly realistic, not quite so doctrinaire as Kerista. We have our own Manifesto describing our alternative values and aims."

The blue vinyl of the dome shielded most of the sun's brightness, but the afternoon heat still beat through.

"Our Moora Moora is a hamlet style pattern. We are still manoeuvring our way through the local Council rules, and many locals think we are smelly immoral hippies poisoning their cosy rural neighbourhood. Make no mistake, we're struggling with ourselves all too often, our limits, our preconceptions of right and wrong, our differences.

"We fund ourselves as a community, we are self-sustaining. Mostly we are professionals or skilled workers, and we take pride we haven't dropped out in any sense of sponging on resources we don't earn. We continue to ply our trades proudly either inside the community or outside in the wider culture, and usually it's outside."

It was an inspiring talk, and a spirited exchange followed. Jim Cairns and Junie were in the audience, sitting with the rest of us. Leon and the Pialligo gang were there too.

I left with Rose, and we studied the timetable boards on the three domes. Today's listing was spent, but another board had started for

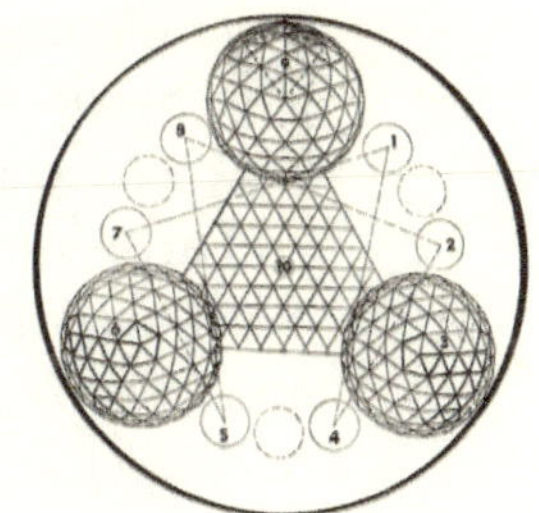

tomorrow's events. A notice attached said no more printed timetables would be issued; the noticeboards were now the main information source.

"I want to do the 'Meditation for Beginners' tomorrow. It's something I've been thinking to look into for some time now."

"Yes but it overlaps the 'Designing Sustainable Agriculture' session with Bill Mollison. Jim told me he had brought Mollison here to ConFest by invitation, so it must be significant stuff."

"With so many options, there's going to be conflict, silly. You need to make choices, set priorities. Where's your freedom?"

"Yes, you're right. Well, how about I have Jo while you do your meditation tomorrow?"

"Thanks, that was my next question."

Today was a good day.

———

I don't know who you are
Just that your name is Georgia
But it was so good to meet you
You wandered by seeking Rose
Who wasn't here
So instead we sat
And chatted on.
    For forty minutes we shared our thoughts
    We relearned our studies
    And replanned our careers
    We travelled the world's undergrounds
    Took jobs in strange places
    And argued the favour of Freud and Greer
    We shared little things
    And some large we played down as small.
Jo fell asleep in my lap
So I bid you goodbye

———

Rose and I had decided to try the marketplace for a late lunch on the third day. We were to meet near the domes.

I arrived and they weren't yet there. ConFest time was that elastic time that many tourist and third world communities boasted. I peered into one of the domes. About fifty people were inside on the grass, set into a step-forward Yoga pose. I'd never tried Yoga. It was so stylised and stressful to me, but that was an unfair judgement. Some day I should take a class.

This place was full of people exploring, trying something different, defying assumptions. Simply not the same world as back in town. Home, no-one trusts themselves to join up life's dots. The emerging picture may be too unexpected, threatening.

A lot of noise was coming from the other large dome, and I looked in on a group of high legs. The owners were lying on their backs, heads facing out from their tight circle, legs all close together, high in the air and kicking wildly. They were all laughing furiously, the noise rising and fading, and breaking out again. It was a laughter workshop. One day.

The board at the small central dome read *Mysteries of Tarot.* It wasn't the usual subject board for the dome sessions. The workshop leader must have made her own sign, because it was carefully painted in scrolled lettering and decorated with stars and flowers. A dozen were sitting inside listening to a talk by an old woman, with striking brilliant white hair so long it fell to her thighs.

Jo ran up to me dressed in a way I didn't recognise. By a moment later I realised they weren't clothes at all, and that she was body-painted in an all-over suit, trousers, jacket and tie. All she really wore were her sandals, and Rose, grinning broadly, was carrying Jo's clothes.

The largest food provider by far was the Hare Krishna collection of tents. I say a collection because the Krishna area was a sprawling mansion, an interlinked set of canvas room spaces, disappearing into depths that were not public. What was most obvious, were the large eating space, the serving counters, and the view vanishing into the cooking kitchens themselves. The Krishna complex was not far from the other marketplace sellers, but distanced a little, that way not fully integrated into the rest.

That the Hare Krishna folk were at Cotter was obvious to every ConFester. Periodically, well an hour or two before common meal times, the shaved and orange-robed devotees of the Krishna sect would snake around the whole festival campus. With drums and tambourines, they chanted loudly and in unison their fanatic Vaishnava mantra:

Hare Krishna Hare Krishna, Krishna Krishna Hare Hare,
Hare Rama Hare Rama, Rama Rama Hare Hare.

The chanting troupe was always loud, and many thought it was unpleasantly intrusive and aggressive, and not consistent with the Cotter spirit of harmony, peace and joy. Workshops would stop to allow the ruckus to pass. "Bloody Krishnas, I wish they would go away, or at least shut up," was the frequent response.

The matter was raised at several Morning Sharing sessions—seeking a "ruling", if an organisation honouring only consensus could ever issue a ruling—to silence the disruptive and discordant chanting. Always it was an unsolvable issue, first because the Krishna folk themselves didn't attend the general sharings to explain or negotiate, but mainly because total tolerance and achieving self-protection will always be incompatible goals. It is the art, or rather the pragmatism, of politics to be the fumbling adjudicator in

                                        Down to Earth

conflicts of interest, and the ConFest was heatedly opposed to shows of internal politics in any form. ConFest believed in the single principle of discussing for as long as we needed to finish with a consensus. Was this what Leon had been calling anarchist?

The Krishna chants continued all ConFest.

For many, however, the Hare Krishnas were one of the best features at ConFest. The food was good and it was plentiful and it was free. We didn't eat there. Were they trying to recruit? They were just doing what their beliefs led them to: provide generously for those who had a need.

Instead, we walked past the Krishnas, and we ate a kebab, a wrapped flatbread filled with beans and avocado and cheese. It wasn't food we recognised, but that is what the ConFest was about—experimenting, trying something new, being open, expanding our minds. We made a mess of ourselves mastering these kebabs, and the taste was unfamiliar, but dammit, it tasted good.

A noisy roar of voices was coming over the riverbank every few minutes, but we couldn't see what was the cause. Coordinating kebab and hand and face was taking all our attention anyway.

By now many festival people were hurrying over the bank to get down to the Cotter River itself. Dave, black shorts and black cap, trotted past carrying his camera. "Hey, Brian and Rose, you have to come."

"Why, what's on?"

"The Information Tent calls it the 'River Tribe', and it's on now."

So we followed to the bank. About two hundred people had gathered and were slowly waving their hands high in the air. It was quiet now, but one old man was out front, white hair and white beard, leading the theatrics, and the throng were in his control. More were falling in behind the crowd, and quickly including themselves into the group trance.

On the edge of the bank stood a figure robed in black and wearing a nuclear attack gas mask. The ConFest clown, still painted, was on the bank as well, his coloured parachute folded and under his arm, and they were both waving all newcomers down towards the river.

Most were willing to throw themselves bodily into the group happening. The leader started a "Ho Ho ..." rhythm softly at first, and getting louder by degrees. The tribe joined him. As it got more frenzied, it was recognisably the roar we had been hearing on and off for the past ten minutes. It was even louder than earlier, and must by now be carrying through much of the camp.

It reached its loudest and held on for a minute or two, until a sweeping wave from the leader stopped it. Quiet reigned again. Hundreds of arms waved in tranced silence. The same as before. But the crowd was larger.

Bodies were scurrying across the bank and joining in greater numbers. The word of a "big event" was spreading like fire. Women and kids came. Old men came. The skinny came. The dressed and the naked came. They came as they were. Dave's daughter was holding onto his shorts as he stood photographing. Miri was with them, pointing.

The "Ho Ho ..." began once more. And more again. Eight or nine times more the jungle trembled in fear, and the chant had morphed to a rolling mix of "Ho Ho" and "Ha" and "Hoo". The crowd was now more like a thousand, and many couldn't hear the leads or words from the snowy messiah at the front. Instead, by now, the crowd got their cues from his flailing arms and tossing head.

The white-haired one dropped the sarong which was all he had, and beckoned. Clearly, unashamedly, dramatically signalled everyone to join him. Thousands of eyes opened wider in a group shock. Delight. Alarm. Fright. Blushing or drained white, everyone had a reaction.

Noisy animal abandon, communal trance, hysteria in the crowd, that had been a powerful experience so far, but now it was crunch time. Awake out of this passionate dream, or embrace it. The uninhibited acted at once, but the majority paused to do their urgent emotional calculations, and then they progressively allowed themselves to be seduced into the overwhelming experience of the group decision. A thousand naked bodies stood in synchrony, bemused with their own daring.

The hooting had restarted with a passion. The tribe had seen off the unexpected enemy and were tight again, ready to march forward. Two more howling sessions, and the passion grew and the crowd grew.

Our leader turned and walked into the Cotter. There were rocks, and there was good flowing water. This was more water than yesterday—the dam was releasing more today.

But he could still stand, even at the middle. He stopped and called furiously once more.

"Come on," I said.

Rose and Jo both were startled. I shed my shorts and shirt and Rose joined me. She had less option now, and Jo was already bare. The clothes we abandoned. If we ever returned alive, we might find them later. It didn't matter. I scooped up our decorated daughter, we merged into the back wall of the River Tribe, the tribe stumbled into the Cotter and jostled around trying to fit everyone in, and all the while we kept up a lower level of shrieking, uncoordinated but supportive, on and on until we were all standing in the water.

The sun was still mid-afternoon high. Our Moses man raised his arms for silence. Then once more he led the naked mob into a howl of hooting. Then a second time. Now, I swear I didn't see the leader signal anything different, but on the third howl the passion of the orgy broke all its limits. Everyone present continued roaring, hooting, yelling without restraint; as one we pelted the water, we scooped the water and flung it high, we splashed with every ounce of effort we could find, we dunked ourselves under, we covered our neighbours with double hands of Cotter, and two thousand medallion bearers just kept howling.

———

Volunteering for some work was a part of ConFest. At the start of every morning at the common Sharing gathering, many of the tasks needing volunteers for that day were mentioned, so everyone soon absorbed the cultural expectation that to volunteer was an essential ConFest experience. The volunteering tent was adjacent to the coordinators' tent, and helpers staffed it all day. I had put in enough effort during the setup days, and also I had kept an eye on the radio sets and their batteries. I felt under no debt for more. However, ConFest is a "throw yourself in" adventure, so I still volunteered for a two-hour shift on front gate duty.

There were two gates. Little ConFest traffic arrived via the rural back road, Paddys River Road. Police had diverted non-ConFest civilian traffic on that road many kilometres back. So the back gate a kilometre up was closed, and the road was used for car parking, and had been filled early in the ConFest. Much of the camping area was car-free.

The main gate was at the Uriarra Road intersection a kilometre back up the hill towards Canberra. Many people left their cars parked on the roadside outside the barrier, along either Uriarra Road or the Cotter Road, and a designated runabout car helped them ferry their tents and supplies down into the campgrounds. A few with large camping vehicles and the occasional house-bus chose to stay at Casuarina Sands, which was outside but had facilities and flat ground that could accommodate them. Those people walked down each day.

Nominally, the main gate stayed closed to vehicles after dark. However, there was always the exception that needed access: an emergency car, a special visitor. Crews stayed day and night at the entrance-way, and a large marquee tent was the gate office.

The gate was also the money collection point. Some had pre-registered their ten dollars entrance, and we admitted those on their receipt. Kids under ten did not pay. We gave all entrants one stringed medallion, made of light coloured fired clay, with a cameo motif the triangular layout of the three ConFest Domes. Everyone at the ConFest wore their medallion always. By now, several days into the festival, a minority walked some of their day partly or all naked, but they still wore their medallion. It was a talisman, a bond, a symbol of belonging, and could become one day a treasured memento.

The aim was to have a minimum of two people on gate duty, and at the busiest times there were more. With just one on the gate, the risks could be greater. Yesterday, there had been the forcible removal from gate duty of one man who had generously volunteered to stay on duty for many, many hours at a time, in fact, almost continuously since the barrier started. He hadn't registered as a volunteer with the volunteering office, but he became accepted as the resident gatekeeper.

The coordinators' tent had begun to notice possible differences between the medallions consumed and the collected entrance money. It had taken some time to spot this, and then to be more suspicious, because there hadn't been any attempt to count the medallions in the first place. The firing kiln down by the river had blindly produced "bucket loads", in retrospect, an error of judgement. Considerable money had gone astray, but proof would never be available.

All this I knew, because I had been radio checking in the coordinators' tent yesterday when the issues were being raised.

Since yesterday, the communications from the office below to the gate up here had improved markedly. The gate answered calls at once, excuses were never made, the sets were always on and working now.

The spirit of the ConFest was explicitly one of openness and trust. Episodes like the gate hassles of the first few days threatened to spoil the joy and trust, but the only answer we would accept was to be wiser and more secure, and to then revert to the same simple trust.

The theft was wrong. Or was Nietzsche right, God is dead, the best human is the strong arrogant one, and fuck all the meek, they deserve their misery?

I relieved Tim who had been on the gate for four hours, and was quite tired. He explained the guidelines for admission, and how the money was stored. Handover done, Tim walked back down headed for the food market. Judy was staying on duty with me. The two of us sat beside the big cloth sign draped across the tent. Some artist wit had been at work: "No strangers here—just friends yet to meet."

———

I was still tired from last night's big band music on the stage.

"My friends," started Jim, "today is the last day of our wonderful experience here at Cotter. Every one of us must be in awe of what we have created together, what we've seen, what we've learned. We have shared a spirit so different from what the world out there lives every day. We should congratulate ourselves thoroughly." He paused while the applause ran.

Leon was not here. Gone home.

"When I called you all here, I wanted to explore with you what ways we could find to change our sick society. Because our society is sick. It leaves us anxious and alienated, over-consuming, brainwashed, with little personal freedom to be our real selves. We've listened this week to some eminent forces for change in our world. Bill Mollison has a vision for revolutionising our farming and land use so

                                    Down to Earth

we no longer pollute and destroy our earth. Rather, we must turn it back to a flourishing healthy mother for us as it used to be in past ages.

"We saw this week with our own eyes the healing power of Wilhelm Reich's therapies. We saw how we can remove all those body armours that lock us up, devastate our sexuality and reduce our free and joyful functioning as emotional and spiritual humans.

"James Prescott from the States has spoken on body pleasures and the origin of human violence.

"Peter Cock from Moora Moora commune in Victoria has shown us models we may use to enrich and restructure our relationships and escape the sterile nuclear small family so common now.

"The Findhorn community in Scotland have lovingly revealed for us how their modern version of spirituality nourishes their community and inspires them to great undertakings together, creating nurturing gardens, building supportive homes and offering healing.

"We've had fun here, but that isn't enough. Now we must go forward to make a plan, a plan to change our culture at large. We must take our discoveries, our newly realised alternatives to that repressed and controlled life out there, and take our ideas out. We need to reform what is. That of course is revolution. We must be the seeds for that revolution. What we know for ourselves, we must show to everyone. We are the new society." More cheering.

Two people were handing out copies of a document as Jim spoke. "I have here today a manifesto of change. Take this *Cotter Manifesto* with you. Study it carefully. It summarises many discoveries we have found this week, and it lays the foundation for a more complete strategy of revolution in our culture."

I looked at the page. It was on Footscray Tech paper.

"Lastly, I want to announce today that we will gather again. I will prepare a place and a time, and we will come together again to celebrate who we are, a Down to Earth community, and to deepen our strategies for social change. There will be another ConFest."

We heard what we wanted to hear, and the applause was deafening.

Autumn

I had two circular magnets I had extracted from some small damaged speakers. Jo was watching me holding them, interested. She stood in the kitchen near the refrigerator, and she held out a hand in request.

I smiled at her. "Watch."

I put one of the magnets on the refrigerator door, where it stuck. Jo looked astonished, eyes wide. I pulled it off again, and gave it to her. She looked at it in her hand, then walked to the fridge, and stuck it to the door herself. She grinned briefly, but that quickly became a full child laugh. Repeatedly she stuck the magnet to the metal door and took it back off. What she had discovered was delighting her. She put it on the floor, picked it up, put it on the fridge once more.

The laws of reality get confronted sometimes by new evidence. That everything always falls down is amended by a new physic that can push and pull other ways. The ecstasy on my daughter's face was priceless. The thrill of learning new things. Understanding them.

I handed her the second magnet, and we experimented on the two pulling together, and even pushing away.

Dave – Canberra

Mid-Winter

Dave turned the 'Bondi Junction' bus into Condamine Street, and headed for the park on Sullivans Creek. It was eight o'clock. The Winter Solstice Fair was to be from eleven until three, but he needed to park the bus in a favourable position before the crowds arrived.

This fair was a new event, and definitely not a very official one. The idea had grown out of the Full Moon parties that the Canberra women had been staging since Cotter had finished. Some of those had been along Sullivans Creek, and they often drew twenty or forty. But midwinter in Canberra deserved a daytime party, not after dark, and a public hippie fair was advertised around the counterculture networks. Anarchy in practice. "Solstice" was a suspect concept to the larger population, shades of pagan forebears and magic intentions.

The bus idea was Bev's, and she had persuaded Miri and Rose into using the blue house-bus as a tea house. *Bloody women, they talked me into this.* He didn't believe his own talk; the tea house was a brilliant plan.

He settled the beast on a level spot holding a commanding position across the small site. The big diesel motor rumbled unwillingly to a stop. Locking up, he headed off for a long steady jog: keeping fit was a passion. He followed the track along the creek down towards the university. The ANU campus he had known well once. Life moves on.

Returning, he unlocked the bus and carted out the three handmade trestle tabletops with their folding legs. All had been protected for travel by some old rugs, because Dave was proud of his timber panelling. Out came five long planks and a dozen four-gallon drums. By ten minutes later, a serviceable set of seats and tables had been arranged outside the bus.

Miri and Rose and their two girls arrived in the Corolla after ten, and he helped transfer boxes of extra cups. The usual house-bus stock was enough for the three of them plus a visitor or two, but not for a fairground of customers.

He left Miri to sort out her kitchen, and went to the drawer at the back of the bus. Out came his *piece de resistance*, a cloth banner he'd salvaged the day the ConFest wound up. He set about tying it between the rear of the bus and the tree nearby, where it would make a light windbreak against the wintry breezes. By lunchtime, it mightn't be needed, as the short Canberra winter day can be quite delightful, quite sunny and comfortable, for a couple of hours. "No strangers here—just friends yet to meet," it read.

"So where's Brian? Isn't his birthday tomorrow?"

"In Cairns for the week," said Rose, scrubbing a table. The trestles had been stored in the back shed at Sandford. "The Navy are having consultations with a shipbuilder up there. His Defence job now is on the new class of Patrol Boats, and they have decided the construction yards might be too small for what they need."

"How are you getting on these days?" *Dangerous ground.* He didn't get Rose's version so often, but Brian was struggling.

She'd cut that long hair.

"It's not working. I don't know how his head works." Rose turned and went in quickly with her cloths, pretending to be finished.

                                          Down to Earth

Dave took Sunday and Jo, and left Miri, Bev and Rose to run their enterprise as they wanted. The house-bus stove boiled the water, the oven heated the muffins, and the sink handled the washups. Lemongrass tea, other herbals, Ceylon tea, or Nescafe. Cold fruit slice or warmed muffin. And a thriving business.

Ali sat nearby for a while singing to his guitar, and he had an entertainer's talent. "*Puff, the magic dragon, Lived by the sea, ...*" Tribes of kids gathered around.

Little do those kids know what they're hearing, thought Dave. The rascal Puff, and Jimmy Paper and the other fancy stuff. Tally-Ho papers and hookahs. It's like Santa Claus—don't disillusion them too early.

"*Give me a home among the gumtrees, with lots of plum trees, ...*"

Dave crept past the kitchen staff and found his bodhran stored under Sunday's bunk bed. He and Ali played for an hour until the kids grew restless. "*Though the carnival is over, I will love you till I die.*"

The arrival of the Canberra clown took over where the singing stopped, and thirty children and a few not so young stretched a multicoloured parachute to catch unpredictable and unlucky transparent skydivers.

———

Late Winter

Dave fastened Sunday's belt, closed the rear door of the Corolla, and sat his big frame in to drive home. His daughter would be asleep within a hundred yards. It was a thirty-minute drive from old suburban O'Connor to the shack at Sandford.

"I like Mum. I can talk with her."

"You always did like my Mum," replied Miriam. "Why is it significant?"

"I can have fun with her. She accepts me."

"Mum told me she wasn't so sure about you when we were first going out. She learned to relax after she understood you a little better."

"Really, I didn't know that." He did.

"Well, parents want to protect their kids, I suppose. They want the best for them. When I moved to the farmhouse, she worried a lot about me, and I had to prove to her I was OK, I was safe, and I was looking after myself. When she was learning to trust me and saw me spreading my wings, you bounded into the picture too. You were like a whirlwind. She worried for me all again."

"Do you talk to Mum about that?"

"Sure, we always talked lots, and you know that, but we shared important ideas too, not just what we did each day."

They passed the War Memorial. He was taking the airport road home.

"I could never talk with my Mum," said Dave. "We never trusted each other to talk about anything."

"I know that, love. But I do. I know Mum took a while to accept you as someone good for me. When I came back from the big gig carrying Sunday, she thought all her hesitations were warranted, that we were creating grief. You hadn't even met my Mum then, remember? She knew you only from what I'd told her."

Miriam had hinted once she felt Mum was a bit psychic. He paused. "So I guess I was a disaster at that time."

"Yes, but we came home, and we both got stuck into what we needed to do. We set our life up together, we scraped up enough to buy the farmhouse. You were there for us when it counted."

"Miri, I loved you."

"Joseph loved me before you appeared. He left me hurt and confused. Joe only knew about Joe when relationship issues became important. Mum had watched what'd happened, and she feared I was on another troubled love affair."

"Miri, I love you," he repeated. There was no moon. They had passed the airport and were approaching Queanbeyan by the Oaks Estate way.

"Davey, my dear, I know you do." Only Miri called him that. "You love Sunday and me dearly. I love you and I trust you. It took Mum a little longer to realise how good you are for me. Now she knows, and now she is happy. She still knows you have some pieces in you that are incorrigibly hippie, she knows you can be bull-headed, but she does trust you and she's happy for us."

He fell silent. He slid his left hand under Miriam's bottom on the seat beside him—this was a common intimacy. They had had this conversation several times. Why did he still need the reassurance? *Dave, Accept. Enjoy.*

The car radio was playing softly, a new Crosby Stills and Nash, 'A Song Before I Go'. The new AM station 2CC was playing so much better music.

Almost home, the Corolla pointed down the long narrow slope on the 'Flat Road. Miriam and Sunday both slept.

It was too late that Dave caught the wombat form in his lights. Striking the solid body of a wombat can demolish the front end of any fast-moving car. The first tiny moment of instinct turned his wheel leftwards, and then the awesome image of the rock embankment lit up in every cell of his body. He corrected sharply to the right, deciding to roll over the animal and take their chances that way. Too late: the left wheels fell into the drain gully cut into the stony ground. At speed, the crippled car spun, nosed into the bank, and tumbled drunkenly down the road.

Brian – ConFest: Bredbo

Summer

On the Monaro Highway eighty kilometres from Canberra going south, lies the sleepy town of Bredbo. The Murrumbidgee hides somewhere on the right, and some peaks of the Snowys foothills are past the river in the distance. Bredbo is the only town of any note along that road for the many ski-field trippers from Canberra and from Sydney. To the left lie the Tinderry Ranges, but few venture that way. It's the Snowys that are in most travellers' minds. Those Snowy Mountains, Australia's poor attempt at ski Alps, are further to the south-west.

On the long bitumen rise south out of Bredbo, as the car is still winding back up to speed, there is a dirt side road that heads westwards, and it crosses a bush bridge over the river. The festival site property gate is then on the right. *Mount Oak.*

I was alone. The track grew less distinct as I drove in, until I was following a fence-line on my right moving parallel to the river, northwards. Billowing dust rose behind the car as it lurched from knoll to gully. Anything leftwards looked too mountainous to take the car. After a total dirt distance of about seven kilometres from the highway, the fence turned right to allow access to the Murrumbidgee. A creek lay ahead anyway, so this was as far north as the property went. This spot was less than one kilometre from the highway directly across the river.

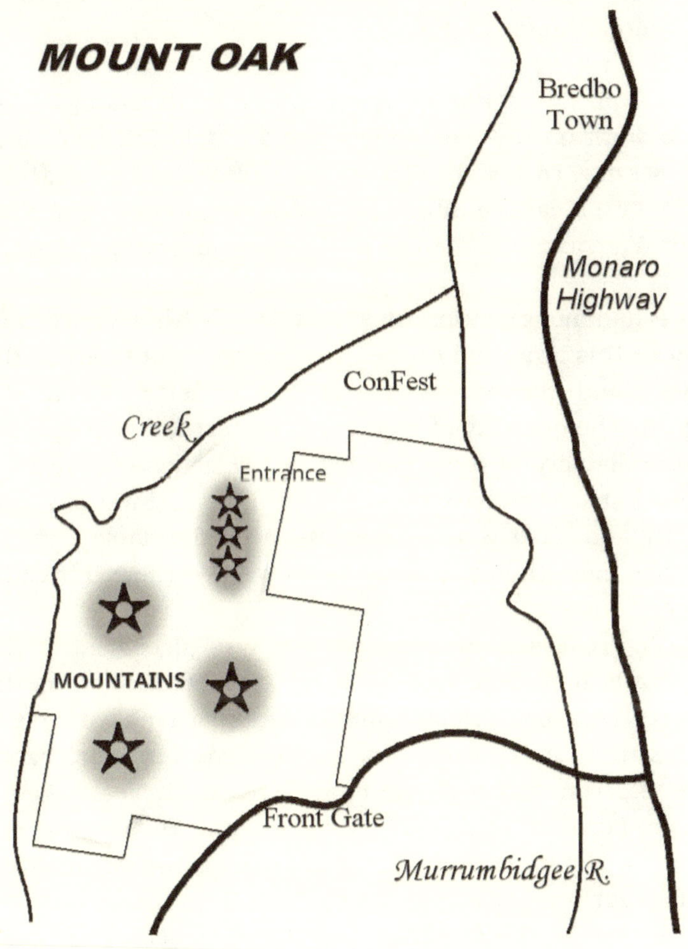

Three other cars were here at Mount Oak, near the river. A huge load of second-hand timber and corrugated iron lay on the ground beside a truck. Several bodies were sitting at the river on rocks, drinking beers from can.

It was still more than a week before Christmas Eve, when the festival was to launch, even a couple of days before the proposed setup time. My plan for today was to check the site, to pitch my tent, and to judge on what day I would come back here to join the pre-ConFest team. I was to bring radio gear, more than for Cotter.

Several days on, I duly returned. The three walkie-talkies from Cotter I had converted with fresh channel crystals to work on the newly regulated 27 MHz Citizens' Band radio service. I'd bought three more units, and I'd fitted my Mazda with a car-mounted CB radio and nine-foot steel whip aerial. We could use the car in the communication network as well.

I had no intention of persevering with rechargeable batteries this time, and I hoped they didn't want to argue the ideology and the practicality of this decision during the ConFest. The quantity of recharging required, and the primitive unreliability of any charging in the chaos of a festival site, had shown recharging to be unworkable. First aid, gate security and other coordination jobs needed reliable communications more than the hippie mind wanted the eco-friendly answer.

The real issue to solve, for me, was placement of the entry gate. If it were to be several kilometres back at the property entrance, radio communication wasn't possible. I had heard of the repeater concept, but repeaters were hand-made experimental gadgets, ham radio stuff. Yes, I was a ham, a licensed radio amateur operator. But I was not making up any repeater station to try to use on a dusty paddock far from power.

If instead the ConFest control was closer to the main site, we might have communication back to the coordination tent. No-one had set up any gate barrier yet. I needed to get the location agreed before they made any gate. I had seen, along the fence coming in, one suitable bottleneck in the terrain that could give us some access control.

                                    Down to Earth

At the coordination tent was a ground map of the growing site. The marked place for entry gate was, I saw with some relief, the obvious narrowing in the track that I had wanted. That was a problem I ought to have addressed a few days back, but now it was of no more concern.

That off my mind, I went on a tourist walk. The structures the team had put together in the past few days were inspiring. The ConFest kitchen was almost completed, roofed, and ready to commission. Worker meals from tonight would all come from the big kitchen, instead of from a small makeshift one close to the river. The plan showed the temporary kitchen was to be turned now to a ConFest cafe right at the river. A Hard Rock Central sign was on it—there were many seat-sized rocks in the feeble Murrumbidgee stream.

Down by the river, too, was a pitched-roof open-walled building designed as a children's workshop area. Again, mostly completed.

I walked on. The ground was dry and dusty.

A large corrugated iron water tank sat on a rise above the festival central area, but not too far from the kitchen. Black piping lay around to be run in a trench to the kitchen later today. A small digger was working on the trench as I watched. I found out a lot as I walked around. A water tanker was to make several trips in tomorrow to fill the big tank. It was the primary drinking water for the festival, and a battery of outlet taps was being screwed together today for public use.

One dome and its blue vinyl, from Cotter, lay in pieces. There had been no effort yet to assemble it. A massive marquee tent space showed on the plan for Friends of the Earth, "FOE". Nothing was there so far.

I had no special jobs for now, so I helped for the afternoon putting up several tents that were to serve for workshop spaces and craft areas.

By nightfall, the first bongo drum was rapping, and I knew the spirit was awakening at Bredbo.

Dawn saw me sitting on a rock at the far side of the Central. A few smoke trails arose in the valley, but not many folk were abroad yet. Why was I here? I was the hippie with the Government job.

I kicked my feet in the small flow of cool water. Everyone here wanted a better life, for themselves and for the communities they lived in. They had a purpose, a drive, a need for change, renewal.

For many people their purpose in life, if they have one, is tied intimately to their belief in their god. Their faith hands them a purpose: live well, look after others, honour your god, and earn your passage to another life.

At the ConFest, many instead spent effort to "find their own purpose", so it could energise them, give them passion. Bill Mollison last year had his passion. Cairns was a driven man, stiff but driven. It seemed to me a search for the elusive.

Does life at core have no purpose? Surely we yearn for one, need one? We admire those who have a strong purpose, a dedication. How do I make my own purpose?

What energised football teams, churches, nations, the zealots and thugs of all persuasions? From outside of each regime, all was illusion, quaint and often dangerous. I'd been on an inside once, deep inside. So now, which tribe was my tribe?

At eight thirty was the daily coordinators' meeting, the planning session for the day. Attendance was open—if you wanted to be contributing, you joined in. This was no closed power group. We started with a minute of silence, holding hands.

The coordination hut was a marquee tent, with two walls raised as sun-shades. It sat over a steep small embankment, so the marquee was trimmed to fit awkwardly on the uneven ground. The bank formed a seating slope, a small amphitheatre facing inwards, and twenty or forty people might sit there. Today we had more than thirty, and I sat up the slope, but still under shade from the morning sun.

I guessed there would be a hundred bodies here by now, and a third of those were in the morning planning meeting. I'd seen it at Cotter. This was where we were creating a city.

Leading the meeting this morning was a tall wiry bloke with a European accent and a tee-shirt reading 'Yoga'. "Good morning, Today is my turn here. I'm Andrew. Look around. These are your workmates for preparing a feast, a festival, for many people arriving in a few days. How well we do our work has a great effect on the success of the events coming up. Let's throw in our energy and our love.

"Let me say it again for all our newcomers, our tasks are a labour of love. Many of us already have a vision of what we want to do, some of us are reporting in to join. All our projects have one common aim, a good ConFest. We meet here to discuss what needs doing today, to enlist working teams, to learn what compromises we needed to make."

The morning was warming already, and the dirt we sat on was hard.

"Our method always is to work together in peace. We're not a majority democracy. That is the old way, the way we're seeking to escape from. Instead, we try to negotiate and talk until we can reach a consensus that we agree to accept. Sometimes this takes us longer than voting and counting. We persevere until we have convinced ourselves of a common answer."

The ground map had been brought in from outside. "Have we any reports from ongoing projects?" asked Andrew.

The kitchen was up but the benches and the gas appliances still needed setting up. Last night's first workers' meal was cooked with some difficulty, because not everything had been operational. Several volunteers offered work today.

I raised the radio sets, explained what we had and what to expect it could and could not do. They wanted them put into service immediately, with a "base" naturally at the coordination tent.

The location planned for the small workshopping spaces needed moving. Someone adjusted the map. The dome frame would go up today. One team should take the truck back to Canberra for extra roofing materials. Each piece of the ConFest fabric was discussed.

Jim Cairns and Junie joined the group. They sat on the embankment in front of where I was, and two cushions appeared for them to sit on. Greeting our mentor interrupted the flow of the meeting, and Jim then addressed the gathering with his standard homily on alienation and freedom, and the hopes for the ConFest.

The business continued.

"When are we getting better toilets?" For the hundred dwellers so far, two structures had been enough for now, and the drops under them had been roughly dug by the digger machine doing the trenching. But we needed major expansion of toilet facilities, fast.

The large American responded to this. George had a shock of red hair and a chest with a carpet of the same red. "Dunny works are under way." The word dunny is unexpected in American accent. George was sitting next to Junie, and not far from me. "They delivered a grader by truck last night, and it's still out near the entrance gate. This morning we're levelling some space for a gate tent, and grading up some barriers to stop cars driving around wide. We are grading a smoother road right into here this afternoon. By tomorrow, we'll fit the drilling attachments, and drill long drops here, here, and here." He was marking the map.

"How many are you proposing?"

Neighbourly massaging had become a common ConFest habit. Some were rubbing the shoulders of the person ahead of them. Not real massage. I leaned forward and began kneading the shoulders of Jim. He started and then rested a little into it.

　　　　　　　　　　　　　　　Down to Earth

George was replying. "We're still guessing on how many people may come. We could have up to twenty thousand, but we're digging these three groups for now. Each group will have twenty drop holes. The grader stays on-site, so we can expand by adding more compounds further out. In the outer suburbs, if you like."

"What do you call a compound? Do we get hut structures like the two we have now?"

Jim's shoulders felt stiff.

"No," said George, "unless we get a team cracking on framing them immediately. Fenced compounds of five holes by four is all that we plan so far."

There were a few agonised faces around the group. No offer was forthcoming to build huts.

"Lime and paper supply deliveries can wait for tomorrow's meeting," added George.

"Who has a licence or skill to drive heavy machines?" came the next query.

"No need. And not here," said George. "I can do it."

"It sounds like many long days of work, not a day and a half."

"Bet on it." This issue was closed.

The meeting wound up. I was glad of that; the contact with Jim was awkward. He was embarrassed, too bodily tight to relax into the touch in the way most other ConFesters learned. He was older than anyone else present, so we could give him more caution, more space. As we broke up, he turned, and gave a wry smile of thanks.

—

Windy night, unsettled

Moon high over the trees

Summer is here I feel

Smoking fire

More a sacred altar in the dark

Than a warmth

Voices wandering through the silver black.

  It's a small group yet

  Pioneers for Mount Oak occupation

  Resting loving restless between days

  Beyond the murmurs

  A bard solo in the distance

  Soon joined by two silhouettes

  Dancing among the starlight

  Pass it along

  Who paddles the river playing Christopher?

  Or climbs the half-built dome frame

  Past the moon?

Summer's coming fast

Energies are shining down

To warm this earth valley

Even midnight can feel it.

Down to Earth

Dave – Mount Oak

The bright evening moon cast light puddles and eerie forms. The surreal quiet defied Dave's knowledge that a fledgling noisy city was creating itself in the next valley.

He sat beside the rolls of canvas and bedding he had managed to carry here while the sun had still shone. The demons were punishing him, and he needed to stare them down. Alone.

If there's a god, where are you? And why? Why Miriam? Why, when life was so beautiful? Why am I left to carry the guilt?

Daughter Sunday, four, was with Mum, Miriam's Mum, Suzanne, for these few days. He would go back and collect her the day after tomorrow, the real start date for the ConFest, and they would have fun. Sunday still awoke many nights screaming in terror. Holding her close calmed her slowly, but he knew Sunday would relive that nightmare for long ahead. Dave's one comfort was the support and love Mum had given them both.

Sunday was hospitalised but her child's body survived the car rolls with only severe bruising. But the collapsing roof had crushed Miriam, and she had died instantly. Dave recovered from the concussion, and the broken ribs and arm, but he lived to grieve over life, death, love and wombats.

He could feel Miriam's body, trusting and warm, curled into his, and the ache was unbearable, unfathomable.

He opened his eyes. A little moss was below the boulder he sat on. The only moss on the Bredbo property? The big rocks had lichen, but moss needed some damp, and a little dampness was seeping in this gully.

Mount Oak was a dry, dry land, an Aussie outback hard dry land. Eucalypt, dirt and some rock outcrops, hilly. Rain hadn't fallen here for a long stretch. Sheep had taken every skerrick of pasture grass that may have been here. Dave had found some of the sheep when walking here today. Emaciated, they trudged forlornly ever searching. His own acres at Sandford were a fertile paradise compared with this.

There had been a makeshift sign saying "Mount Oak" at the gate, so he supposed that really was the name, or some prankster might have bestowed that name in the past few days. Well. Mount Oak didn't have oak trees. Unless they meant sheoak Casuarina trees, and there might be some of those near the river.

He had come early to join the setup team, but it was too hard. So he would study the place in his eyes and his head, rather than dig and paint for the erupting festival. He could construct a philosophic foundation for the ConFest instead of wood and piping. He had no reserves left in his soul and his body for the physical. Or was it the social?

From where the ConFest was starting, he had struck out to the west, and quickly he had come to the dry creek bed that steered him south of west. It had to be the

northern property boundary, as a rough fencing on the far side held back wandering sheep. For a while, the going was sandy with loose rock, but soon he needed to scramble up large boulders and rock waterfall areas. A startled dark wallaby bounded up from its foraging. The shallow creek valley had become a gully with high banks, and he wondered if he might need to return out the way he was going. Evidence of flood marking and debris were high up the bank.

The hilly shapes beside him grew more complex, and he found himself in a creek bed that was twisting like a serpent to fit to the tortured hills. It was darker, more sheltered, and it was here he had set his pack down.

Some bedding, some food, camera and notebook. It was enough. This gully would be a base camp. From the little flask he made tea, sipped it slowly, and ate his bread rolls from home. He tried to listen to the quiet.

As dark fell, the moon was still high, and it fed silver into the gully. The gnarled shapes of the box trees made a surreal landscape. Reaching for his pouch, he hand-rolled a fag, just tobacco, lit it, and crawled into his makeshift swag.

Disoriented, startled, he woke abruptly. The moon had rolled over past the embankments, and the magic forest of a moment ago was blacker, heavier, spookier, lower. The small torch was beside his head, and carefully he fumbled, picked it up and slowly pointed it to where the slight rustling was coming from. He switched on the torch, and the face of a fox looked straight at him from six feet away. The first instinct was to think of his father's wartime .303 rifle, but that was in lockup at home. The animal froze for the moment, then ran into the dark at speed. He tried to sleep again, but sleep was slower this time.

In the gully, the sun rose late. What woke him then was yet more animal life disturbing the camp. A goanna watched him stir, and looked intent on standing its ground. Goanna bites are germ heaven. Think fast, Dave, what is the smartest etiquette for negotiating with a goanna? But the big scaly beast chose then to turn aside in disdain and walk around, its body and heavy tail whipping sideways with each ungainly step. He ran his fingers through his crew-cut hair, and willed himself ready for the day.

Two food bars served as a breakfast, and he placed more of those and some fruit and a water canteen into a small pack for the day. Oh, and the camera and a compass. The bedroll would stay here in the gully at the bend. Hidden wrens in the light undergrowth were making that subliminal busy twitter that gives them away. He headed further up the creek, and there were a series of tight bends where untold ancient torrents had forced their twisty way through the mountain ground. The creek bed straightened, and it now led southwards. He had been skirting a big hill on his left perhaps eight hundred feet higher, and the hill marked the north-west corner of Mount Oak.

Miriam had loved their Sandford acres. She would have so enjoyed this trek to the back of Mount Oak.

He sat on a rock. The creek, still dry, was nonetheless more friendly. Trees hung over the water that wasn't there. The rocks of the bed were giving way to a sandy rubble. A kingfisher was looking down, eyeing everything closely, waiting. To the right it was flatter for a distance, and sheep ran there too. He presumed it was a different property. The left side rose steeply. It was rough pasture country with scattered trees, huge boulders and quartz outcrops and some erosion gullies. A second hill, even higher, lay south of the one on the creek's elbow, and Dave decided to leave the creek and trudge to the top.

By an hour after noon, he was at the top of the property. From here it was clear Mount Oak was mostly occupied by a square range of four mountain peaks. The Snowy Mountains he could see in the distance, but these here would not rate as alpine, only as foothills. He was on the south-west peak, and the other three were about two hundred feet lower. The four summits, about a mile apart each, and with

                                    Down to Earth

their plateau valley between them, represented most of the whole property. Aside from a narrow access strip from the front gate in the south-east where he had driven in yesterday, the only flatter land was that far north-east pocket facing the Murrumbidgee River. The ConFest was being built on the only sector of Mount Oak that was possible, because all the rest was mountain.

The whole property was about five kilometres by four. He sat in the narrow shade of a large flat stone slab, and imagined that any other country once used rocks like this as altars to their ancient gods. The summer sun beat down. A red-bellied black slithered across the ground a little distance away and retired to the shade. He didn't fancy negotiating with snakes either.

For the second night he slept again in the gully at the elbow of the creek. This land was rugged, no doubt. Dave understood rugged. He could imagine being here again in future times, with Sunday when she was older.

———

He missed the first day, Christmas Eve. He was in Canberra with Sunday and Miriam's Mum. Mum had surprised him by offering to join them at the ConFest for two days, after she got a few jobs in order, cooking the food early and preparing it to go to Bredbo.

So it was that Suzanne and Sunday and Dave drove into Mount Oak early on Christmas morning. They stopped at the canvas gatehouse. No faces of friends, just strangers. He paid their two by ten dollars, and collected the roneoed map and event sheet for the day.

A tent city of thousands opened out ahead, spreading from the river village on the far right, up the slopes, hillocks and gullies into the foothills direction he had roamed a few days earlier. Ten thousand? Twenty? The new metropolis of Mount Oak ConFest was awake for the sunny morning. Over some of it hung dust, dust tossed up by moving cars on the freshly graded tracks. Not many, but enough to make a spoiler to the anomalous summer morning beauty of dry countryside and canvas colour.

The day's program had two items he marked in his mind as the big ones—a gathering mid-afternoon by Jim Cairns on 'Mount Oak, Purchase Options', and the fire dance after dark, as tonight was full moon. If Suzanne wanted to "see for herself" as she had pleaded yesterday, well the full moon celebrated in hippie style would be an abrupt and challenging induction.

'Our Planets. Ancient Knowledge Versus the Very New'.
This afternoon? No.

Dave had set two tents as close to the main village as he could manage, squeezing among the earlier settlers. The three of them had wandered a little, tourists so far, and had then put together their picnic version of holiday dinner. That ConFest kitchen food they could address on a later day.

The afternoon was still hot nearing four o'clock. Jim and Junie stood talking under a yellow box tree on the sloping ground near the river. There were several large eucalypts around, each ragged in the Australian style, and offering only a pretence of serious shade. It was the best available. A dozen people were waiting around, and the group was growing. As the address started, perhaps three hundred had gathered, standing first, then shuffling themselves gingerly on to the rocky dirt. Jim stood. Junie's David hung back watching behind, hat and camera.

Dave recognised several in the crowd, but today he wanted to sit with himself. Sunday and her Grandma were sitting at the Hard Rock Central. He could still see them from where he was. Sunday sat in the shallow stream. Suzanne was on a rock keeping an eye, but also deep in conversation with an old woman on the next boulder, the woman bare-breasted, and wearing snowy white hair set in a confident very long ponytail. The old woman he couldn't

recognise, but Suzanne, he was deciding, he'd underesti-
mated.

It was an accomplished piece of oratory. Jim spoke of
the yearnings, the hunger for true freedom we have, the
forfeit of those freedoms so many make. The forces of our
culture persuade us to surrender to oppression and dullness.

Damn it, thought Dave, that woman with Suzanne
looks so sexy with hair as feminine as that. Age notwithstanding. A lone drum was practising further along the river.

Witness the recent State elections in Queensland, Jim
said. The incumbent National Party had banned the freedom
to strike, demonstrate and even gather in public. There had
been street struggles, which the television had gleefully sent
to air. But the majority population had then accepted its
subjugation, signed away its freedoms, and re-elected the Joh
Bjelke ultraconservatives for another term of office.

We live encased in emotional armour. All of us are
inhibited, crippled through fear of freedom, fear of sexuality,
fear of authority. Eva Reich at Cotter told us of the work of
her father in healing our blockages, restoring the freedoms
we humans deserve to have.

We need a new way, a new life. We need to study and
plan and take action to change how we live.

Jim spoke of yesterday's keynote talk by Stephen
Gaskin, from The Farm settlement in Tennessee. Hundreds
had settled there to create a new communal life for themselves. They took on a mission to be an influence to export
their views and their lifestyle into the broader American
community.

Findhorn community in Scotland in many ways are
aiming to be a similar educating and politicising influence in
Britain. We had listened to the Findhorn delegation at length
at Cotter last year, and while they're not here at Bredbo, they
will be back in Australia speaking in the coming March. Last
year we heard of the heroic struggles to found Moora Moora
community in Victoria.

Look around you, asked Jim. This land is typical of much of rural Australia, over-farmed, undernourished, harsh and wasted from grazing. Imagine what it might be. If we could control its water and its fertility, we could turn it into a place of beauty and bounty.

Neville Yeomans whose father founded the Keyline irrigation principles is here with us this week, and his design skills could lead us to make even a place like Mount Oak a garden of paradise.

Bill Mollison is talking with us tomorrow. Let us hear from that great man how the philosophy of Permaculture could transform the rough ground you now sit on.

"I have a vision," he called. "I have a vision in my mind of this place becoming a university for the people. It can be an oasis of human happiness, to show what we can achieve on the land with right agricultural principles. We can make it an example of human community, of freedom and emotional healing."

The crowd applauded. Jim waited.

Does "I have a vision" measure against "I have a dream"?

"This vision can be possible," he said. "The owner of this property has given us an option that we could buy it. Mount Oak could indeed become a centre of renewal, a college and community of happy and energetic people. If we here at Bredbo this week should decide we want to create such a place, it is in our power. I want us to consider this. Are we willing to buy Mount Oak as a Down to Earth project, a centre for all alternatives, a 'communiversity' of the new society? It would be a grand aim. It should be our future."

Jim swept his arms around. "I want you to think on this. Let us meet again here tomorrow, and we can continue these thoughts. We can dream a utopia. Let us consider the possibility of buying Mount Oak for Down to Earth."

Fuck, this is just a chess game.

Brian – ConFest: Bredbo

By the morning of Christmas Eve, the population of Mount Oak had jumped to eight thousand people, and they were still coming. The dust of incoming cars lay like a pall.

Any normal town or city grows by slow measures, and revisiting after ten or twenty years may make the growth look dramatic. But I saw the ConFest explode from a few hundred residents to thirty times as many in just two days. The week of planning and construction now had its meaning.

Jo and Rose had arrived last evening, and had set up their camp some distance away, so Jo now had two tent bases. We had agreed to schedule times as parent. For this morning, the three of us made a cooked breakfast together on my little stove. I regaled them with incidents of the week gone, the arguments, the mistakes, the people I had been among. I don't think it carried as much interest for them. I stopped chatting on.

Rose had a day sheet, like the original Cotter ones. For this festival, the sheets were printed again, after much debate. The notice boards outside each venue had been some problem, as many people didn't even know of some places, and even then they needed to visit each board to be sure what was on there.

Those in the Information Tent did their best to maintain a timetable for events held at each place, and a large notice board there showed a chaotic list of pinned and scrawled postings. The handout was again the most reliable way to inform everyone. What it did imply, was that events not added to the timetable before midnight would not be listed on the morning sheet. The subject had triggered much angst. The best answer was still elusive.

"Have you had to cope with the long drops yet?" I asked.

Rose's eyes opened wide. "Yes, we have. This morning, someone added some hessian cloth around the outside wire fence, but last night we didn't even have that. I wanted a poo last night, but I couldn't handle the idea. This morning, I just had to go. There were two men and three women in there together. We squatted over our drop holes and tried not to look at anyone. It was awful. What on earth did you people do all week? Those facilities are disgraceful."

"Well, each drop has a hessian and wood cover over it to keep out flies," I said. "There's a lime drum for dropping some in after you finish. And there's a wash tap alongside when you leave. It's crude but it's enough to provide the necessities, and it's enough to preserve public health."

"It's not enough to preserve my decency or my dignity. Nor Jo's." Jo grimaced.

"Rose, we've had the long drops ourselves the last three days. It made me nervous, too. But our inhibitions are merely what we are taught since we were little. Perhaps we can desensitise ourselves. When we can talk and joke with those beside us, when we have confronted our fears and gone through them, we just may be better off."

"I don't think so. Not me. But it looks like I get no choice. This is going to be a long few days."

She still has her rules. The human race uses rules to keep life together, assumptions under presumptions, Earth on the shoulder of Atlas, who stood forever upon what?

———

                                     Down to Earth

Morning Sharing was to be a daily event. Nominally it was the plenary gathering to give a soul to the day, but those attending were always only the dedicated minority of the camp.

Andrew from Melbourne Down to Earth group conducted the first Sharing. He stood in the warm breeze, caftaned, adorned with tassels. He had no microphone system and had to call loudly, the crowd of nearing a thousand falling quiet, sitting, straining.

"We are here again, ConFest number two. We have safely arrived, to do it all again. Let us all cheer ourselves." He led the clapping and the yelling. Many stood to add to the effect. Bredbo ConFest was under way.

We sat. We held hands and formed a connected whole.

Jim Cairns addressed us for a few minutes, welcomed us, reminded us in a precis version that we were here for fun, healing, experiment, and to look at how we might create a new society. I had heard it.

Several of the organisers explained what facilities were running, what work-gangs were still seeking volunteers this morning, what hours and expectations applied to the ConFest kitchen, the practical trivia of how the ConFest ran.

The crowd had questions and problems. How could noise be reduced overnight? Were pass-outs available to go back to town? Toilet paper rolls were blowing in the wind. One of the water taps had no water flow.

Questions, disagreements, responses. Reminders for the main ConFest events scheduled for today.

Sharing lasted forty minutes and finished with communal hugs. For many it was a bewildering introduction to ConFest routine. It worked every Cotter day. It helped weld the ConFest into one body of participants, and even those who were not present received second and third tellings of the Morning Sharings.

——

"In the fifties I was a marine, and the military abducted me to serve as a rifleman in Korea," started Stephen Gaskin. Jim had introduced him to the seated crowd of more than three hundred squeezed into the dome. The midday sun made the dome a hot place to sit.

"Then in the sixties I was an English professor in San Francisco, and the hippies abducted me to serve as a philosopher. In the seventies now, I am a soldier of life, a teacher of freedom, and a hippie commune theorist. For the eighties I am becoming a farmer."

He was probably in his mid-forties, but the gaunt Stephen Gaskin sported a greying beard, trimmed to be narrow, stringy and wispy like some chinaman's beard, but denser. Two plaited tails hung from the back of his head, but the forehead was balding. He would not be easily mistaken.

"Jim has invited us here to tell the story of the Caravan and the Farm. I will tell you that today. Tomorrow Della Ray," and he pointed to his partner sitting at the front, "will explain the great work we are doing in natural and spiritual childbirth".

"For several years in San Francisco in the sixties, we had a very productive weekly talk group that had grown out of my creative writing class at the local college. We called the discussions simply the 'Monday Night Class'. We wrote, we thought, we experimented with ideas and spirituality—what is reality, what is life? Up to fifteen hundred of us at times. Some were artists, some were the young professionals, but more and more were just the hippies who were pouring into San Francisco. This was the time of the Haight-Ashbury hippie explosion.

"When the flower power days fell apart into disillusionment and squalor, our group was still strong. We still had a message. We wanted to make a difference. Then the funniest thing happened. The hippie story turned inside out. It went like this."

More were crawling in, jostling, finding space.

"The hippie phenomenon sorely contradicted the conservative majority in the States. It threatened them. It was big. They saw sex, delusion, drugs and inability to accept their society. A delegation of pastors and researchers came to 'Frisco to study the hippies, to see us for themselves, to talk and negotiate with the enemy if that was possible.

"The first group they spoke with was us. We were well-spoken, we explained our dreams, our ideals and philosophy, our spirituality. That we had a spirituality disarmed them, and the delegation reported so well about us that I was invited to tell our story all across the country. They lined up a whole tour of speaking engagements.

"We now had our opening to make that huge difference."

Jim left quietly.

"I decided to travel on the speaking trip in an old school bus we had.

"But many of our Monday class wanted to be in on the fun. So I said, you want to come with me, then you get your own buses. They did.

"At our peak, we were a moving caravan of sixty vehicles, and we kept together using CB radio. I addressed meetings in forty States. Can you imagine the logistics of moving dozens of buses each time?

"The sight of us on the highway and rumbling through towns created much fear, and they arrested me merely for being the leader of this roving band of nonconformists. The FBI followed us closely, and they stirred up problems and rumours in a scare campaign. Helicopters have trailed us. TV networks have hounded us."

Stephen picked up a dozen large photographs of the bus caravan, and passed them down for handing around.

"Our odyssey," he continued, "covered eight thousand miles, criss-crossing the country. I spoke at colleges and churches about the changes sweeping the nation, and about peace, love and understanding. We had a mind-blowing experience on the road. We had friends to learn and to love, up close, we had disputes to resolve, we had authorities to negotiate with, and we had to find places to park all our fleet. Mostly, we had one another, and we were not the rabble they branded us as—we had strong ideals and aims. Our health and our discipline held. We realised we had now become an intense nomadic commune, an intentional community on the road. We had turned into something new.

"As we travelled, we started looking with a zealous passion for a place we could call home. In 1971 we settled in Tennessee near Nashville on a thousand-acre property, and we name our home simply 'The Farm'. We began with one house, and we lived in the buses."

He paused to give out another set of photographs, this time showing life on the farm. A couple showed Ina May Gaskin talking with her pregnant clients.

"Tents followed the buses. We met our neighbours, made friends, we became a part of the fabric of that area. We salvaged and scavenged from around us for materials to start building some structures, and we learned the farming practices that worked in Tennessee.

"Today, fourteen hundred people live on The Farm. We are an outwardly-directed community—we still want to make our difference in the world.

"We are self-sufficient, we promote nonviolence, and we live collectively. The Farm has become well known for many things, from natural childbirth and midwifery to creative arts and alternative technologies, and healthy diet and vegetarian cuisine.

"We have a real life on The Farm. People have babies. The farm breeds and uses horses. We build houses, supply our own water, run our own school. We are becoming respected players in health food, consumer electronics, textiles and niche publishing markets."

—

                                          Down to Earth

South along the river away from the main dome was the Massage Village. Did massage have a suspect reputation? There had been a massage area at Cotter. Massaging a friend's shoulders at a Sharing meeting, well, that wasn't a real massage.

I should try.

First along the river was the Aboriginal camp, flying the new Indigenous flag, a yellow sun before red earth and black sky, or black life over red earth, interpret it as you will. I had seen that flag first five years ago at the Aboriginal Embassy protest camp outside Parliament House.

Bredbo lies at a northern finger of the Monaro Plains that start down at the South Coast. The first settler whites found many peaceful Indigenous people living tribally across the plains and into the highlands. They had been here for unknown thousands of years, and they ate well from emu, kangaroo, Bogong Moths of the mountains and prawns of the coast.

As everywhere when white met black in this country, the blacks suffered. The Monaro claims not to have had the savage pogroms that sadly happened in some places. But the relentless march of white land use and a black inability to handle the Europeans' diseases saw the last of the full-bloods die out early in the twentieth century, at least among those still living locally.

I was stepping from one noticeboard to the next. The Cooma Aboriginal Community had supplied them. A black woman, Ruthie, had arrived and she stayed politely near me. I recalled seeing her near the dome talking with Junie yesterday.

The Monaro, or the Brisbane Downs as they tried to rename it once, was a long way from administrative Sydney. From the 1830s the arriving settlers, with bullocks, servants and rations, and cattle then sheep, pegged out competing claims, and sent back to Sydney to register and pay the ten pound Crown Licence. This was wild frontier country, both the plains and the highlands. Now it was simply whitefella country, and trodden all over by the cloven hoof.

Ruthie fetched a tray of damper squares. "We had a damper ceremony last night," she said. We sat. "We aren't many from here."

"You?"

"Across the river in the ranges past Bredbo. For part of the year."

The black communities who had cautiously included themselves into the ConFest, at Cotter too, she said, were mainly small groups from other places around Australia.

———

I walked on, and found the massage place, among the gum trees, with a huge tarpaulin tied to the trees. There were about twenty tables scattered under the tarp and under the trees. A bench had bottles of oil and hand wash soap. Some tables had towelling or sheeting, some bare vinyl. Several folk were face down or face up, naked, being massaged.

What were the etiquette, the expectations?

"Are you part of a class, or can anyone come in?"

"We do have some classes, but mostly you come in and use the tables yourself. Sometimes an instructor is around to give you some pointers. If you wait around, some of us are happy to do a massage for you. Would you like to stay? I can do you if you like, in twenty minutes."

I waited at the side to watch. Two patients—Is that the word?—had kept knickers on, one man, one a woman, but the rest lay on their tables naked. Two of the masseurs tossed a towel over their patient, and uncovered just the area they were working on. The day was warm, and I doubted the covers were for keeping out the cold. Most worked quietly, but some chatted.

"You can lie up on there, if you like. I'll be with you shortly."

                                            Down to Earth

Decision time. I stripped, stood a moment, and lay face up on my bench. Go for keeps.

I don't remember so much about my massage. Yes, it was both challenging and wonderful. But it was the conversation beside me that dominates my memory. That masseur was an elderly gent, not the hippie look. His patient was a red-haired lass perhaps forty years younger, and naked under his fingers. He thought his day was lucky. They had been massaging while I had been waiting. As I lay being pummelled and stroked and made oily all over, I was also eavesdropping on this mismatched pair.

"This is a great massage. I needed this," she said.

"Oh, massage is always good for us. Good for the aches and pains, good for the soul, good for digestion."

"Hmm ... ahhh ... Arrr, that is sore there."

"You know what, you do have a lot of tension in your body, all over."

"I know, I get plenty of stresses. My body gets itself into knots."

"So what do you do for that?"

"Oh, easy" she replied, "I just lie on my bed and turn myself on. I find a good orgasm gets rid of heaps of the tensions."

———

The Bredbo ConFest was a harder-edged event than last year's Cotter. The resident crowd was larger. The land was dry, hot and harsh, and the facilities provided were primitive. A more determined effort was made this year to be staging major workshops and discussion.

Jim talked each morning, on his themes of alienation and the need for social and personal reform, on the possibility of buying Mount Oak as a community of learning and social experiment. We came to call it Jim's Tree, the favourite spot he used as his meeting ground, with the Murrumbidgee River behind him. Jim standing and delivering with the

Aussie bush scene as backdrop, became imprinted on our minds as the iconic memory to keep of Bredbo.

Jim's audience fell a bit each day, and on later days he retired into the dome for his talks, where it was stifling but not sun-scorched, and a smaller crowd could feel more intimate. The ongoing community posed for Mount Oak, a curiosity at first, was becoming a difficult sell.

The huge marquee tent of the Friends of the Earth was a larger venue than the dome, and they held several workshops each day, for crowds that often overflowed. FOE presented its own events, variously on ecology and wildlife subjects, world climate, and on political action as a tool for change, but other presenters used the tent as well. Bill Mollison's proposals on the popular new area of Permaculture attracted major attention, how to plan the plantings on a property for best benefit to the land and to the dwellers. Neville Yeomans explained the principles of Keyline irrigation, sustainable use of land and its water, using the contours to position the roads, lakes and growing areas.

130   Down to Earth

Many at Bredbo yearned for the romance of living "back on the land". Many already were.

In the dome and at several side venues, classes each day delved into healing therapies, philosophies, arcane and familiar. Iridology, reflexology, massage techniques, gestalt, reiki, hypnosis, crystals and pyramids, sprout growing and moccasin stitching. Dream interpretation, stretch exercises, creative writing, and a dozen flavours of Yoga. I should attend 'Singing for Cowards'.

Sometimes workshops appeared at other locations, not near the river. A guitar workshop was to be at the Music Village. I looked at a pinned notice advertising a mid-morning meditation session for beginners, and the location was to be up the slope among the campers. "Look for the red marquee with Yin-Yang flag on a pole."

Meditation was a part of my daily regime for the years I had spent in the monastery. We rose at the bell every morning, in silence, showered, filed into Chapel by six, and chanted the morning prayers. We then had about forty-five minutes of "meditation". Our novice-master introduced us to the proposed topic, reading aloud a biblical or religious text for several minutes. Our method we referred to alternatively as "contemplation". We spent our time in thinking on the assigned subject, absorbing the moral, being edified, praying. Meditation always had a target, a purpose. After the meditation, we had a daily Mass, if a priest was available.

That was my earlier life. Monastery life. It hadn't worked out.

Meditation versions offered at ConFest were different beasts, eastern rather than western monastic, and it was time for me to explore. I walked up to the north of the range, sticking closer to the dry creek, and passed a group signed as Anarchist Village. A black flag flew.

Ten of us gathered at the Yin-Yang flagpole. A raked space in front of the red tent was the workshop spot. Two old logs bordered the small area, and we sat either on the dirt or on a log. Two hosts introduced us to the workshop: Niraj wore braided hair and an Indian sarong tied across her front, and Ravi also had at his waist a sarong, a Javanese weave. Ravi then assumed all the control.

We were to sit for the duration. For those who could manage it, Ravi demonstrated how to sit cross-legged, how to rest arms on knees and hold hands forward, palms up. This was the "Lotus Position".

"Well, it's not quite the lotus position. The legs should be wrapped tightly up to the body." He spread his knees further apart but staying on the ground, and moved each foot up onto the opposite thigh. None of today's novices could manage to copy him.

"This position is the most effective for true meditation," he continued. "We try to hold the shoulders stretched a little, the spine straight and upright, so even if the jaw falls a bit the head is still high. The left hand should rest on top of the right one on your lap. In this posture we stay motionless for as long as possible, and we can slow our heart, reduce our muscular tension, relax."

We shuffled.

"For today, I suggest you sit cross-legged as best you can manage. Find a position where you can remain upright and still for the meditation."

I stayed on the log. It was barely comfortable after a couple of minutes.

"In meditation, we try to clear the mind, breathe, empty the busy clutter of life. It's a higher state of consciousness. The easiest way is to focus on one thing, not thinking in a complicated way about that thing, just being aware of it. When other thoughts intrude, as they do when we are still learning meditation, we try to let those go again."

Ravi fell silent: that was the end of our guidance. I sat as upright as I could, but even at mid-morning the summer warm was becoming daunting. I tried to focus on my daughter, see her as present. No story, no action, no talking, just here. A crow cawed high overhead. I brought my attention back to Jo. My poor daughter Jo. No, Brian, no judgements, no values, stay with the presence. And don't talk with yourself.

My back hurt. How can the pain of trying to sit straight be a help to calm and peace? Jo appeared again. Where were she and Rose this morning? I dispensed with Rose. I shuffled on the log, as my bum bones were uncomfortable. Back straight, Brian. Jo. Jo.

Slightly I open my eyes. Ravi and Niraj sat unmoving in lotus posture. I closed my eyes again. Think of Jo. A drift of marihuana moved across us. The blurred yells and laughs of the ConFest campus below made waves of background. I bent my head back and forward for a while to get some relief from the ache, and then straightened up for another session of keeping to the "rules". Jo. I wanted to cry, half from pain of sitting here, half from the worry of Jo. What was our future? Let that pass. Empty the details, Brian, sit. I peeped out again, for a moment. Is this all there is? I hurt. Do I belong here?

We sat forever. No break, no other guidance, no movement. What had started as curiosity and tentative keenness had collapsed now to anger and pain. I stood and quietly left, and I saw that several others had gone before me. It had been an hour.

I had trained as a teacher once, a qualification I had forfeited now, but I knew plenty to be sure that leading newcomers to a subtle art like meditation could be done in some more effective way. If I wanted to learn to meditate, I should find another swami.

I headed down to the market. I could find Jo, and we could both get one of those tofu burgers? I needed to check the radio sets again.

—

A bit before dark, I sat with George on a log of a fallen tree, partway along the track that led upwards to the sound stage where Santana was to play tonight. It was not yet time for the music. That ubiquitous "other music" from the Hare Krishna chants and tambourines was floating up from the kitchen area.

My landlord Mike had spoken of a George who stayed on his farm property, and I had today realised our red-haired grader man was the same bloke. We shared a few pleasantries.

"You want a toke?" I asked.

"Oh, sure, that'd be great." In American accent.

I unwrapped a small plastic bag. The dope was twigs and some leaf, no sign of a head, a bit pathetic. I brought out some tobacco to mix, and rolled it in four Tally-Ho papers, double thick and lapped to be over length. George had matches, and I offered the lumpy log to him for first draw. He looked at it awhile, lit it, drew and held the smoke. He handed it back, and I followed. There was one word for it: it was shit. We both knew.

We burned it down. He produced his own stash, and used a mechanical roller to make a perfect little version, and we started again.

"Where'd you get it?" he asked.

"I grew it. I used some seeds, and rigged some growing lights under the house. It grew spindly, not very bushy. It's a few months old now, too." I wasn't even in that house any longer.

George's weed was the real product; perhaps he found it at the Hemp Embassy along the creek.

Jann was walking past, but I stopped her to talk. Her wavy hair was easy to recognise. I had been at a talk she gave yesterday in the dome. She was a radio engineer at the NASA tracking station at Honeysuckle Creek, barely forty kilometers from Bredbo but over the Tidbinbilla range.

                                      Down to Earth

Yesterday's had been a captivationg presentation, starting from the Greek and Roman gods of the planets, astrology, and Ptolemy's knowledge and Galileo's. All those she correlated with the secrets and anomalies now being found by the radio-telescopes, and by the tracking of the rocket probes.

NASA had more rendezvous planned with several far planets, and some are launched and travelling already.

"We can see so much," she had said.

Most puzzling was a series of anomalous signals, feeble, being studied at Honeysuckle. Were they "messages"? The dome crowd had been abuzz. The radio source was Saturn or possibly its rings.

ConFest had its own hippie scientist.

George was wide-eyed. "I missed that," he said. "I wish." He asked for Jann's contact details. "I have a friend who should know this stuff."

Jann Cassin, she said. Just call Honeysuckle's main number.

George had rolled another log. We were mellow by the time we walked on to the Santana performance.

———

The population moved out yesterday afternoon. Last night I had collected the remains of the set of radios, dusty, knocked, one missing. I would pass all that to someone else for next ConFest.

It was now the third of January. We were no longer a city of fifteen thousand. Perhaps one per cent of that were still here. The vacuum after the air was sucked.

The constructed features remained, but they had no function now. It was remains of a ghost town. The big ConFest kitchen had its cookers stripped and it stood forlorn. The dome's vinyl fluttered heavily, but its crowd was gone. No children laughed, but the children's workshop still had some streamers and balloons. The shade trees by the trickling Murrumbidgee River were bush trees again, like the millions of other gums across the country.

Red George was using the mechanical blade to bulldoze the dunny compounds, and my lungs hoped the dust clouds were dry and clean. He had drilled three fresh long drops we could use from now, because Mount Oak, despite the implosion, was not finished with. We were wondering about that residual promise of an afterlife, a resurrected life. The black veins of plastic still carried water. Some life was still remaining.

I still had a few tent neighbours scattered near. I had settled here early before the ConFest, and I had set my home in the inner suburbs. It had been close to activities all the festival, but being close together now was more important, and several relocated to cluster into the tent town of the stayers.

Did the ConFest make a clear intention or promise to buy Mount Oak? No. It was a dream. Jim was still calling for donations and support. It was clear he wanted to proceed, but few registered any commitment or dollars.

———

Cairns had left. Morning Sharing had vanished. We were as lost as the sheep that had lived here before us. The ConFest process was an addiction, and I was still here, as bemused as the others.

Six of us pooled our resources and found enough to cook a stew on my gas stove. Brandi and her Canberra friend Libby were like me, all extending our time here to see what happened. We still had homes and work and commitments back in town. We could commute in an hour. Back home it was still summer holiday time. Redhead Sammy was from Victoria. He didn't say much, but he was wondering if a community here might be fun. The other two, I didn't hear their story.

Was there commitment anywhere? Not really.

But if anyone of effective leadership and substance were to get involved in the Mount Oak dream promoted pleadingly by Jim Cairns, then they would not be among the motley crowd left behind. They would be elsewhere organising, arranging their affairs, not sitting on their bare bums around the Bredbo stew pot. Several of us were bare—nothing but our hats. The nudity was a badge of graduating. I've been here, I've coped, I've faced the difficult tasks, I've passed.

I'm likely getting burned, too.

I headed out with Brandi to walk across the hills into the far areas of the Bredbo property. Few among us had any idea what lay there away from the inner festival site. The maximum heat of the afternoon would soon be past.

Behind the ConFest precinct, the ground rose to a high ridge, but it was the southern peaks closer to the front gate that we wanted to explore. Boots on, we walked between the fence and the ridge, beyond the abandoned control station. The canvas structures were all gone, and only earthworks remained.

We were looking to that peak ahead towards the property gate, but we first headed to its right, skirting the target for now, still climbing however.

Brandi was an immigrant from the States, here eight years now, and loving her new country, but still carrying most of her old accent.

"I'm not sure if I can still have clear passage back home," she said. "I was arrested in a protest rally and spent a few days in prison, and I still have unpaid fines."

"Crikey, woman, are you a criminal?"

"No. Well, yes, in a way, by their reckoning. I burned a flag."

I looked straight at her. "Looks like you burned your bra. So you burned the flag?"

"Oh, I've burned a bra, too. That was another time, another story." Brandi grinned, then cut it short and frowned.

"It was in the Vietnam anti-war protests. The United States was an angry and divided country a few short years ago. We were very opposed to the war. Protest was everywhere, it got rough, and there was a lot of violence. People died in our demonstrations. I was there. I lost a dear friend: she fell dead not twenty feet ahead of me. The police were crazy, you can't imagine." She stopped talking, short of breath, but needing to stay with her memories, too.

We had an anti-war movement here, too, I said. I told her of the Melbourne moratorium march, how we scared the country. But we never killed people here in our protests. My story didn't compete.

We had found ourselves in a plateau hammocked between a choice of four peaks. Any semblance of pasture grasses was chewed or dried to nothing. Nothing but dusty soil with some rocky outcrops, particularly up the slopes. Scattered eucalypts stood waiting for better times.

Now we could see where the highest point truly was, not the hill we had intended. It would take us an extra couple of kilometres if we wanted to conquer the high one instead.

"I'm game for it," threw Brandi. There were still several hours of light left in the day. So, tackle the tall hill we did. A naked man in walking boots and cap, and a woman in hat, boots and denim shorts. "Enough to scare the sheep," she said, starting to puff. The grin was back.

"You said you had two kids in town?" I asked.

"Teddy and Lucy. They're teenagers. I drove them home two days ago. They'd had enough here. Both are good kids, and they are fine looking after themselves. They'll go watch *Star Wars* again. I have three more children back in the States, older. I have one grandchild back in the States, too."

"You're a grandma?" She was older than me; why couldn't she be?

"Sure, a few months ago. I haven't been back home, but he looks so cute," she said.

We shared pocket histories as we tramped upwards.

"So do you hear at all from Gerri?"

"No," I said, "she'd met an Italian market gardener who lived out in the Dandenongs, possessive and old-fashioned, and she was planning to marry him. I've lost contact with her completely."

But don't ask about Rose.

When we reached the top, we were masters of the world, a broad scene laid out in all directions. Sitting for a while, pumped with achievement, we just looked. No words. The rock was warm.

Brandi handed me her water bottle. "You know," she said, "we could christen Mount Oak, us two on this mountain. Were you going to suggest the same?"

"Well, it was crossing my mind."

"By my observations, it's been crossing that mind walking up the hill."

I fudged. "We've been enjoying the company and the walk, and the surreal sense of where we are."

"Well, I think celebrating this spot would be a memory to cherish. Crazy and fun. If we finish up buying Mount Oak, we'll have a good claim to infamy. If we ever dare tell."

Why should we never dare tell?

"The first obvious problem," I said, "is that we've come here with nothing. How do we prevent you getting pregnant?"

She giggled. "It can't happen. I'm pregnant now."

My eyes opened wider.

"I'd been attending the Quaker family meetings, and I stayed some nights with a friend I met there. The fling is over, but I'm pregnant. It doesn't stop us."

It didn't stop us. Our useful resources stretched to a pair of shorts and knickers, and an unforgiving flat boulder, now losing its midday heat.

Boots off, she lay back on the rock. We were both sweaty from the climb and from sun cream.

The rough stone made any comfort impossible, but we did succeed technically in failing to get Brandi pregnant again. Symbolism one, romance nil. But mission signed off as completed.

It was time to get off that mountain before the day finished. No moon tonight.

"Brian, you're a funny chook," she said. She wouldn't explain. Her smile was beautiful; we held hands as we strode.

We'd both leave tomorrow.

Sammy – Commune: Mount Oak

Late Summer

All the Bredbo stayers from last month's ConFest went up to the Goulburn meeting. Today the fate of Mount Oak settlement could become clearer.

Sammy was a Bredbo stayer. He had no car, but there were several cars going. It was a two-hour trip, and he persuaded the others to stop in Canberra to get a few bananas and apples and some bread. They didn't know how long the meeting was to be, but if they needed to stay overnight then they would need food to survive.

Jim Cairns had called the meeting to discuss Mount Oak, and he was holding it off the Mount Oak property. It was an early February Saturday.

Perhaps it was at Goulburn because of big George, thought Sammy. George lived at Goulburn, George who drove the digger.

The farm was not easy to find. At the old stone church, they had doubled back.

Gunningbar. It was a sheep farm on a gravel road twenty minutes from town, and it looked run down and dry. From the dusty drive up to the house, he couldn't see any sheep.

"Hey Sam, welcome to the farm. I thought you might not get here." It was Dave from Canberra. Dave looked at home. He had been here before?

"Dave, glad to see ya. I thought we might be lost, too. And we stopped back in Canberra t' get some fruit. Where is anyone?"

"A few are here already. We are all down at the shearers' house on the other side of that rise. Follow that track. You might need your fruit and more. They are talking about staying tonight and possibly the following night for those who want. We can all bunk on the shearers' hut floor. Mike has a huge pile of woolskins for when many people stay over."

"Ya mean this is a common event? People stayin' 'ere?"

"Oh, yes. Mike has many weekends here with work parties. It's an inspiring yarn. I'll fill you in later."

Sammy did get the fuller story. He got it from Brian who strolled up.

The farm had been a real and thriving sheep property once. Late 1800s. It still did run sheep, and Mike the owner grew up here.

Several years back he had despaired of making his fortune from the sheep, and had taken a Government job in Canberra, an hour or so south. Mike had two sprats, twins, but he was a single dad now. So he owned a modest old home in Canberra, did the work and school there, and did the sheep farm business on some of his weekends.

"That's no way t' run no sheep farm," said Sammy, puzzled.

"He knows that. He knows it'll never be the old thriving and efficient farm. But Mike loves his farm. It's in his blood. So he's trying every tricky way he can to make it work sufficiently."

"What ya mean?"

"Some weekends he just brings the kids, and they do what they can. Mike does the jobs he knows how to do by himself. The twins are good at being house help and cook, and Mike gets the real farm jobs done.

"Many of the weekends are special. He has a reputation around Sydney, and even Melbourne, of running enjoyable weekends of farm work. He has lists of young people willing to drive here and work on the weekend at jobs he arranges."

"Oh really! Does 'e pay them? Or charge 'em?"

"He asks they bring good farmhouse food. I know he brings milk and jam and some staples, but his workers bring most of the food like a big roast or bread, fruit and vegies.

"Everyone pitches in. Any day might be toe clipping all the sheep or mulesing, or it might be fence mending or digging weed. It might be rebuilding the falling veranda. The big event of the year is shearing. He has a couple of real shearers and a whole house of visitor-workers. I think Mike's shearing season is the only one around where the real shearers have surrendered to Mike's rules. Women sorting and working in the shearing shed. And—horror—women cooking and eating with the shearers."

"I heard ya been 'ere yourself. You been 'ere for shearin'?"

"For shearing, no. But I have been here on two of his work parties. I live at Mike's Canberra house—I think I hadn't told you that. Up here I've re-strained some fences, and I have helped in cutting and mulesing."

"Mulesin' should be banned."

"Well, that may be. Mike is old school, and he struggles to make it all work. New ideas don't get a hearing."

"Then how come 'e's a Jim Cairns man? Why's 'e with us?"

"Come on, Sammy. Are you perfect and consistent in all parts of your life?"

"Hmm, one or two parts a me life would be good."

"Yeah, we'd all like to have our shit together, eh? Anyway, this is a good place to have a meeting. This property is dry farmland like Mount Oak. Mike is a ConFest man—he was the clown performer wandering around both Cotter and Bredbo. But the main reason they chose here is that George now lives here in Mike's shearers' hut. George invited Jim and Junie to have the meeting here. His way of saying, you come to my place this time?"

It was not true George lived in the shearers' hut, at least not anymore, Brian corrected. George had moved into a crazy new out-building Mike had built a few months back (with work party help, of course). He called it a "yurt". Yurts were Mongol tribesmen's transportable dwellings, but this round wooden assembly Mike had made was too complicated and heavy and hard to assemble. It would never have interested the tribesmen.

George was now camping in it with his girlfriend Maxine from Canberra, and he was studying its construction in detail. He was promising to prepare a new set of simplified plans, and he was damn well going to build that second yurt himself here on the farm.

It was getting too much, too distracting, for Sammy. He preferred life in simple slow pieces. He needed the next couple of hours to skip by instantly, to start the public meeting. Jim's message had said two o'clock.

Was the Mount Oak property really to be bought? There were many waiting for an answer.

Where was Jim Cairns?

Weeks Earlier

As he woke, Sammy realised that Mount Oak today was going to be extremely hot. The sun had barely come up. Sleep had been unpleasant and fitful.

There were foreign smells of burning debris, shouts of impatience and irritation, sounds of tent pegs and rattling canvases, the backwash of a hectic ConFest that had wound up yesterday afternoon. There weren't many left here now, but the scene was a battleground.

So is this what I wanted?

What was there to go back to? Life was empty in Shepparton. There weren't any friends there. The shifts at the cannery earned him a dollar, sure, but he didn't know anyone there at work. When he had work, he thought bitterly. Sammy could not see why returning to his little flat there should hold much appeal. More people here at the ConFest had spoken to him than in a year of living in Shepparton. He lay back in his tiny tent and closed his eyes. Staying in bed wasn't going to last, though—it was getting too warm.

"Hey Sammy, wake up."

"Huh? No, I'm not sleepin', just lyin' here thinkin'. 'Morning, Alfredo, an' thanks, I need to be up."

"Get out of there, Sammy, the day has started. Have you decided yet? You've been agonising about this community idea for two days. You're in one big funk."

"Yeah, ya so right. It keeps goin' round and round in me head."

"That dreadlocked head?" Bushy red display of whiskers, too, but it was the dreadlocks most recognised.

"Round in this dreadlocked head. What about you? You def'n'tely stayin'?"

"Sammy, this is a big adventure like never before. Mount Oak is going to be famous. It will be an example for all Australia on what cooperation and community can be. Fuck, man, you heard Jim down by the river. Everyone can be free to be truly themselves, no-one owns the property, everyone cares. They're planning Keyline water supply and Permaculture and wonderful gardens. Out here on the banks of this dry patch of the Murrumbidgee! The whole Down to Earth movement wants to use Bredbo as a New Age demonstration community. Sure as hell I am going to be in all this from the start."

"Ya think it's gunna work?"

"I'm sure of it. Jim Cairns is setting up a big trust to run it all."

"'E hasn't said where 'e's gettin' the money from."

"Sure he has. He's inviting everyone to put in donations to the trust, until there's enough money to pay for this property. I know a few people staying on. Come over home, the billy's on. And get something on your feet. I have seen some dangerous ulcers here on feet and legs."

———

Sammy and Brian had wandered around the Gunningbar farmhouse and its farmyard trappings. No-one was about at the old house, and their concentration was on the talking, not so much on the scene. They found Jim Cairns down in the shearers' hut, and a meeting was in progress on personal alienation and responsibility. Several of the Mount Oak gang were in the group, plus Dave and some others Sammy didn't know, even if the faces were familiar.

"Mike. He owns the place," whispered Brian. "I'll introduce you later. There's your George from the yurt, and his friend Maxine." They sat on a pile of woolskins on the floor, merged into the group.

The informal gathering wound up about one. A camping gas stove was on the veranda outside, and a large kettle had been boiling. Mugs were found for tea. A few people drifted away, and some found themselves something to serve as a lunch. Sammy stole a few words with Jim, who shook his hand warmly.

The business of the day got under way early afternoon. Fifteen were from Bredbo community, which was more than half the permanents. Together there were about thirty people. Mike slipped out.

"As you know," began Jim, "we gathered at Cotter to look at ourselves and our society. I called the Cotter ConFest into being because I believed many people are seeking something better. We called ourselves Down to Earth. We found something better at Cotter, but we didn't finish with a strong plan to make changes in our broad society.

"Last New Year, I again summoned together the people of Down to Earth to meet and celebrate at Bredbo. I chose the Mount Oak property, two-and-a-half thousand acres. Bredbo was a more difficult place, it was a genuine Australian place, and still we celebrated our life and our vision for the future.

"At Mount Oak, I led several studies on whether that might be a place where Down to Earth may find its base. Could we settle a community there, tame that challenging land, and make for ourselves a centre of community, a place of learning, a bountiful garden, a demonstration to the larger world that it is possible to live in peace, in freedom? We could live without the tyranny of alienation and possessions and boundaries. We could be a seed of change in the greater world."

"How many people do we know want to be living there, Jim?" asked one of the Sydney visitors.

"This is very early days," he replied. "We don't own this property yet. We only have an option to buy. I believe fifty people are staying on. After we become established, there will be many, and many have shared with me their excitement on the Mount Oak project."

"About thirty of us are still there now, Jim," called Fire, "plus a few Canberra people who still have tents on-site, and who come down to visit."

"Thank you, well there are thirty early settlers now at Mount Oak, waiting for the time we know it's bought."

"Jim, where's the purchase up to?"

"Many people have made promises of money to me. It's not enough yet to proceed with a contract. The asking price is sixty thousand dollars. I haven't yet received pledges enough to cover a deposit that would allow us to go ahead."

"Can you tell us how much we can rely on so far?"

"No, I can't tell you that. I'm still talking with several generous people on the matter."

"Are we close?"

"I can't talk on that."

"Jim, many people are wary of making a broad community investment in Mount Oak. It's too difficult. Maybe we should be thinking of a property somewhere more amenable to turning into this ambitious college of new living you're proposing?"

"Allan, it is Allan, isn't it? Allan, we had many long debates on the Mount Oak property during the ConFest, and we remained with the target of founding our base there."

"But each day at those meetings, and I was at them all, there were fewer people present, and fewer who had any enthusiasm to tame that ruined Bredbo farmland."

"Allan, the society we imagine, we yearn for, is a fellowship founded in freedom. It behoves no-one to deny us the freedom, those of us who do indeed wish to proceed with the Mount Oak vision, to continue with our dream. The naysayers should leave, and those who believe should remain free to do as we choose. There's no compulsion to join us, but don't shout down a dream you don't share. Please don't be a part of the alienating forces we are trying to overcome. Those of us who indeed do wish to settle Mount Oak, allow us to seek our funds, to buy our property, to found our community."

Sammy looked around nervously. Brian had his head down. There was not an eye anywhere. Maxine, an octopus, was leaning all over George, and George was enjoying with eyes closed. Mike was missing. Sammy felt alone.

"Jim." Another voice. "Who will own the property?"

"No individual will own Mount Oak. I will set up a foundation that will hold the ownership for all who wish to join in. Anyone is free to live there, joining the community there."

"There is no such foundation yet?"

"I will establish a New South Wales tax-free foundation, the Down to Earth Foundation, when we need it. First, for legal reasons, I'll buy Mount Oak in my name. I will transfer it to a trust as early as possible, for everyone, and for all time."

Sammy stood up. Jim looked across. "Sammy?"

"I have somethin' t' say." Sammy shook. His cheeks burned.

"I want to belong to Jim's Mount Oak community. I live there now, and I want to stay there. It's that vision Jim has. I want to contribute what I can." He handed Jim a small piece of paper and sat down.

Jim looked at it. "I believe Mount Oak project will now proceed. I have in my hands a cheque written to me, for more than half the asking price."

It was all Sammy owned, all his life savings. He was thirty-six, had never married. Sammy had not had a girlfriend to spend on. He had lived frugally, and while his incomes had been small and erratic at times, the expenses in a simple life were even lower. The clapping and applause filled his ears, frightened his soul. He kept his eyes closed. He could keep his tears better hidden.

Mike hadn't been at the shearers' hut meeting. When the now electrified group broke up, they emerged to find the smell of roasting flesh wafting across from the paddock alongside the farmhouse. A whole sheep was on a large handmade spit, and the fire under the beast was well established. It was some wonder no-one had noticed the smells earlier, but perhaps the wind had changed during the afternoon. Indeed it had.

There were some hungry bellies on the farm. Few had managed any lunch, and the day's excitement had peaked and was settling into euphoria still tinged with disbelief. The drifting aromas were a torture.

"I don't eat meat, ever," said Nancy.

"Well, we've lived vegetarian for the month," added Sammy. "Except'n Johnny who sticks t' himself across the ridge. I know 'e traps some rabbits."

"Did you bring any food?" she asked. "We were planning to drive back today, but now it feels wrong to leave."

"Hey, Mike, whose idea was this?"

"Hi, Sammy, I own the sheep. I reasoned most would stay tonight, and there seemed little other plan to prepare any food. So ..."

"But most of us are vegetarian."

"Many of us are hungry," said Mike.

"But," and Sammy stopped. There was no answer to make.

Jim had left, but thirty hippies dragged together a huge bonfire near the spit fire in a side paddock at a humble old Goulburn sheep farm. Thirty bellies ate heartily from the pulled away carcass of a crossbreed eater. Several drums appeared, and a trumpet. There was no moon, but merriment continued until many of the dark hours had passed.

—

Early Autumn

About fifteen remained on the Mount Oak community. Overall health was fair.

The Murrumbidgee had flooded a few weeks ago, and the road in from the highway had its concrete bridge span washed downriver. Access into Mount Oak now took an extra thirty kilometres via a back track nearer Cooma. The sense of isolation was crippling. But some green grass had come with the rains, and then the countless rabbits.

They had chosen a plot of ground not far from the improvised water system as the inaugural garden, and it now had chicken wire around to keep out the raiding wildlife. Comfrey, rosemary, basil and other herbs were growing, and it was all bordered with sunflowers. Much work was still needed. They had planted a few vegetables, but there had been no success on that score yet. They had started buying lime and fertilisers, despite objections of a few.

Many buildings built for the ConFest still stood. The flood-waters had swept across the children's workshop, a large building low near the river, and many of the roofing sheets had torn off. Flood debris was clinging in the rafters. Higher structures were intact, including the steel and vinyl dome, which served as accommodation for visitors. The ConFest kitchen still stood, but a structure that size was overkill for the small remaining community. There was now an alternate open-air kitchen with a cooking campfire, and the old kitchen had become the commune office and telephone place.

The current main project was to build a thirty-foot-high new A-frame building. The rafters were up, and corrugated iron was stacked nearby waiting to go on top. So, life might have been tough and basic, but this wasn't a layabout community. It needed effort to live and eat, to build their experimental family of supportive people, and to set up an improved hamlet and environment.

But Sammy knew, they all knew, that they were for all useful purposes quite alone.

Four of the community sat on the log that always lay by the kitchen campfire. The fire burned day and night, and was the nearest thing to a soul that Mount Oak had.

"So who wants to go t' the Fyshwick market on Thursday?" asked Sammy. The market was the usual vegetable source, and vegetables made up most of the Mount Oak diet. He went every fortnight, driving the ute. Some of the community had no licence to drive on the highway, although there had been times when they overlooked that trifle—a risky trick, because tiny Bredbo town had a reputation for often having a police car patrol.

"Yeah, count me in," said Fire. He had been Mex, but at Mount Oak he had rebirthed himself as Fire. Fire was a solid worker around camp. We needed more folk like him, thought Sammy.

"OK, good. We 'ave the market jobs this week, remember. We need to get there early." The Mount Oak boys (Usually it was the men, recalled Sammy. We need to talk that through before long.) had an occasional contract to do some fruit-stall work at the market. The work was scrappy, odd jobs, stacking, cleaning. The traders were happy with the Mount Oak people. They were willing enough labourers, and the return was in leftover vegetables and fruit. Barter. Cashless. Taxless. It conserved their precious dollars.

"Which reminds me," said Nancy, "can we get a fridge here? We always lose some of what comes back." Nancy did at least her fair share of the communal cooking.

"I've been looking out for a kerosene fridge," said Fire, "but I think they have disappeared these days. I'll keep trying. I left notices in several places in Canberra a few weeks ago. There are more spots I can try."

"Are we never going to get any electricity running?" Nancy was dragging a piece of wood into the fire. She lifted out the billy that had been boiling contentedly. "It's ocker tea. Anyone?" She counted two nods, and poured for three.

"Hey, we know a grid connection is more money than we can contemplate. Solar would be good for one day, but that isn't cheap either. The panels are getting cheaper, but last I checked they were about a hundred dollars a watt, and one or two hundred watts of that is out of our budget, before we even look at the batteries. Perhaps we could omit batteries, just get some daytime power."

"Fire, stop. Too many numbers. Just tell me we can't do it. But didn't we score an experimental wind generator?"

"We did, before you came back. Some bloke living across in the Tinderrys near Jerangle and attached to the CSIRO research office in town called in. He runs a wind turbine consultancy and imports them as a sideline. He had this old unit they had been trying, but he didn't want it. So one day he turned up here, unloaded it, and said it was ours, but we had to get it working for ourselves. We pestered him to load it back in again and drive it up to the far ridge for us. We didn't get any more information from him. Something about gift-horses, we judged. It's still up on the hill.

"None of us has much idea how to make it work. We haven't tried yet. For now, we have no fridge. The weather is cooling. Vegies going off should be less of a problem for winter, so we have some time to solve the issue." Fire sipped slowly.

"We need a hilltop party tomorrow," he continued. "We should check the generator to see if it is intact and could be working. Then we'll need some way to mount it high enough to catch the wind. From memory, I think its swivel function was built in. Yes, we should get on to it as a proper project. If we let it drag on unsolved like the water tank issue, then we're making the oncoming colder months that much more difficult."

The tank left from the ConFest had been a disaster, and arranging a replacement water solution had taken too long to address. The communal mood had been too depressed, too disorganised, to solve the problem initially, and bucketing water from the pitifully low river stream had been a part of the primitive life they managed for the first month. They had bought an old water cart from a nearby farmer, and had made special appeal to Jim Cairns for funds to buy a small petrol-driven water pump. That was still the Mount Oak water supply system.

Jim didn't visit Mount Oak much lately. Just for the policy meeting here, after Goulburn, and one other unannounced visit. They had invited him several times last month, by letter, but he hadn't come.

One reply explained that the existing owner held the land as crown lease, not freehold, and the first stage of purchase was to be change-over to freehold. That process wasn't yet under way. In the meantime, he insisted they should build no permanent structures. What about our A-frame? thought Sammy.

A surreal unease pervaded the little community.

———

Nancy had left yesterday. Sammy had liked Nancy. Not that there was anything emotional. No, Nancy was just good value, no nonsense.

Why was it all so difficult here? Where was the support from Canberra, from all the ConFest people? Where was Jim?

He had covered the sleeping bag with a woolskin Mike had given him at Goulburn. Sammy had been unwilling king for one wild night at Goulburn. Now he wanted to stay in bed. It took a little later into the mornings now to be warm. He was hot, and then he shivered. Another fever? Would anyone know?

Man, what had he done? At Shepparton, he had a job to go to most months. He'd had a place to live. Sure, it was quiet, sure, it was lonely back south. Was this life now any better? Where was the friendly community? Was there any security?

There was no going back. No money still in the bank. He was chilled again. His head throbbed.

Sammy pulled his frame into an infant curl, and his eyes stayed closed. He pulled the rugging around his chin and wished the world out there would vanish.

—

Mid-Autumn

Sammy arrived at Paddington with Dave.

"Hey, great to see you again, brother." It was the Reverend Tom. "We need all our wisdom here today. It's a difficult time."

"Hello, Tom. I need a hug. And this is Sammy from Bredbo. It was Sammy's cheque that made Mount Oak commune viable."

"Brother, I've heard about you. We all have. You are brave and very generous. Has Dave brought you?"

"Hi. This is all a bit overwhelmin'. Dave drove down to Bredbo early this mornin', and collected me from there. The others from Mount Oak couldn't get 'ere, but I'm to represent 'em. I'm representin' all the Mount Oak settlers."

"How many are there now?"

"Well, some people drift in and out, but I s'pose there'd be a dozen who are at Mount Oak full-time. We are the hard core."

"How are you all feeling?"

"Oh, we're a rough bunch, mostly. Like me, I s'pose. We're still tired after the high of the festival. There was so much cleanup after everyone went home. We could do with some support.

"Actually, we divided into a couple of groups, and there was some tension. Well, two camps plus dancin' Carol up by 'erself. We didn't have any water running or stored anywhere for a month, so that was making life difficult."

"But we installed a huge supply tank for the festival, the one Benny Zable painted. It should've been left full."

"Brother, when the crowd had gone, the tank'd split its side. I don't know, a car may have hit it. It couldn't hold any water. We were drinkin' water direc' from the river."

"Straight from the 'Bidgee?"

"It was that or nothin'. We 'ad buckets. The river was close on dry, and we know it got a bad water report before the ConFest, but it's all we 'ad. We now 'ave an old tanker cart to store in, and a pump from the river."

"That's a worry. The main tank was to remain operational after the ConFest. It should've had a reasonable supply left for a few people, and the aim was to bring a run down from up the slope. The property owner had reported there's a spring up there somewhere."

Dave interjected. "Tom, Yeomans isn't working on the Mount Oak Keyline plan now. You didn't know yet? During the Bredbo ConFest he was offering to do the complete design for Mount Oak. That was before he realised the size of the task, quite how barren Mount Oak is, and how it wasn't the right place to be developing, and community support was lacking. He withdrew his offer to Jim after the ConFest finished, until Mount Oak is shown to be viable."

"No, I didn't know that. Sammy, and Dave too, come in and get a cup of tea. There's a kitchen in that corner."

"Hey, this is an amazin' church here," said Sammy. He wasn't liking the previous topic. "I've never been t' Sydney."

"Oh, then welcome to Paddington. This place is the birthplace of all the ConFests. In this very hall; it's our original home. This hall is where Jim and Junie still serve wrap food on some Paddo Market days."

"Is that why we're 'ere today? Home ground?"

"Yes, of course. We have some difficult negotiations to have here."

"Difficult?"

"About where Down to Earth is heading. What the ConFests have meant. On what we need to do better next time."

"And about Jim?" Sammy looked concerned.

"Jim and Junie are here. We are all here. We need each other. We work together."

"And about Mount Oak?" He was even more cautious now. He had that feeling again—to run away and hide.

"Especially including Mount Oak."

Brian – Canberra

Spring

The work crew was Mike, Marcus and me.

Mutt Marcus lived here all week while owner Mike earned a civil salary in Canberra. A neighbour from the stone church up the road checked the dog in its lockup each afternoon, and Mike repaid with deliveries sometimes from Canberra. But today was a weekend and it was a sheep day. When called to duty, Marcus showed his rounding-up skills are clearly from kelpie instinct. Despite the scrappy farm training the dog had received from Mike, he was still a usable assistant.

The dog's job for today was to keep pushing the terrified sheep up into the funnelling fences that pushed each animal in turn into the dip. Mike had been up early, and had filled the dip from the old tanker truck. The tank had been filling from the dam overnight, using an old donkey-driven pump, until around midnight when the fuel ran out. I heard it time out, from bed.

Mike had added the dip chemicals this morning. Organophosphates, he said. "Try not to get it on you, but it's not easy. Just do the best you can."

The sheep dip structures were very old. The fencing had been repaired in several places, but a new dip was too much time and dollars.

There were two holding pens for the incoming animals, the large one now full. We would do half the farm mob today; the balance were for next weekend. The second pen was small, and twenty or thirty sheep at a time were drafted from the first pen. That second pen narrowed to a raceway one beast wide. As the animal moved forward, the ground rose slightly, and that hid the abrupt plunge that awaited. The aim was to shove, trick, or terrify the animal into cresting the rise until, too late to reconsider, it fell or sprang forward into the dip water.

Every sheep had its own way of being difficult. Some were new season additions to the flock, but it was obvious most had a blinding recall of last year's passage through this alleyway and the hell that lay beyond. It was a frantic circus task for the dog and his owner. Marcus behind, snapping, barking, darting back and forth, packing them up and keeping them tight, doing what his genes designed him for, psychological warfare. Mike beside and outside the laneway, but leaning over and shoving, abusing, and pushing fingers where sheep had a problem, until each animal had only one option, over that rise.

Some sheep recalled too well. Mike jumped the fence and used all his body weight to crudely throw the animal onto the down-slope.

I, too, leaned over the fence, but further along at the water dip itself. I had to guarantee that each sheep was fully wetted all over with the magic and toxic water. Using a long-handled fork, 'Y'-shaped at the end, I pushed each victim under so it went to the bottom, and I held it there for a long couple of seconds.

The insulted and stricken animal, after a swim for dear life, scrambled out and fled into the holding yard to discuss the ordeal with its mates.

It wasn't a normal working party this week, just Mike and me. Not even the kids. It was late afternoon when I returned to the house to think about a meal. The return of the dipped mob to their paddock, the cleanup, Mike was attending to. Dog stayed with master.

Mike had set out lamb chops for thawing. Some vegetables from town were in a paper bag. Add half a flagon of claret, and I had the makings of a Saturday evening meal for two farm blokes. I set about scrubbing off my organophosphates and sheep grime.

It was well dark and the fire was burning when we sat to eat.

I'd lived at several share houses around Canberra in the six months since I left my first refuge at Mike's house. Sitting together now, the two of us, it was more intimate than on any of those days with him back in Canberra.

We yarned and laughed about the meat-eating vegetarians of early in the year. "So how's the whole Mount Oak project going now?"

"Sad story," I answered.

Mike looked at me.

"Jim's continuing with buying the property, but only a handful of settlers are still down there. Poor Sammy left last week. He's disillusioned, and says he won't be back."

"But didn't Sammy put in almost all the money? That's why we were celebrating?"

"Yes, he did put in the funds. I don't think he is asking for it back, either. He just wants to be out. Gone down to Victoria, I think. Mike, tell me about the clown act. Why do you do it?"

"It's my inner chaos coming out." He laughed. Mike may have rural in his blood, but it was not chaos. Some feral, but not bedlam. Quiet deliberation.

"Brian," he went on, "it's the joy that bubbles out when I play with the crowd. I need the joy, the laughs."

"You are so good at it. I have watched you at Commonwealth Park on Sundays ..."

"I have a contract to do one Sunday each month."

"... and the crowd at the park love you. The kids run from everywhere, and their oldies are not far behind. The parachute trick I like best."

"That's one of my best props. Have you joined in the parachute shake?"

"No, not yet. But why do you say you need the joy? Need?"

"Life needs fun, forgetting the heavy stuff, letting it go." He ate for a while.

"I was very depressed for a long time before you came," he continued. "I was immobilised, useless. I had to pull myself out of it, and I got involved in some new activities, and the clown act is part of that." He paused again.

"We used to live on this farm together. She was a city girl, and this was a dead-end place in a blind-alley industry to her. Sally was right, but I came from here, I belong here. So we rented a Canberra house and commuted. We tried to compromise."

"It didn't work?"

"It got more complicated. She threw herself into the excitement of the Labor Party campaigning in '74 after the double dissolution. It was a hotbed of intrigue, feminism and journalism. She loved it. She wanted to be an action woman. By a year later it all blew apart, when Labor was so dramatically dismissed by the Governor-General. She ran off with that firebrand McMungo and left me with the kids.

"We share the kids now, but I was barely surviving for a long time. The farm up here fell apart, and that part I'm still trying to put together."

Every clown's face hides tears.

"I wasn't very functional when I came to your place either," I said. I had simply bolted for two months, hitch-hiked to Darwin. When I returned, I never went back with Rose.

"I knew that." He looked at me. "Now I take life as it comes," he continued. "I make good out of it. I make the weekends here good. The Willing Workers organisation finds me various fun people. With active young people around, the pain is gone. Sometimes I find a warm bed companion, and I enjoy that if it happens, but it's a jolly weekend anyway. I get the chores done."

"You get on enough with Sally?"

"Yes, we're OK enough now. Funny thing is, after she came down from the dramas she put into her life, she with-drew from the political scene altogether. She imploded. She lives on a potters' collective on the fringe of Canberra. Not a very good potter, I suspect. I don't care anymore. She has to sort her own soul out."

We sat for a while.

"Brian, a couple of things I've been meaning to ask." We had never stopped and talked together like this back in Canberra.

"Try me."

"Talking on souls, and purpose in life, whatever inspired you to join a religious order? I've always thought it was so far removed from the Brian I know."

"I've wondered too. I was idealistic. I bought the religious heroism side, the life of dedication. And it was a schoolteaching order. I dreamed I could not only teach in school, but I could befriend kids, give them insight on how to handle life. Handling life felt so hard. No-one quite got it, I believed."

That the order could have been a runaway place, a refuge? Not a topic.

"So is that what you found?"

"Neither. The claim to a perfect life I never saw borne out, just frustration for me, and people in there as problem-atic and flawed as anywhere. As for the teaching part, well I qualified as a teacher, but I hated the school environment, the chaos, the wearying confrontations. And I doubt I have any secrets of life worth a peanut for someone else."

"OK, It's been intriguing me."

Another pause. An ocean of old memories, the flotsam of a faraway time.

"There's something else," he said.

"Sure ..."

"This is a little difficult. I don't want to offend you. Have you ever thought you might have some epileptic symptoms?"

My eyes opened wide. "No, not at all. What prompts that?"

"The way I see you sometimes simply stare into space, disconnected. Then you come back as though nothing had happened."

"I'm not aware of that."

"I've seen it. It's eerie. I thought it could be a minor epilepsy symptom. Thought I should ask, sorry."

It didn't make sense.

"Mate, I sort all stuff out by writing. A diary. I never told anyone before."

A diary?

———

Mike drove us back through Goulburn into Canberra. He had to collect his daughters for the week, and I would have occasion to see the artist commune myself. He was proud of the two girls, and they were doing well with their dancing class.

We turned left from the highway near the Territory border, a few kilometres from suburbia, and drove along Majura Lane, a dirt road leading behind Mount Majura to the airport and Pialligo. We passed the rifle range, and slowed and turned into a gated property bearing an old sign *The Willows*. Three hundred metres ahead, beyond the settlement buildings, were many weeping willows, marking a substantial creek. I left Mike to make his handover negotiations, and had myself a short walk around.

A plane flew in low, low enough to have made any conversation impossible, and I could feel its roar thudding through my body. This spot was on the flight path for the airport a kilometre away.

This settlement long pre-dated Canberra's founding in the 1920s. The main building held farmhouse versions of kitchen, dining and sleeping spaces, and a wooden veranda covered with grapevine. The wire fly-screen door squawked on its springs and slammed like I recalled my grandmother's had.

Next to there was a slab hut, in fair repair, its hand-hewn vertical timbers no longer all keyed into aligned weather tight position. Slab huts were late 1800s structures. Desiccated harnesses and cobwebbed bridle gear still hung in high hooks. Old stables. A potter's wheel stood in here now, and benches with craft paraphernalia and blocks of clay. I saw no kiln anywhere.

Another small outhouse, now a solitary bedroom, I presumed, looked like it may once have been a milk separator house, or a butcher's blockhouse. I was inventing.

Damn. This place could have been an alternative to Sandford or Bungendore once. But they were past dreams.

Leonie – ConFest: Berri

Early Summer

They didn't drive straight to the Council chambers at Berri. It was still three hours early, and they had planned it that way. Lee thought they could skip the tea-break too and instead head right into the park. First things first. Charlie was OK.

Berri was an irrigation town in Riverland country on the Murray. The river snaked into a large bend here, but the town was not in the bend. That land was too low, too risky to have houses and commerce. The area captured in the bend was left as native floodable parkland, and the town was mostly on higher ground to the north-west.

The river bend park was too far out and too unkempt to get much patronage. But it was still the bend that identified Berri. The Aboriginal word "berybery" meant "bend in the river".

Berri did at its southern edge still front to the river. Riverboats used to stop at the jetty, and there was the hotel and accommodations on the town side of the road, and a well-used beach and a promenading track on the river side.

But back to Berri's "Martins Bend" Park. The northern border was an impenetrable band of scrub, and inside that was old barbed wire fencing. They stopped and checked that out.

The single entrance in was a long track through various eucalypts. Then on reaching the river, myriads of bush tracks fanned out until each again met the bending watercourse. Altogether, the park was a hundred hectares or more.

Only Jenny had explored here before, and that was last week. She and her partner Rick had been scouring the River-land looking for some spot like this. It was Jenny's report that had brought today's more formal expedition. She, Chas and Lee were back in Jenny's old camping van to look more closely. Was this the right candidate for a ConFest site?

The Riverland Council had offices in Renmark further up the Murray. Once every four or five weeks Council met at the auxiliary chambers in Berri. Today was that day. Chas and Jenny were to meet with the Town Clerk and his parks manager later this afternoon. Might Council be agreeable to a national group planning and running a large festival in its Martins Bend Park? Had Council agreed to jamborees or festivals there in the past? It could be an easy answer.

They would need to offer a more detailed proposal to Council later. Jim Cairns's imprimatur was needed, too. Today, it was just an informal indication of favourability that they sought. Even a faint nod would be some help, because Jim's national reputation and influence were powerful black-mail when needed. If Council was outright disinterested, well, they would need to continue site-hunting.

From the van Chas was taking photographs. "Bloody River Gums. Hope we see no strong winds."

"But these trees are so majestic, they'll make excellent shade for festival camping," said Lee. *Better than the scrub in the desert country I grew up in.*

"No, River Reds may look big and shady and impres-sive, and many of them can grow very old, five hundred years or more. But they can be a worry to camp under. They have a reputation of dropping huge branches the weight of a truck, without notice. Do you want to be camping under that when it comes down?"

She didn't answer.

                    Down to Earth

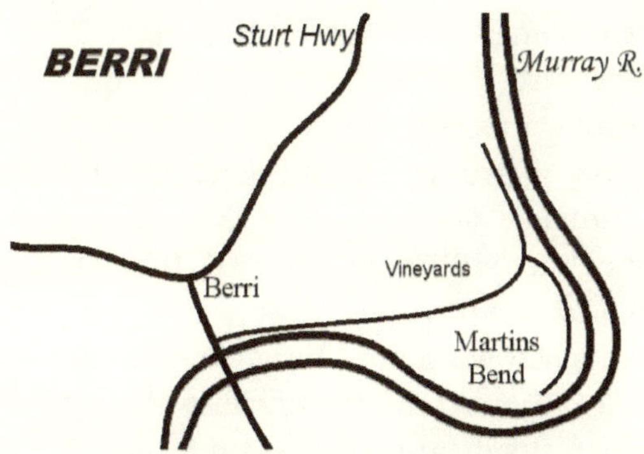

They pulled up near the riverbank and walked. Most of the trees were not red gums, anyway. Lee found a can of drink, opened it and gave it and a sandwich to young Charlie. Jenny headed off separately, lost in her thoughts.

"Well, the site certainly is large enough to house a ConFest."

"No infrastructure of use." Just two forgotten toilet blocks.

"Yes, there's town water here."

"What, one long thin pipe for thousands of people?"

"One thin pipe and a big holding tank is how engineers have designed city water systems forever. We can soon arrange water storage. Water on tap is a big step up on what we started Bredbo with. Bredbo began with zilch, and we made it work."

"OK, I can accept that. What about electric power?"

"Nothing. If needed we could bring in a power plant like we could have used at Bredbo."

Jenny had returned. "What this about power?" she said. "There's a caretaker hut further around, and that has to have power. A ConFest doesn't need much power."

"OK, we'll go up and look at that. Do we have enough cleared spaces for the big constructions?"

"Like a sound stage? I think so. That area there could be fine. There'd be still plenty of audience space for it."

"The remaining dome still at Bredbo could fit on that other side. Not sure how we get that here, but I'm sure we can solve it. Call Canberra."

"So, could it work?" asked Lee. She'd been to one ConFest, a smaller local one at Cambray in Western Australia. She had still been married then, but somehow she'd managed to escape for a week.

"I saw this last week, and I made my decision then. But I wanted confirmation from someone else today," said Jenny.

"This spot fits beautifully," said Chas. "I think your weeks on the road have been well rewarded. This park is saying 'Yes Please'. I need a few more photos first, to be sending off to Jim. We need to get it past Council, of course. And we need a good map from them." He fetched from the van his fiddle, lifted it from its case, and walked around playing a jig. "We need to sing the site in."

"So then let's get out of here. I want that cuppa tea in town."

———

Easter

Two days before Berri ConFest was to begin, the groundworks were well under way. Lee had arrived yesterday to help as she could. Charlie was with a friend in Adelaide, and would arrive here in a few days.

The day started with a meeting in the coordination tent. They were Adelaide people mostly, and many were the team Lee had come to know in the past couple of months. She wasn't a praying person, but the planning meeting had a touch of a prayer gathering. Touchy-feely stuff, communal hugs, chants and handholds. *Get used to it, Leonie, it's the way it's done here.*

Council had insisted they have a pan service for toilets. Sewage was to be carted away daily. They would deliver forty units today. The large map showed four areas to take ten each, and anyone first spotting the delivery truck from Council should direct it to the coordination tent for instructions.

Dave and his mates from Queanbeyan had freighted the Bredbo dome by train two weeks ago, and the dispatch papers were here. But the local train siding didn't have those carriages here yet. Assign two people to follow up. Pester the railways, here and Adelaide, to find out where the carriages were now. Perhaps they're lost on some other siding? In any case, track the consignment down. If they were anywhere close to Berri, hire a truck and arrange to pick it all up

where they were. Conscript a work gang as needed. Try to get the dome steel and skin here by end of today. Because the dome should be standing by tomorrow night.

Today the sauna should be built. A digger would excavate into a bank and a team would top that with iron sheet. Lee volunteered for labourer work on that.

Summer from Adelaide arrived with huge stack of ConFest booklets, a twenty-seven-page introduction and guidebook for all the arrivals. The booklet was a new idea for

Berri, and was the brainchild of the busy Adelaide crew. Chas passed copies around for appraisal.

The gathering wound up with a chant of "Aum".

Her sauna work would not begin until this afternoon, so Lee found her way to the signs workshop, under a tree on the riverbank. A large truckload of offcut wood had been dumped there from a timber mill. Much of the wood was for firewood during the ConFest, and there were various piles on the site, but there were also some pieces that could serve as signs. Pots of white water-based undercoat and blue, red and black paints were sitting on a bench, and an assortment of small brushes.

It was obvious walking around the ConFest grounds that the signs work had been going on for a day or two, as labels and direction posts were nailed up in many places. Some painters had been content with plain lettering, and some felt obliged to unleash their inner artiste. Bloody hard to read some of those, thought Lee, but any sign was better than no sign. A notepad listed signs still sought or suggested. Paints 101.

"So what is most needed?" she asked Stevie, who wore a paint-spattered frock.

"We need signs back in town and along the highway. They should go up tomorrow. Otherwise many ConFesters are going to be wandering the streets of Berri asking directions of every local. Can you remember where the several turnoffs were back at Berri?"

"I have a car, I can go out on a scouting trip. I have a map. Leave it with me."

Fifty minutes later, Lee sat among paints and boards, undercoating four pieces she had picked from the pile. Plastic paint is a wonderful invention. She would do a few more from the list too, more *Toilet* and *Kitchen* and *Water Tap* signs.

The ConFest preparation project was more complex than she had imagined. Some people must have the project manager flair, and could hold in their minds all the component tasks. For this morning, she felt more content to be doing her smaller part in the greater scheme. By lunchtime, she had left four street signs and several others drying on the bank.

The ConFest kitchen, now running, served lunch for everyone. It was simple fare today, but Lee had seen what the kitchen was planning for the five ConFest days. Each morning uncooked breakfast foods and tea would start the day, but later in the day was to be a choice of a soup, a cooked plate or a raw food plate, different daily.

CONFEST 79   MENU

	Sunrise	**Sunset**	
DAY 1	Fruit Juices Porridge or Muesli or Fruit Salad served with hot or cold milk, yogurt, or apple sauce Herbal Tea.	SOUP: COOKED: RAW:	Cream of Vegetable Soup or Gazpacho. Bean Loaf with yogurt sauce Steamed Greens in garlic drag Assorted Salads, Bread. Spinach Rolls or Stuffed Capsi. Honeyed Carrots, Persian Cucum. Assorted Salads, Bread.
DAY 2	Fruit Juices Porridges or Muesli or Fruit Salad served with	SOUP: COOKED:	Potato & Leek Soup or Spinach & Walnut Soup Ratatoulie or Stuffed Capsi.

She sat eating her free soup and damper roll. The Kitchen Village today was a hive of activity, with stall construction for five other food suppliers. Several commercial caterers from Adelaide, and one from locally, were intending to sell food also. There could be a lot of good nosh by two more days.

Noonday was hot. A digger had cut a part of a box shape into the riverbank. It wasn't a clean plain box, because two stepped benches remained carved in the dirt, and these would be sitting space. A timber-framed front wall had been added, and roof framing.

When she arrived, two men were nailing corrugated iron to the roof and the wall and the pieces of side wall. As the iron enclosed the box shape, the sauna room got dark, and just one half-height doorway remained. The wall had one more breach, for the hotbox pipework. The wood-fired hotbox was fed outside, and the flue pipes ran through the wall to heat the sauna room. It was crude, primitive, and enough to serve a few days of hilarity.

The door stayed off initially, and Lee and two other second shift workers first covered the rooftop with soil and grass clods, then worked inside to pack down and smooth the floor and the earthen seats. She helped Maxine set an edging of board to each seat to give strength against breaking away too early. There would be many hot and sweating bums using this steam room soon.

By later afternoon, she had fixed a hessian sheet as a door, and while the test firing was setting the mud used as seals, she checked her door and the walls for leaks.

The first full firing of the sauna would be tomorrow, and they would keep it burning all evening, as a celebration marking the end of the setup days.

"Well, I'm hungry," said Maxine. "Want to see if the kitchen is open yet?" Curry was in the air.

Lee could spot a feisty woman. Over a hearty stew, they learned some of each other's story. Maxine lived in Canberra, independently, choosing life her way.

"I spend some weekends up past Goulburn," she said. "I have a dear friend George who lives out on an alternative sheep farm, lying low."

"Lying low?"

"He was a US operative, and still has health and drug problems that come from his Vietnam days. He's a big man, Lee, larger than life, even in hiding. He's not allowed a gun now, but he practises his accuracy with a crossbow. I like a real man."

                                   Down to Earth

Maxine looked up, broke off, and ran into the market-place. Moments later she returned holding hands with a bemused and stocky man, sporting ineptly cut short red hair and a bushranger beard.

"Sammy, this is my friend Lee. My newest friend."

"Hello, Sammy." His handshake didn't have the "big man" feel Lee thought was Maxine's preference. But she did recognise him; she had noticed him this morning carrying buckets of water to dampen the vehicle dust on the track.

Sammy first went to find his own food.

"He's a darling," said Maxine. "A gentle soul. He lives on nothing, yet he helped buy the Mount Oak commune. I was there. I haven't seen him for a year."

Back with his bowl of curry, Sammy sat with them on another log. Seating generally was logs, some hay bales and scraps of old carpet thrown on the ground.

"Now, tell me what you have been doing. I heard you left Mount Oak. Where are you living?"

"I went back t' Victoria. The winter was cold at Bredbo, but I don't want to talk about that. I have a warm cabin behind me brother's house near Numurkah, where 'e has 'is family farm." His eyes were down.

"You have some work there?"

"John drops me off each mornin' in Shep' when I have cannery work. It's better than years ago when I lived by myself."

"John is OK to live with?"

"Maxine, 'e's me brother. I live at the back, but 'e's always there. It's good. Sometimes I eat with the family, and sometimes we have some friends there as well."

Lee chose not to move into the conversation. Maxine reached to hold both of his hands in her own.

"Sammy, I want you to be happy. You deserve that. Tell me you are happy."

"Well, I'm happier than I managed at Bredbo. I guess I am."

"Do you have some friends, someone to talk with, have a beer with, watch the footy with?"

"Sometimes in the house with John we watch football with some friends." He withdrew his hands to finish eating his food.

"John's friends?"

"Yeah, I s'pose."

"Are some of them nice people to know? Do you enjoy their company?"

"Yes, I do. Of course I do."

"What brings you back here to the ConFest? Don't you find that difficult after leaving Bredbo?"

"But Down to Earth is where I know some people. I have friends 'ere. I know you."

"Yes, you do, you have many friends here. We love you. Have you found any old girlfriends here yet?"

"No, not yet." He dropped his eyes again. "I just got 'ere last night."

Maxine glanced at Lee. It was a question. Lee gave a wry smile. *You have to play this one yourself, Maxine.*

"Sam," Maxine said. Soft. Slow. "Is there anyone here among the DTE people you have been really close with? Anyone you have spent a night with, had an affair with?"

"Not in the Down to Earth lot, no."

"These are your friends, you said so. Do you have a girlfriend back home, or in Shepparton?"

"No, not just now I don't."

Careful Maxine, some menfolk's friends aren't girls.

But Maxine was pressing ahead. "Oh, my friend, have you ever had a girlfriend, a lover?"

His face blazed redder than his beard. Maxine took his hands again. A tear ran down from one eye.

"Sam, look at me." She was frowning at his forlorn expression. "You have never had a lover?"

"No."

"A beautiful, generous man, and no-one has discovered you." They sat without words for a full minute.

"Sammy, will you spend tonight in my bed? I'd like to be your first lover."

"Well, I don't know 'ow to answer that."

"You could say Yes," suggested Maxine.

"Yes, I would like that."

Lee made her exit.

———

Thursday morning early, day one, Lee was down on the grass by the river. The leader was Andrew, a massage and Yoga teacher. The program read 'Relaxation Session'. At least it promised not to be a pseudo-religious activity. She was getting used to those, but not by ready choice.

Andrew guided the group through simple breathing exercises and slow movements. A mist still hung on the river. Smoke and toast smells wafted past. Early bathers splashed further along the bank. Far in the distance, a morning saxophone played fragments of melody. Lee let the intrusions stay there, not bothering her.

Andrew finished the gentle introduction to the day, apologising that he needed to be at the Morning Sharing ceremony at the main stage. She made her way to the Sharing too. It was to be every morning at nine.

A huge crowd had arrived before her—she thought a thousand or two. The stage had a public address system, and it needed it. She had been at the morning coordination meetings in the setup week. This was the grown-up version of those little planning meetings. Shake hands with those beside you, introduce yourself, smile. Andrew, in his caftan, introduced the speakers, held the ceremony together. He explained the main events of the day. Jim Cairns was presented to the cheering crowd, and he would later speak in the blue dome on Marxism and Wilhelm Reich. Tonight's full moon would be celebrated at the fire, as the big stage music will be tomorrow night. Questions were fielded, volunteers were requested.

Lee wandered off at the break-up of the Sharing, and sought out the Women's Tent. The women's liberation group was planning a street theatre event for the weekend, and she wondered if she might join in. Finding places was simple, as good signs now stood around the site. Walking past the Raj Neesh complex, the aromatic smells from their kitchen floated in the air, and their workshop sign advertised an afternoon of 'Witchcraft and Natural Magic'. How was she ever going to fit in all these things? A penny farthing bicycle wobbled past, trying to stay stable on the gravel path. Through the treetops, she could see a fluttering kite.

She was alone, but it didn't matter, it was all exciting. Charlie would be here Saturday afternoon, and the temporary freedom would be over, she would be Mum again, still Leonie, but Mum too. She was missing Charlie.

———

It was the biggest night of the festival, a comfortable summer evening one night past full moon, and on the main stage the first band was warming up. Dark had descended on the river valley, and the aromatic smells of hippie living were wafting all over.

"All you folk," came the PA, "let's sit on the grass in lines behind one another, and we can give ourselves a good back and shoulder massage."

A wait.

"OK, wasn't that so much fun? Now turn and thank your friendly therapist. The music will start in a few minutes."

"Oh, hello," she said, "I know you. We met at Brandi's place in Canberra. I'm Lee."

They sat together on the ground listening to the band. It was rough paddock grass in the daytime, and getting a bit trodden. But it had been mown by Council a few days ago, and with the moon now trying to rise and in the light thrown from the stage, it was quite the best place to sit. They swayed to the beat, aware of their loud coloured clothes, the magic of the evening, the company of like-minded people. Mostly they were increasingly conscious of each other so close. Each was quite alone, each felt the presence of a close stranger, an unknown, a mystery. A friendly mystery.

His name was Brian. All she knew was that and his presence.

For twenty or thirty minutes they listened. To the music, and to the developing vibe, the charge.

He looked across to her face in the half-light, and hesitated a moment as she returned the look. Then he cocked his head slightly in the direction of the camping area. She smiled and gave a tiny nod. They stood up together and started walking back to where they all "lived" these few days, and they made their way by the breaking moonlight to his tent.

He lit the hurricane lamp and set it in a corner. They faced each other and she waited. He peeled off her clothes slowly, until she stood vulnerable finally, uncertain, naked as she had ever felt. No words. No kiss. Was this some mistake, a joke? Exposed, but in the shaky shadows of a small tent. Was he continuing?

She'd forgotten his name again. Panic was hovering in the dark corners of the tent.

She gambled on the initiative, and began the same ceremonial on him. He accepted silently, closed his eyes. Right move.

Naked, he drew her down, beckoned her to join him, covered them with a sheet for bedcover. They lay, crushing gently together, and he buried his face into her curly hair. "Thank you," he said quietly. Where was the cocky assurance now, the bravado? She waited.

"It's been lonely here," he said.

Lee moved her free hand down his back, held him, felt him relax. He placed his lips on hers. Soft, exploring, enquiring. She opened her mouth slowly, allowed the volts to race downwards, lighting a hot lust from her lips to her knees. Eye-to-eye, exchanging the decision, the lust, the ache, the need that had no words.

He sighed and relaxed again. She was happy to have him just enjoy her, slow or urgent as happened. It was like a ceremony, a spiritual event. Alms to the needy? No, that was cynical, and cynical did not belong here. The intensity was intoxicating.

Lee wasn't sure she could ever be seen walking from this tent. But going anywhere this side of dawn was not on her mind.

———

He had driven off to Adelaide next morning, to collect a daughter from the airport. On this same afternoon, Lee's Charlie was arriving with her friend.

Brian had made some curious comment before she left his tent after sunrise. He wanted to know if she knew any of Dory Previn's music. She hadn't. Track it down, he said, and listen to 'The Lady with the Braid'. The lady talked to his soul, he said, scary honest.

A modest mid-morning gathering in a gully was listening to a standing speaker. A sign was nailed to a tree: "Other Souls Beyond Our Earth.   Don German, Aquarius Prophet."

No.

Lee did try a workshop under a canvas shade, 'The Runes of the Druids'. It wasn't really interesting or exciting, and much of the blame for that was the presenter himself, speaking uncertainly, not having a clear story to tell. She wandered away to the marketplace and bought a chai tea, something she had never tried. But then Port Hedland and

Down to Earth

Mount Magnet didn't have the fads. Funny stuff, this chai. Perhaps it was an acquired taste. She was restless.

She strolled down to the river beach, through the Arts Village. A demonstration was in progress making mud bricks. All males. She kept going. Water spilled nearby, flowing down the bank, and two children were sitting in the puddle, covered in mud, happy as kids can be in mischief. Do their mothers know? Did it matter anyway? She wondered what mud felt like rubbed into skin. Her skin still tingled.

Fifty or so were down on the beach, and the sitting space was more dirt than sand, but no-one cared. Some were swimming, some sitting about, a few standing in bewilderment. Lee had seen naked bodies at Cambray, and it had frightened her. Not for her. Here at Berri, nakedness again was a part of the scene, voluntary, if you dared. The beach had the most of it. Some swimmers wore togs, most didn't. She sat on the ground, watched, while her resolution stayed paralysed. The sun was warm by now.

Maybe now is the time? In five minutes. If I'm still here.

Putting her head down, she closed her eyes. *Now.* She removed her tee-shirt, put it beside her, desperately hoping she looked calm and nonchalant. Unbidden, her arms folded themselves across her breasts. Slowly she commanded they unfold and sit on her lap. The heat in her cheeks must be giving her away? Only then did she open her eyes.

Nothing had changed.

Nothing further than an inch away had changed. No-one stared, grinned or noticed. No guardian of conduct came across to upbraid her, cover her up. She straightened her hunched body.

After the fear was relief, even a letdown. As she sat there, after the relief was power, a tiny victory. Well, it was a big victory really, and it wasn't a win against anyone out there, it was a private win. The hot cheek feeling faded and the hot sun took its place. She surveyed the crowd again; she belonged here now, a little. Lee dressed again and went in search of some lunch.

Thinking hungry reminded her. Tomorrow, when Charlie was here, she also wanted to do the pasta-making workshop. He would just have to join in.

———

Charlie wanted to play in the Children's Village. Lee had done a shift there yesterday, and had no guilt or worry on Charlie staying a while. The other kids would handle him. It was the sauna she wanted to try. Having helped build it— well, being a labourer under orders—she wanted to enjoy a return for her efforts.

Smoke was puffing from the smokestack. The hotbox was burning strongly with offcut wood from the pile. Patrons dropped their clothes in a heap and entered, tip-toe, nervous, excited. Other reddened sweaty folk were staggering out, many to slop down through the wet runoff to the river for a cooling dip.

Lee stripped, smiling. Cracked this one, she thought. She'd been back to the beach today, with Charlie, and she'd decided the Berri beach was a laboratory for exploring and studying human inhibitions, a workshop, hundreds of works in progress.

She hobbled to the hessian and plastic door drapes and pulled them aside enough to clamber inside. It was quite black, bracingly steamy. It was also full of low laughs and chatter, disembodied. "Er, help ..." was all she could manage, and the ghosts laughed.

Voice 1: *Just move slowly forward until you touch someone.*

Voice 2: *There's space over here near me, but I'm up one level.*

Voice 3: *Always room for one more.*

She knew the layout, and she groped, held arms, fell across knees, and found a spot to sit. The seat was muddy

    Down to Earth

wet, squelchy, and hot on her bum. On more than my bum, she thought. Breathing was an effort. The smell was a mix of eucalypt leaves and human sweat. Someone male on her left welcomed her with a shoulder hug, and a pair of hands behind her—female?—then began to massage her neck. Conversation in the blackness rose and fell, sometimes to steamy quiet. Some left, and newcomers jostled in, as blind as Lee. How long should one stay in a sauna? She wasn't sure, but it felt good once she had settled in. New bodies sat around her. One groped for her hand, and held it simply as a blind bond. She copied the handhold across to her other side. Murmurs along the row suggested it continued across. Someone sat at her feet, her legs straddling them in the dark. The shoulders didn't resist her fingers.

A hand ran fingers through her curly hair, damp and sweaty. She rolled her head unhurriedly in an answer of accepting and enjoying. The hands slid to her shoulders and needed no oils. Those hands wandered progressively lower, over past her shoulders, circled her breasts, cupped them gently, waited—for rejection?— and continued slowly moving. *Fuck.* In the dark, Lee's eyes were wide open. *Do I want this? Do I cause a scene or stay with it?* She did nothing. Fingers delicately circled her nipples, tweaked them, and they spoke up with loud false promises. Her body had been awake since two nights ago with Brian, and it had its own agenda. The hands slid back over her shoulders slowly, paused there, and withdrew, and a slow kiss was planted on her curly head. That was it.

Five minutes later, she made her way out into the cool and plunged into the Murray. Sitting on the bank, still undressed, she struggled to make sense of the ceremony. A legal assault? *Leonie, this is a ConFest, we don't do legal.* Was it a man or a woman? Should that matter? Was it an opportunistic sleazebag, hiding in the dark? A New Age gentle experiment, loving and harmless? A gift? Were they laughing now, or guilty or sorry, or grateful? Was it just how hippie massage is done, so enjoy? Where do our conventions come from anyway, sexual and privacy and personal space? Do they make sense?

A lass in braids and bangles was playing a ukulele and sitting at the water's edge a distance away. The strident gaiety of the music pulled Lee's thoughts back to now. She was dry now, and she put on her shorts, carried her top, and headed up to collect Charlie. Her nipples still buzzed.

———

Up past the Massage Village, Lee took a different track to her tent. A kick-boxing exercise was in progress, and she and Charlie hurried past. Then, camped facing the track was a Volkswagen Kombi van. It had been clad with timber panels, and on the back were extensions, shelves, little balconies, leadlight glass, a few hanging cook pots and some flowers. A caricature of a genuine gypsy van.

It sported a canvas veranda decked with market trivia: mobiles, Indian brollies, earrings, stones, cloth bags, incense. *Sparkling junk. Hippie version of mindless consumerism.* Under the brightly-coloured canvas gypsy shop, the side door of the Kombi had been fashioned into an inset booth, a decorated alcove, and in there sat a bearded real gypsy.

A dozen kids hung around him, jostling in the shop space, endangering the hanging chains and pendants, and all enthralled by the gypsy and his revelations. He was waving a ten-inch crystal tipped wand, real crystal with magical healing properties, and he was explaining how to feel for yourself the great powers it had.

"You have to hold it like this, close to the body, and wave it in a circle. Watch. Little circles like this. Can you feel the warmth in you just under the crystal?"

They could. Enthusiasm in kids is wildfire. "Amazing." "Yes, I can really feel that."

"But remember, you must always move it clockwise. That makes the healing energy double. So important."

More wands appeared. Several kids tried. They were healing each other to keen excitement. Six parents stood behind in bewilderment. They shrugged eventually, and reached each for some dollar coins.

Lee had kept Charlie at a distance, and now skirted around. She hadn't come to ConFest for this.

Leonie – Canberra

Late Autumn

A month after Berri wound up, Lee and Charlie arrived into Canberra on a late Friday afternoon. Brian picked them up from the Ansett-Pioneer bus depot in Northbourne Avenue. She had phoned twenty-four hours ago, before she left Adelaide.

"Thanks so much. I know you had short notice, but I was a bit stuck. I had booked the bus, but I wasn't very organised, and when I tried to phone Brandi, I could get no answers. So I turned to you." She suspected it was transparent. She could live with that. Brian didn't seem to be minding. He was hugging her. Tonight seemed secure, anyway. Charlie stood by and waited.

They collected the one case from under the coach. "This bus depot is so small. Adelaide has a large terminal in the city now that services all the bus companies together. It was impressive." What do you say when you drop in like this?

"I know the new Adelaide terminal. I went by bus for the Adelaide organisers' meeting a few months back, and I was amazed too."

The meeting Lee had missed. She'd gone back to Perth for that week. The Perth week had been a bad week.

"This is my car. Here, put the case in the back." They got in and Brian headed for Curtin. "What brings you to Canberra again?"

"Oh, it's just my time to be travelling around. I have some friends I made here last December, when I stayed at Brandi's place. You do remember meeting there?"

"I remember. It was Brandi's birthday. She lost a baby last year. The birthday was her way of being happy. I met various people that night. But I do recall her introducing us."

Brian, then we slept together at the festival, remember? You and me, remember? Shit, this could be awkward. Was he holding a loyalty to Brandi? No, that made no sense—she knew he had stayed with Summer in Adelaide for a few days after Berri.

"But I didn't go meeting with others from that party way across Australia to throw them straight into bed, did I?"

He thought that was an answer? It would do. This man needed interpreting.

Brian turned and grinned. "Hey Charlie, are you hungry?" Charlie grinned back.

The house in Curtin was like the few Lee had been into earlier in Canberra. Brick veneer, no front fence, lawned and treed. Clones of this filled Canberra. All very sufficient. All very generic. What all good Canberra folk wanted and could afford. All raised their kids in. All trotted off to work from.

"Do you own this place?" He was offering the way in. "It's a good house."

"Well, kind of. Yes, we rented it some while, and then we were buying it, but now we will sell it soon. This was Rose's and my place, and we split up a year and a half ago. Rose and Jo have lived here since then."

She knew Jo. Jo had been at the Berri ConFest for the second half, and Brian had to drive to Adelaide to collect her from the plane. Lee had watched various of Brian's movements during the festival.

"A few months ago I moved back in because Rose now has a Government flat at O'Connor. We plan to put this on the market in six months, and we'll split the money. Rose wants to buy something herself when she can. She says she wants a place with no memories."

Brian set up Charlie in the second bedroom, leaving him there for a moment. He cocked an eye at Lee—she'd seen that before—and put her case in the main bedroom. "Is that OK?"

Of course it's bloody OK. "Sure, I can handle that … It won't be for long. Either I'll find a place to settle down somewhere in Canberra, or if it doesn't work out, I might go on to Sydney for a while." That much was truth. For today at least. She could even go stay in what had been grandfather's country up north of the State.

"Lee, it's fine. I could handle some company. You might be willing to help out on our new bulletin, too. The *Canberra Down to Earth Newsletter.*"

He prepared to cook a chicken stew. "Oh, you're not vegetarian, are you? Good, I hadn't thought of that. But many of my friends are. It goes with the territory. There was no meat food available at Berri market, did you notice? Charlie will eat this?"

Charlie was parked at the television. She looked into the next room. No, he was asleep at the television. "Charlie is no problem. He is a good kid, and I'm asking so much of him just now. He seems to be coping, but we do need to slow down."

"Lee, you have been wandering around from city to city. What is it?" Brian was frowning.

"It's a long story." Yes, it's a long story, she thought, all difficult stories are long stories. But not now, not straight after that bus trip. "I promise I'll tell you all. But not tonight. Is that OK?"

"Absolutely. Sorry, no more questions. Just a cold moselle and some food." He was browning the chicken first.

Huh, Lee would have thrown it in with the vegies. She was no inept cook, but there were times you cheated and simplified, and now was that sort of occasion. But the wine was welcome.

"At least tell me about this newsletter," she said. *Yes, tell me your stuff. I can handle the talk tonight if it's that way around.*

"Five or six of us are meeting here in the morning to kick it around. I think Brandi is coming. We have some ideas we want to be saying in the Down to Earth network, and we're thinking a newsletter might be our best vehicle. Newsletters we understand. I apprenticed myself into newsletter publication with the local Learning Exchange a few years ago, and some of us have worked with *The Other Way*, an anarchist-leaning magazine organised by the commune across town. I even wrote some articles in that one."

Personal, indigestible, he mumbled quietly, and paused.

"Adelaide Down to Earth have their quarterly newsletter. I helped with the issue before the ConFest."

"Yes, I get a copy of the *South Australia DTE Newsletter*. Victoria DTE have their own, too, a big one. And Sydney. I get those as well. Queensland ran a newsletter for a little while, but I think that may have folded. Perth has one I think, but I've never seen it. They are so far away."

"So why one from here? I would've thought Canberra was on the small side?"

"Well, it's all a bit complicated."

So he's got long stories, too.

"Have you heard any rumblings about Jim and Junie in Adelaide?"

"All the South Australian people were playing cagey with Jim during Berri," she said. "They needed Jim to help secure the Martins Bend parkland for the festival, but they tried to keep him away from all the rest of the negotiations and much of the planning. I couldn't get to the bottom of it, because I came into the whole story more recently than Jenny and Chas and all the others in the team. I went out on a site finding trip, but I was missing for much of the festival preparation time."

"Summer?"

"Summer was in it too. It felt a bit like a conspiracy."

"Lee, Down to Earth is a divided camp. Well, it's Jim and Junie and David and then it's everyone else. It's been a frustrating experience."

"So why are you involved?"

"Because I can still see more passion here for alternatives and truths than elsewhere. Life has endless possibilities, and most people refuse to see, can't allow themselves to see."

This was too apocalyptic for Lee.

He gave her a run-down on the unhappy story, a story many people around the country must have known long ago. *Damn. If I would only settle down and live a sane life for a while, I might know these stories, I'd be in the loop.*

"We have here the tape recordings for the planning meetings for the last year or so, including one here in Canberra at a house out of town we call Sandford. I've taken pains to be delivering copies to each State team. The idea is that we could check back on what we'd agreed, because so often we believed things happened at cross-purposes to what we had laboured to a consensus over.

"But reels of tape are so impractical to play back in different places around the country. We need an easier way to publish our decisions, so we can keep being sure we all keep to them. It's as if we have agents among ourselves white-anting everything."

"Who?" she asked.

He just looked at her.

"Oh." She felt tired again.

"It's been like this since the beginning. We are being played with. This stew is ready. There's bread in the bread bin. You'd better wake Charlie."

Early Winter

The women's refuge door clipped shut and a weary Lee stepped out to the Torana parked in the street. One bruised new resident had arrived late last night, with two traumatised little kids. The doctor had visited this morning, and Lee had started some legalities that would be handled later today. It was so wrong. But when she walked out the door, the refuge stories stayed back there.

The Torana was old and had seen far better days, but it was transport. Two panels were of different colour, and a touch of rust showed brown in the passenger door. Two-door model, sought after in its day, but a pain for getting kid and clutter in and out. Brian had test-driven it for her, had poked under the bonnet and looked under. At $700 it was good value in her budget. Budget? Huh. She needed money to have a budget. The $1300 from Charlie's father was about gone. Tomorrow might be a good day to walk the streets of Queanbeyan checking all the shops for a job, any job. Not today.

But she did have to get work, fast. She had moved into the old house two weeks ago and rent was due again at the end of the month. It wasn't a proper lease, at least, but she still needed to pay that rent. Lee took the house in Queanbeyan rather than Canberra because past the State border the rents were cheaper. And, well, Queanbeyan felt more comfortable. She barely belonged in any city suburb, and Canberra suburbs especially.

Charlie was at school. It was mid-morning now. She had delivered him to primary school in Yass Road earlier, although she didn't finish her refuge shift until ten. It had turned out a bit awkward. She had rented in Queanbeyan, started her son at the regular primary at Queanbeyan East, and then took on the refuge work back in Narrabundah in Canberra.

That hadn't been her plan—she had intended offering herself to do duty at Queanbeyan refuge. Every women's refuge had its own ground rules, and at Queanbeyan, they couldn't handle boy children of staff. So she had approached Narrabundah, and they welcomed her. Charlie was OK to be there when Lee was, and he could sleep over when Lee was on night duty. So that's how it was now.

The car stopped in the driveway, and she sat still for several minutes. At this moment, she didn't want to be home. It wasn't quite home yet, anyway. So she stepped out, locked the car, and walked away from the house, heading for the centre of town. She knew where she wanted to be for now.

Not many used the overgrown foot track along the riverbank. It came out by the low-level traffic bridge in Morisset Street.

Morisset Street was an accidental main road these days. The big bridge over the river was in Crawford Street, the main highway street one block parallel to the south. It had been demolished last year, however, and the earthworks and the new constructions had disrupted all traffic flow since. Four more months they were promising. Queanbeyan had no option but to suffer.

Below the low-level bridge was the caravan park, even lower. Remind me, someone, not to be here in flood time. She sighed. She'd done her time in parks. This park had a few vans of travellers, but it had even more ramshackle shanties of longer-term residents. But the river itself looked a bit grander from the middle of town.

The RSL was on the far side of the Crawford Street bridge construction. The Queanbeyan Returned Services League. The "Queanbeyan Rissole" to many of Canberra's office hordes who wanted a cheap club lunch with the mates. Lily had spoken of the RSL, friend Lily who related to Lee's fire and passion. Lee didn't understand the culture of service clubs: Perth and even Adelaide didn't have them. Lily wasn't an RSL person, but she had suggested visiting to experience what the club was, what had happened there. An educational visit.

                                    Down to Earth

So she wound her way around the barriers and the working trucks, and climbed the RSL steps. The entrance was almost formal. This was money that had built this place. The RSL had burned down two Christmases ago, and they had taken the opportunity to rebuild in grand style, at some millions of dollars. It was a crime to spend so much.

The uniformed door attendant stopped her, and as she was a nonmember they asked her for a driving licence. Hers was still a Western Australian one. Which reminded her, she hadn't yet sent in the car transfer documents. She lived across the border.

Lee was admitted because her licence showed she didn't live nearby. "Did *not* live nearby." Were these people crazy, or what?

The decor was lavish. Polished wood was everywhere. The carpet covered even the walls. Rows of dining tables and the longest drinks bar she had ever seen. A performers' stage with a surfeit of large black speakers and overhead lighting. Along one wall an extended display of medals, guns, military maps and war photos. This wasn't her world. She turned and walked back out to Crawford Street.

Was it money or war that was being glorified? She despised both. Men doing what men always do, setting the world to their way. It was always men.

So why did she imagine Brian could be different? She felt angry and weary, and she wasn't sure which was stronger.

She found her way across the construction area and scurried into the Central Cafe, where she had been heading all along.

Central Cafe was different. It had once been elegantly decadent too. Now it was old, with character, history seeping from its walls and its cubicles. This was her third time here, and it was quickly feeling like a home place, for her soul, if not for her body.

Her friend Lily had brought her here. She worked at the Queanbeyan refuge, and that was why Lee had originally wanted to be there too. Lily was sister and mother in one.

Lee had tried to talk with her about Berri ConFest. Lily would mutter, "A drum, a drum," and change the subject each time. She was sure Lily had been to one of the ConFests. There was a story somewhere.

Lily was always busy around Queanbeyan. It was many years since she would have called herself young. Yet, besides the women's refuge work, she had a plant nursery where she lived out beyond town limits. On market days, she sold her wares at a stall she had labelled *StarFlowers*, and Lee and Charlie had sat with her on her stall last Sunday. She kept a Tarot pack at the stall, and if she ever had help (and Anton her friend did assist sometimes) she would do card readings for customers.

But what everyone knew most about Lily was the striking tumble of all white hair, brushed, loved, falling to her waist. She was always recognisable.

She came often enough to the Central, to meet with Anton in a late evening. Did they live together? Lily and Anton were partners, that much Lee knew.

It was Anton who used the Central as a home base. Anton was here two or three evenings each week, always in the company of several male friends, and Anton was the gentle alpha.

Now, Anton had only one arm, a left arm. The last time she was here, Lee had watched in awe how the friends embraced. Anton would every time hold his left hand forward for a handshake, normal except for the left-handed-ness, and his friends always had a response that worked. Some shook left-handed, and others twisted their right in an exaggerated inverted grasp. Always there was a broad and knowing grin from both. Anton's arm was part of their bond, their secret from elsewhere.

All Anton's friends, and she had trouble recalling the names, were of a type, tall and dark stubbled. Not a pound of spare flesh was seen among them, although a couple were bending a little with their age. They sometimes talked for hours, Lily had said, and Lee had heard them last week break to a language she didn't identify, but the cafe owner had known it.

"Hello, Thomas," she said, "do you remember me? I'm Lee, a friend of Lily."

"Lee, of course, my dear. And I'm Tomas, no '*h*', but it matters little." Yes, it sounded different in Tomas's accent.

"Tomas, sorry, I'll remember. Can I have an espresso coffee from your fancy machine, please?" Espresso was the word on the machine. It wasn't espresso Anton's men had been drinking. That was a darker brew, aromatic, and it came from the kitchen on special request.

"Espresso, most certainly. A small cup of black coffee, or a cappuccino?"

She had a cappuccino last week with Lily, and she was an instant convert. At the counter, Lee watched Tomas do his wonders with the new steaming and hissing machine.

Central Cafe was empty at late morning in Queanbeyan. She sat in a booth and nursed the cappuccino.

It was Brian that filled her thoughts. She had stayed at his house for a few weeks. They had been comfortable and stabilising weeks, and it took little time to realise that Canberra (well, Queanbeyan was Canberra) was where she should put down some roots. There were good people here, people whose friendship was genuine. Excitement ran, and the passion and the politics being thrown into the proposed Canberra newsletter was part of that exhilaration. There was support, too, and she could handle some support and stability.

And I have Brian.

The subliminal comforts of a body bumping up in the deep of the night, the sharing of skin.

Sensual and caring, once she allowed for …

Well, she wasn't sure what she was allowing for. There was another vulnerable dimension in there somewhere. A cat's soul? She should play that Dory Previn cassette again tonight.

That man with no dress sense. That man with no OFF button.

If he was from Mars, was he delivered here by error?

She still knew she needed her own spot, her safe place, and the first move was to find this cheap rental. She had been in Queanbeyan a fortnight now. He had stayed one night, and she and Charlie had gone back to Curtin once. So the party wasn't over.

But it was Brian's proposition of this week that had turned the world around. He was out of town now, on ConFest stuff, so she had time to play the week back at her own speed.

"Lee, we have been enjoying our company together," he had said. "It's clear we could have the makings of a deliberate and loving affair, if we want to choose that."

Lee had tentatively agreed.

"I would like to make a proposal that isn't standard, but it is what I would like. Knowing by now some of how you think and feel, you also might like what I want to say. Would you consider joining me in a relationship, a love liaison, where you are my partner and I am yours? But also where I reserve the right to own my own sexual self, my loving self, and be free to relate sometimes with other people? To explore who I am? Where you in quite the same way had that same personal freedom to be relating to other people, experimenting with life?"

She had hesitated only a moment. He should talk in English. Then she answered, "Yes, I'm in on that."

"That was prompt."

He paused.

"Imagine being in a room with a large party of friends, enjoying your own corner of the party, even flirting or making assignations. Imagine then the other of us is across that room, enjoying the party the same way. I would like to be able to lock eyes, acknowledging that that is my mate over there, and it's OK. If there came a collision of loyalties, our agreement would be that we are partners who will protect each other, privately or publicly. I don't seek a pledge of forever, I don't want a pledge of only, but I would like a pledge of special and of honest."

"Yes," she had said, "that's what I would like, but I've never known how to put those pieces together. No-one has ever put it like that, with that, with that ... brutality."

"We might discover it's foolhardy," he added. "But you would be willing?"

She had been willing. Living around Canberra was where life needed to be.

——

In the deep of the night, the coach, half full, had changed drivers outside a dim shopfront on the highway through Holbrook. Few passengers woke, or at least few stirred. Lee had watched the handover, silent to her in her seat, and the bus continued its haul to Canberra. Sleep was unlikely. Thoughts tumbled in chaos, and yesterday's court drama in Melbourne kept replaying. Was life gaining traction, or was all still out of control as ever it was?

Life for a white-looking curly-haired kid in the dusty few streets of Western Australia's Mount Magnet was raucous and rough, but perhaps she had been happiest in those days. If only she had known that then, to savour it. Because by adolescence, the awareness had settled on her of how biased and exploited was the bottom stratum of mining town life, and it was more than a headstrong lass could take. She had run away at age fourteen the first time, worried she was pregnant, and a few more escape attempts followed.

At nineteen, established in Perth as de facto manager in a small coffee shop, and that on her street skills and hard work, she had fallen for Charlie's father, a young mining man.

She had vivid recall of their few years among the new mines appearing in the Pilbara, mines vastly bigger than any before, complete mountain ranges of ore. They had lived in turn at Port Hedland, and Tom Price, and lastly Newman, and each town she despised. She despised the town culture of bored women and feral kids, depending on whether the wife (well, let's call them wives) scored a mine job as well. She missed the counterpoint of black and Chinese presence she grew up with. Increasingly she despised the mining for itself. The rugged outback was being sacrificed to the grasping companies who cared for nothing else than the tonnage and price.

Charlie's father, the rising company engineer? Well, that didn't work for long before the suspicions and resentments crowded in about them.

There were the two kids, though. Charlie, dear Charlie, and then young Kerilly.

It had exploded on a break they were taking in Perth. She had gone into the city one morning alone, and that was itself of little note. But her purpose was to join the marchers protesting the gross and rapacious mining being condoned by the Government of the day, indeed welcomed by the Government of the day. The motel television on that evening's newscast had a clear shot of Lee with one fist raised and one hand with a placard. Abruptly the miner had understood how impossible was any further tolerance with his fractious wife.

By an hour later she was homeless. She was bruised and her eye was swollen. In the dark of evening she had escaped with a terrified Charlie and found a room in the nearby hotel. Her once husband had already checked out when she called back mid-morning to negotiate over Kerilly.

Young Kerilly, curly like Lee, was tougher. She had better chance to survive than Charlie, had he been the one left behind. But this was desperate spin, and she knew it to the depth of her soul. They were both her children, and she loved them savagely. She knew she must nourish and protect them, both of them.

And she had lost one.

She stared out at the earliest lighting of dawn. Tears rolled down. They were coming to the city outskirts of Canberra. *Please, be there.*

It wasn't yet breakfast time, but Brian was waiting at the depot, and Charlie and Jo too. No-one else even knew she had gone to Melbourne. It was thirty-six hours ago she had left, and one Friday missing can be hidden from most friends.

"You OK?"

Lee shook her head, closed her eyes. They spoke no more until they drove up to the house at Curtin.

"A cuppa first."

When she was ready, she asked the two kids to come in and listen. Some adults would not have done it that way, but it was her way. Her eyes were red. "Kerilly stays with her father. The judge was so awful." She sobbed more. "He asked to see Charlie. Do you think I would have dared to risk Charlie too? He asked me where I lived, and if I had any income. So I had to explain the part-time job at the burger shop in Uriarra Road. I didn't dare mention volunteering at the refuge. He wanted to know who I lived with, but when I tried to explain about you and me, he just got stroppy."

Another pause.

"Charlie stays with me." Charlie was sitting on her knee. "Kerilly said she wanted to stay with her father, and she stays. The judge found the father was better positioned to be supporting the children. However, as Charlie has been in my keeping and there seems to be some stability in his life, he will let that arrangement stand. Provisionally."

She held Charlie closer and the bitter tears ran down her cheeks. "*Provisionally!*"

She could see the distress and puzzlement in Charlie's face. She kissed him on his head. "It means we have a great life together, you and me, and we better go do it." She cried.

Late Winter

It was mid-morning, and Charlie was at school. Lee was suffering a slight hangover. She didn't drink much, but last night she'd been home alone, with Charlie put to bed, and she'd been thinking too hard. Had she crossed some line? Well, she had certainly crossed a line, but was it that line too far?

A short refuge shift was starting at eleven, so she didn't have the luxury of feeling sorry. It would have to solve another time. Not even tonight. She started the Torana and headed for Canberra.

She'd promised dinner for three tonight, and cooking was fun. Cooking she was good at; she was going to cook well tonight. Brian was coming over, and Jane.

He had mentioned Jane a couple of times in the last month. Jane had been at the same massage class Brian had taken. He had called it his special project. One of the Canberra chiropractors, a bit alternative, and his hippie girl-friend, had started the personal massage classes, and the daring and the hippies had joined enthusiastically.

The classes were scarcely demure and cautious, either, she had been assured. Like the Massage Village at the Berri ConFest, the chiropractor's massage classes were done the proper way, the naked-on-the-bench way. She must enrol for one herself. Everyone learned to work through the embarrassment, even her Brian.

Brian and Jane had taken their friendship from there to home, and Lee had no trouble with that. It was that freedom to explore relationships that was integral to their own bond. It had worked well so far. So far.

Last week she had asked him, "Have you and Jane slept together?" Not that it should be a problem, but, well, a girl does get curious.

"Oh, we hadn't until a few days ago. But yes, we have, once."

"Are you hiding her?"

"No, I don't hide. Is it the sex or the face you want to know?"

He was right. If we had someone else in our life, we didn't need to hide, but then we were not under a duty to explain everything in detail, either. Or should we? Why were there no rules of etiquette for living our way?

It was the face, she decided. "So, why have I not met her?"

He chuckled. "Jane is feeling a bit confused. She knows about you, and I have explained how we see our relationship. She is taking some time to think about it. She is very sweet, though."

"Brian!" Mock indignant. "You tell your Jane she is invited here to dinner because I would love to meet her. Any friend of Brian's is welcome here." So dinner for three was tonight.

Poor Jane, let's hope her sense of humour handles this man. He took her on a treat last week, proudly invited her down one afternoon into the sewage pumping station tunnels a hundred feet beneath Commonwealth Avenue Bridge. He still had keys to such places, from his earlier job. "Brian, love," Lee had pleaded, "you can't do that."

Where do the rules come from? he had asked.

The chief rule we had given ourselves, she recalled, was to own up if we had changed, or our own circumstances had changed. If it might have some consequences for the agreement we had. Learned it with Brandi, he said.

Tonight was *not* going to be the right time to raise our etiquette. Brian and Jane was easy stuff. Brandi, OK. But Lee and Lesley? It had been at last Sunday's refuge staff party. What had happened with Lesley on the carpet in the middle of the room, that was way past mere massage; that had been lusty and passionate. Lesley's tongue and fingers had set her body afire, and she had made a shameless, naked, noisy spectacle. She had stayed on with Lesley for the night. Her "circumstances had changed". Would Brian cope?

She flashed back to Charlie's father. That was a man who never coped. And he never knew the truth of Charlie.

I should be enjoying tonight's dinner, Leonie, enjoying the company. For tonight, I must trust the man I have.

And explain everything later.

— Intermission —

*He still stands by his hippie story, but a name
or two may be wrong.*

*In his story, they bid for a new world, a
freedom, a simplicity, a new human way.
Almost another planet, Le Guin's Anarres,
tough but true. They would save their world.*

They would never save themselves.

Dave – Camp Eureka

C amp Eureka was a commercial holiday camp buried in forest in the mountains east of Melbourne.

"Dave, you knew we were preparing our own State-based ConFest in early summer? OK? So, did you bring your photos?"

"You wanted to see them, so I brought them." He had them still in the car. Andrew was making his bid too early. By tomorrow morning Dave had been planning to have the best of the photos pinned out in a montage on the meeting room wall.

He had driven from Adelaide, where he had been calling on Summer. They had arrived together an hour ago.

"We wanted a good one of everyone in the river at Cotter." Andrew was in a wizard caftan. Andrew couldn't help himself.

"And possibly a shot of the mud bath people," added Patrick. "Berri had a great mud bath incident. Some eye-catching pictures would be good content for our promotional poster."

"Hmm, I did catch the mud people at Berri. I'll find them for you."

Carolyn weighed in. Carolyn ran the Down to Earth Radio Show each week on the community AM station in Melbourne, and had been doing that for two years now. "Andrew, I know we traditionally use a well-thought-out poster leading up to ConFests, either Jim's national ConFests or the local one we are planning. But is a group of naked people skylarking in a mud bath quite the image we want to put out front?"

Patrick answered. "Mud baths could become of the essence of ConFest. The human spirit set free to frolic in new ways."

"We were thinking it was a brave image. ConFests are challenging. ConFests are about questioning our old patterns, restoring freedoms, having fun," said Andrew.

"Of course it's provocative. But I'm not convinced that sensational and confronting pictures are the way."

"Let's see the photos first. We can judge their worth when we see what it is we are talking about."

"Look, I am tired," said Dave. He was. He had driven all day. Silly, probably. "Can it wait till the morning? Then you can see them all—there might be other options for the poster. Shots of Cairns addressing the crowds, and the market stalls. Clowns and entertainers and body painters, too."

After breakfast, Andrew had chosen from the display what he always wanted, a Cotter River event and a mud event.

The others had milled around the wall of photos. Dave was a good photographer, and many of the shots were skillfully taken. The joy of the revellers, the passion of the presenters, quiet reflections at the fireside, Benny Zable's ubiquitous radiation mask, Junie talking with her friends, the canvas suburb in the early dawn glow. Some here today saw themselves caught by Dave at a moment they didn't remember.

Dave made himself a cup of Red Zinger tea, and went for a sunshine break. He had been up early to prepare his collection.

"Dave, this collection is a treasure." Dave hadn't seen Carolyn behind.

"They make a beautiful memory, don't they. A few of them I got from friends, but most of them I took."

"I missed Bredbo. I was overseas. But now I feel I know all the ConFests. How do you manage to get such close-ups, such exquisite expression and intimacy in some of those?"

"It's been a hobby for a long time. I use a modest camera, but I bide my time."

"Well, I think they're wonderful. They could make a grand advert on their own for the ConFest experience. Don't ever lose them as a collection. They have so much colour. You always look black, and your pictures are full of colour."

He paused. He rolled a cigarette. "Carolyn, have you seen many people taking photos at ConFest?"

"That's a silly question. Some people pull out a camera. Or at least the touristy end of the ConFest crowd. The real alternatives never owned a camera. When you wear little, or even nothing, around a festival site, there's no handbag or backpack to carry anything like a camera."

"Have you seen David Dansfield taking photos?"

"Junie's David? Yes, I think so. So?"

"Nothing. Don't worry about it." But it wasn't nothing.

Carolyn had been nominated to drive into Yarra Junction for bread and a few other supplies. The meeting crowd were always ravenous eaters, and more had arrived than had been catered for. She leaned on Dave to join her for the expedition.

"Only if you drive."

"Right, now what was it you were trying not to say? What are you saying about Dansfield?"

He stared out his side window. He didn't answer.

"Dave, what's bugging you?"

"It's David."

"Obviously it's David. David and his camera. Yes, I can recall seeing David with his camera."

"David just hangs around. He stands nearby when Junie is about. Or he's around when Jim is presenting. He always carries his camera."

"Yes, he's often enough taking shots. That I can recall now that I have had time to think."

"He is always fully dressed. Come on, even Jim has appeared without his shirt, trying to come down to join his constituency."

"Mister Dave the man, I suppose you want Junie looking hippie, too?"

"No, stop distracting me. If Junie took her clothes off, the press would thrash her. It won't happen. No, listen to me."

"Sorry," she said.

"I saw David with his camera on a couple of my own shots. I didn't realise what I was looking at until after Cotter, and I was daydreaming my way through all my photos. I suppose it set off some tiny alarm bell in my head."

"Dave, you take photos at ConFests. You join ConFest activities of your own, but you also take your camera. I can recall you carrying a camera. So why shouldn't someone else? Why not David?"

"That's what I tried to tell myself. But the niggling feeling wouldn't go away."

"I'm not sure you're being fair. Would you worry about me if I carried a camera?"

He didn't answer the question. "Do you know anything of David's background?"

"Not much. He's Junie's husband. He's not an alternative like one of us, he's a businessman. But he's OK, as far as I can see, with Junie's liaison with Jim. All three are content to knock around together. Is there another story?"

The road was hilly, windy.

"I hear assorted rumours about David."

"Rumours get us nowhere."

"They worry me. I've heard CIA, Libya, all sorts of offbeat connections."

"I think you are out of order."

"Carolyn, think about it. Post Vietnam War. Australia then had a hostile and uncontrollable Government for several years."

"You call the Labor Government 'hostile'?"

"It was the same people, Cairns included, who opposed the war, and our participation in it. Who helped get our troops pulled out a few short years back. Now it's vacuum time. Some countries, ally countries, have to see us as partly hostile now. What's more, Labor was an unstable Government here. Look, they were lurching from one disaster to another, politically."

"Dave, am I hearing you? You think there is some big story here?"

"I don't know. But it's playing on my mind all the time. From the outside, would you pass up on a fall-in-your-lap opportunity to get someone on the inside of the Aussie Government? A mole, if you like? Foment, distract, destroy from the inside. Then get your friends back in power, as it should be. Bingo, Labor's now out."

"It's not like that. Jim Cairns is a good passionate man. An idealist."

"Was he a target?"

"No! Junie is her own good woman, too. I have plenty of time for Junie, she's a hero for me. She has ambition. Talent. Beauty and strength. There's no-one who meets her who fails to be totally impressed. I have no problem with her affair with Jim, either, it's brave and it's honest, and the press hysteria stinks. We believe in honesty."

"It's not Junie I am concerned about. Or I don't think so. It's David. He has too much time now. He knows every one of us by name. All the Australian counterculture. He has our photos. Where have those photos gone?"

They had arrived at the store.

"Dave, you should let it go." Carolyn broke the brooding on the way back.

"I can't. I followed David around at Berri, and watched."

"What?"

"I kept an eye on Dansfield all during the festival. He ran an orange juice stall. But I have a series of photos that have him taking photos of us all. Those photos are not on the wall."

"I can't believe this. You can't stalk one of us based on vague rumours you can't identify."

"I talked to big George at Goulburn about it. We know for a reasonable certainty that George was an Air America pilot during the war."

"CIA?"

"Yes, CIA. He keeps his cover blown so they won't ever recall him."

"You believe that?"

"Yes. I know of various occasions where he was in conversations with people who knew their subjects, and George's knowledge was intimate and detailed. War stuff. Aircraft stuff. He checks out."

"George is a bragger. Have you been reading too many spy novels?"

"George told me David was probably British MI6."

"I've heard enough. I don't believe any of this crap. You've mentioned rumours you have no basis for, or you won't reveal. You're painting a whole creepy scenario that is outrageous and plain wrong. It's character assassination that should have no part in the lifestyle and principles I thought we stood for."

"Carolyn, I've damaged no-one's character. Other than George, you are the only person I have ever mentioned this with. I don't know what to do with it. You started this conversation, remember."

"No, you did. You asked if I recall David with a camera."

"Yes, OK, you're right. I'm sorry I did start this."

"Well, stay sorry. And bury it."

———

It was late morning when they all gathered. Brian had arrived, and had set up the tape recorder. These tapes were going to have newsletter material.

"Welcome to everyone. It's been a long trip for many of you," started Jim. "Junie and me included. We've just come in from Perth. This is a beautiful place, and let's hope we can meet with peace and be productive. Let's gather around."

Sharine from the Rainbow Region grabbed her cue. "Link hands and close our eyes."

After some pause, Sharine began the customary "Aum" chant. It grew slowly, each voice in the room adding to the hum at different timing, until all had joined. The overall sound came in surges. Dave would reach the end of his breath and start another Aum, but the aggregated sound never stopped.

One female voice began a harmony pitch. Spiritual over-fulfilment, or ego?

It's a petty sin to stop too early, to drop your bundle. It's a giveaway on your lack of spiritual subtlety. After some elapsed time it does become OK to stop chanting, but the insight on that was a magic Dave never could read. So when the volume was fading for what seemed like the real ending, he allowed himself to chant more softly in unison. Until calm. Eyes-closed calm.

"Peace," added Sharine. Eyes opened slowly. Everyone merged to the middle for a massed hug.

"Today I thought we might spend a few moments thinking on the source of our energies and our happiness." All sat back, and Sharine pinned up a kundalini diagram.

"Our meeting here is a living human event. It's like a human body and human spirit. All the Down to Earth community itself has spirit and body, just like any human." Dave shuffled. Jim shuffled.

"In our communal body here, we need to know and love our energy centres, our chakras. Balanced chakras mean a balance in our mind, our body and our spirit.

"Each of the seven chakras from the root chakra upwards must be stable and balanced before we can hope to balance the higher ones. We will never nourish the third eye and the crown chakra if they do not have firm foundations at the lower chakras."

Maslow's hierarchy tossed into New Age? Or perchance this stuff did come first.

Ten minutes of shared exercises followed, trying to give firm foundation to Dave's root chakra.

Jim Cairns said nothing right through. He kept his eyes down, but he went through the same motions as everyone else.

Junie Morosi wound it up gently. "Sharine, thank you for that. Maybe it can help us in our meetings today and tomorrow."

"We should start by outlining what we want to talk about here," started Jim. "A rough agenda, a timetable."

"I think the first item should be Berri ConFest reports. That's what is recent, and it's the top interest of everyone."

"OK, Berri reports. Next?"

"Then we should hear from each region on what's been happening there since last we met," added Summer.

"We need to be considering our forward planning. Where do we go from here?"

"I think that is already a simple and fair division of our purpose here this weekend," said Jim. "Berri now. Region reports this afternoon. Future plans in the morning."

Jim continued. "It's obvious Berri has been a comfortable and successful ConFest. Who wants to give a detailed report?"

Jenny spoke. "I'll give a general report first, but Tom Warrior has financial figures later."

Jenny described the early site search, and the trouble convincing the Riverland Council to agree to Down to Earth using the Martins Bend Park at Berri. How it was finally Jim's intervention that saw the venue approved.

Berri was far from the two earlier national ConFests, and especially from the other main population areas. It was even some distance from its own State capital. So there had been less wide support for preparing infrastructure and permits, and the small Adelaide-based team had worked hard to pull it all together.

Once it got to a week or so out from the festival, early-bird helpers from interstate had started to arrive, and the Adelaide team retired from exhaustion.

Dave started handing around some of his Berri photos from the display.

"When we had recovered enough, a successful festival was happening by itself. We were so grateful. Officially we had a gate count of about four thousand. We became worried we would be under-attended, but the surge came a half day later than we had expected."

"What were the highlights?"

"I was coming to that. Let me give you the lowlight first, and then be clear of that. We had an Aboriginal dance troupe to do a corroboree on the first big night. They travelled from the Kimberley. Aboriginal national elder Burnam Burnam was also at Berri, and he jumped at the opportunity to be an introducing patron to the corroboree. Summer, you were there ..."

"Halfway through the performance," said Summer, "a young male, naked, long hair and a bit unsteady, pranced up to the corroboree group, and placed his penis into the front of the didgeridoo of the musician."

"Aww shit! White or black?"

"He was a white man. The musician stopped playing. Then the dancers left too."

"Burnam Burnam was inconsolable," said Jenny. "I didn't see the incident, I spoke with him later. To his credit, he stayed the next day at Berri, but I know he was heartbroken."

Jim spoke. "Jenny, I was there. It was one of those moments when I was so deeply ashamed—and angry."

"But let me pick some highlights," Jenny went on. "The Morning Sharings were delightful. People were happy. They felt free to speak. Lots were ready to join the daily jobs. The stage music caused some controversy, but generally was very good."

The Kids' Village, the Healing Village, the Craft Workshops Village all functioned well, Jenny reported.

"There were no serious medical incidents. The weather was perfect. We could swim as the river was good. The land was ideal. We had shade. The undercover was good enough for tents. Council mowed just before we started. We had power, with only one short outage. There was water. In other words, the site and its condition suited us beautifully. We even celebrated a childbirth."

"A bit better than Bredbo, eh?"

"Oh, this ConFest was a far happier one than Bredbo. More comfortable. It was like we had arrived! We had learned. We could do ConFests now."

"Three cheers for the Adelaide team and the Berri ConFest." For twenty minutes the upbeat reminiscences continued.

Jenny finished off. "Now we should hear from Tom."

"OK," started Tom. "I agree Jenny and the SA crew deserve a thorough thank you from us all. They certainly set up a successful third ConFest.

"You might recall that at the several national planning meetings leading up to Berri, starting from Paddington, we had taken care to exercise more control on looser areas of our festival operating. This time, we had clear designations of responsibility for various parts of the preparation and running. Many of the on-the-ground issues were in the hands of the local South Australian people, because Berri was so far from many of us.

"We had one appointed poster artist instead of an accidental two at Cotter and nearly none at Bredbo. This is the poster we send in quantity all across the country to be displayed in any library, health food shop, newsagent, clinic or school. People in every State approached the media to promote the ConFest in every way possible. And we arranged to freight the dome to Berri.

"Procedures were set for gate control that functioned better than at previous ConFests. The attendance figures we recorded are more reliable than the numbers we declared for Bredbo and Cotter, because the control wasn't as porous, but also because we had a monitored process for collecting the entrance money. The most effective system we had in place was the banking control. We banked all incoming moneys immediately. As treasurer, I approved all expenses. And I recorded them all."

"I did gate duty for two shifts," said Patrick. "The entry rules and the money collection were certainly strict."

"As Jenny has told us, the ConFest experience was a good one. The festival was smaller than either Bredbo or Cotter, but the result was a lot better.

"So I can now give you the final financial report."

"Give us the goodies!"

"I made copies to hand around today, but you may need to share. If anyone needs another, I can send one later. It's final, but it's not yet audited, and we should decide today if we wish a formal audit. The attendance was 3727 bodies. The entrance was ten dollars, and the gross takings was $41,500. That includes some concessions and artist entrances and kitchen profits. The expense groups show our budget against actual, and you can read those yourself. We can use our miscalculations there to better budget next time.

                                    Down to Earth

"The bottom line is a $13,000 surplus." Tom knew to pause. His training included that.

After a minute of competing comments around the room, Jim seized the floor and acknowledged the result. "I think you should all be pleased with the results of Berri ConFest. I congratulate you on the fine financial result."

I congratulate you?

They broke for a hot drink. This was the easy part, thought Dave.

The Reverend Tom Warrior was still treasurer of the Down to Earth network. But it was Carolyn presiding over the proceedings when they resumed.

"One task we have now is to decide what we do with the $13,000. This isn't a position we have ever been in. What possible uses can we make of our funds?"

Brian kicked off. "We are all aware Cotter and Bredbo national ConFests both posted losses, Cotter by three thousand dollars or so, and Bredbo a little past six thousand dollars. Jim has each time funded the shortfall from his own pocket. It seems to me sensible and correct that if Berri has now made a profit, then we should first make full repayment to Jim."

Several of us had been kicking that proposal around all the last week, once we heard early news of the Berri surplus. Some discussion did follow, but paying back Jim was patently appropriate.

"What else?"

Jim wanted a different narrative. "When we left from Mount Oak at the close of the Bredbo event, we had a Down to Earth plan to consider buying the Mount Oak property. It was to be a spiritual and human and ecological college, where ownership was vested in no-one, and where anyone could live in freedom. Now, Mount Oak purchase is under contract. It still owes money. At this stage, I have stumped up a part of the deposit for its purchase."

First flag up the pole.

"I consider, and I have considered this at length with Junie, that this will be the moment where the whole body of Down to Earth can place its commitment in Mount Oak. This meeting is the main gathering outside the ConFests themselves. It has funds. It can devote its funds and its moral ownership in the project that is Mount Oak. That is what I would ask."

So who speaks now? Dave didn't want to go first. He was burned on this at the Paddington meeting last year.

Where's our own flag?

Tom spoke. "Jim, there weren't many people who were enthusiastic about buying the Mount Oak property after Bredbo festival. This was true not only during the festival at the massed debates, but at various follow-up meetings that followed that festival."

Eureka Stockade.

Jim replied. "Because some people didn't wish to be involved in the Mount Oak project, that ought not give them any right to stop those of us who did want to proceed. This is the point I have presented at length at all Down to Earth gatherings since Cotter. If we live authentically and in freedom, we each should be free to follow what we choose in our lives. If I and some others choose to grasp the Mount Oak vision, please allow us to follow it."

It was a doomed argument. An anguished discussion continued.

"At the moment," said Jim, "Mount Oak is a project of me and about fifty contributors. It's not yet a national DTE project, but you can make it so."

"Those fifty people imagined all DTE was with them for the long haul," said Carolyn. "Perhaps Mount Oak should be given a two thousand dollar grant, half the residual, from the Berri profits?"

"That's crazy, it's a pittance" said Dave. "Without massive funds, Mount Oak isn't viable. It will die. DTE nationally must either commit massive money and energy

                    Down to Earth

into the future if we want to be a part of it. The only other sensible alternative for us is we let it go, give it nothing."

There's no-one here except me, he knew, who has been near Mount Oak for well over a year.

He had never seen a DTE meeting chair apply a gag. But this time the matter was tossed to a vote, and the two thousand dollars was assigned, and there would be no further responsibility from the gathered Down to Earth community to Mount Oak.

It was the only answer, but Dave was grieving. We had cut adrift both Jim and Mount Oak. Can you excommunicate a pope?

So the surplus was divided. Part to Jim as full refund for earlier ConFest losses. Part as a grant to Mount Oak. The small remainder would be start-up funds against the next national event.

Lunch was a sombre affair.

———

It was mid next morning that plans for a future carnival arose.

There had now been three national ConFests, and they had been spaced a year apart, give or take some. Was that how long it had taken each time to recover and then go through the searching and planning all again? Or had Jim engineered it that way? Dave had no illusions.

At Cotter, the ConFest adventure was unique and psychedelic. By Bredbo, the experience was that of a sequel, of such harshly different character as to be sobering. Berri was fairyland again, and smaller. We knew Berri was truly of our own making, thought Dave.

Cotter and Bredbo had been orchestrated by Jim and Junie, and the processes regarding site location and the festival dates were lost in history now, if ever they were public. After two festivals, Down to Earth around the country was becoming more "networked" (and that was the favourite term), and the wish to do ConFest again was conscious and widespread. Jim had been scouting for a third ConFest site, and so had the Victorian and South Australian DTE groups. Jenny and Chas had found Martins Bend at Berri, and with Jim, had then settled on last Easter.

Meanwhile, there had been several regional ConFests that had been put together by local DTE enthusiasts. Jim appeared and spoke. Some local events were not minor, either. Jackys Marsh in Tasmania and Cambray in Western Australia had each drawn thousands. Victoria was about to do another State one.

But the matter for today was national ConFests: Do we stage another? Where? When?

The first question got no air time. Another ConFest would be staged; it needed no justifying.

Carolyn looked serious. "Are we jumping the gun? Why and What are more fundamental than When. Are we trying for a repeat of what we have done? I'm not downplaying how great we found Berri. Do we want more of the same. What are we achieving?"

"Carolyn," said Jim. He regularly used names. It came as formal, but it was his habit anyway. "Carolyn, every ConFest we have, thousands of people come who have never before in their lives been exposed to the wonderful things they find. The ideas and the fun and the freedom are new for them. People come to ConFest as an experiment. They're intrigued by the possibilities, and then they summon enough bravery to try for themselves. After they come, they're changed. They glimpse freedoms they didn't dare know, and they leave different. It helps build a critical mass of enlightened people to create a new society at large."

"So you think we should just do more ConFests, duplicates?"

"Yes, and more come each year because they're curious."

They come, decided Dave, because they are enticed by the messianic reputation of Jim Cairns, former Federal Treasurer, on TV and press.

"I don't know. I keep feeling we need a more specific purpose, a clearer target. Even if we placed an individual theme on each ConFest to give it its own character." Carolyn stopped.

Peter weighed in, Peter from Sydney. Dave hadn't expected that. "Cotter was such a massive detonation in all our heads that it needed no other identity, I suppose. But Bredbo had some strong threads. The central Friends of the Earth tent was a stage to much ecological and activist conferencing. Bredbo was about land too. Permaculture and Keyline irrigation, and Mount Oak purchase."

Ouch.

"Berri?" Peter continued, "Well Berri was soft and mellow. Childbirth and meditation. Spiritual themes. So even if we hadn't planned themes each year, we still had them."

Time to force some hands.

"Last night," said Dave, "I was talking with some of our Rainbow Region colleagues. Don and Tom and Flora. They have some ideas we should be considering."

The Rainbow Region did have ideas. They had been touting them a while back as a prospect for the third festival, the one that had become Berri instead. Jim had always stonewalled.

Donny German started. "I live on Tuntable Falls Cooperative near Nimbin, and I have for six years since the Aquarius Festival. In the Rainbow Region of New South Wales we have many people living various aspects of the alternative lifestyle, and we feel we can contribute a great wealth of experience to the search for alternatives. We have had many meetings to consider this, and we would like today to put on the table our collective offer to host the ConFest for next year."

Instant chatter. Positive chatter.

"However," and this time Tom, a Rainbow man too, spoke, "we have a specific version of ConFest we want to offer. Unlike the three gatherings we have had so far, massed happy festivals on one campus, our Rainbow offer is for a series of intensive workshops on alternative subjects. Each workshop will be several days long, and each will be in its own location, clustered around the Rainbow area. We offer to plan and run the classes. In this way we could supply some real substance, real depth to the search for alternatives, real-life stories, working solutions. We want to offer a syllabus that any Mount Oak college cannot yet offer."

Jim said no. He felt the living styles of Rainbow Region were a hippie retreat from society. There was not there a real revolution to free the broad society, he said, and using Rainbow lifestyles as a model for others wasn't what he wanted.

For the others, the concept was tempting, albeit daring, and was worth doing for this once. The familiar ConFest still had a visceral appeal, but just once done this intensive work-shop way might be good.

The agreed outcome was to accept the Rainbow offer, although Jim now held silence. Could we add a small "real" ConFest in with the workshop format? It was still a year away.

Dave closed his eyes, buried his face in his palms, and sighed.

Where to now?

Brian – Terania Creek

Spring

We needed to put the second Newsletter together. So much was happening, and some of this news deserved to be published and sent around the country as early as we could make it. I say "around the country" rather than merely "on the streets" or "around town" because despite our journal's Canberra title, our real agenda was a national one. As befits a document from the national capital, maybe? Too much hubris?

Ostensibly we published for the Canberra constituency. But Canberra was a small target. The unspoken purpose was a national distribution for some key Down to Earth stories and facts, padded with softer articles to be an easier read. We were *not* admitting that.

"Issue One in July has been well received around the country," I said. We had tried hard to target as many alternative organisations in Australia as we could, magazines, community radios, every DTE pocket. "We searched for information that was accurate and transparent. DTE might despise authority, but I suggest what we published was detailed and patently knowing of the real story, and in that sense our reputation should be seen in time as authoritative."

"No, I don't like that concept," said Summer. Summer had moved in with Dave last week. "It's that word authority that's wrong. We don't have an authority."

"Do you accept precise accurate inside information?"

"Sure, that way I have no problem. Heaven knows, truthful facts are scarce. We have been living among rumour and contradicting versions of everything we do and plan."

"That's why we here are in the best position to publish the facts. We have all the document and now tape archive for Down to Earth. Dave has many of the documents." Dave nodded. "And in this house are all the tapes."

"One point I want to make clear," I started. "The declared publication cycle is for five issues spanning the twelve months up to the next festival. We need to make that a window to say all the things that should be said."

"Why stop then?" asked Lee.

"Same question, why stop after one year?" added Ollie.

"Because it takes a huge amount of energy to do it. We are a small group doing the work. OK, let me put it another way. Speaking for myself only, I am prepared to commit myself for five issues. If after our year, I have energy to go on, that is great. If someone else wants to take it over, that's great too. But I'm just promising five issues."

"So what is the motivation for those five issues?"

"To say the things that are not being said. To put clearly the decisions and plans we agree on. We talk, but we don't believe in any minutes recording what we said? What we do have is the 'archives' that few know of. We move two steps forward and then slither backwards and sideways. Who pulls the strings, really?

"Anyway, let's go on. We have many submissions here for this edition. It's up to us to decide if we want to shape the issue to a strong theme. Last time it was easy: there was so much to say about Berri ConFest, and so that theme was an easy choice. We threw in a lot about where Mount Oak community were up to. What about this time?"

"We have several letters to editor." Dave was looking through the folder of material. "Good reading in those, too. There's an article from the Pialligo commune on running an

                                        Down to Earth

alternative apple orchard. Plenty of news in the interstate DTE newsletters that we can collate into a good few pages. Hamlet housing development article from Nimbin. Some letters from Jim Cairns, too. Two articles on massage. Latest Mount Oak situation from Eureka. A couple of new advertisers, too, and that helps. Hmm, how do we put all that together? One more question: do we want to raise the uranium mining Northern Territory is planning?"

While we spoke, the phone rang. It was Tom Warrior from up north. The Terania Creek rainforest dispute was a bloody one, and we all knew that, as the media were carrying daily scenes of damaged bulldozers, and of hippies being arrested by police to be wagoned to Lismore. The rainforest preservation issue was gaining some traction, if only in securing press, but it was a long way from any success yet for the forces of conservation.

Tom had been talking with Jenny in Adelaide, who had expressed her intent to drive up to join the fray. Two thousand kilometres. Some of her friends were considering joining the trip.

So, between them, they had raised the possibility of merging the planned Nimbin coordinators meeting of the Down to Earth network, with support for the Terania cause. What did we think?

It took less than an hour to lock in. Tom called Patrick in Melbourne and Dan's house in Brisbane. Dave talked with the folks in Sydney. Yes, Yes and Yes. We would gather at the Terania Creek protest site, if indeed we could get access, as early as we could manage, with our DTE formal meeting in nine days from today. Every region would send as many as could travel, and that would constitute a visible assembly of Down to Earth from across the country.

This was the first time Down to Earth had stood up nationally, and we knew it. Native forest and rainforest conservation was an issue that so far had always lost out to the forces of economics, local jobs, national progress and

Government blindness. For the first time, it seemed the preservers might have some slight hope of winning a battle against the loggers. The war once under way might still be a long one, but we hadn't won any significant battles yet at all. This time, we might be getting closer.

In the State elections for New South Wales three years ago, a new Premier, Neville Wran, won office in a campaign of moderate conservationism. This was a remarkable stance for a top politician, and would never have gained winning votes in earlier years. After relentless hard-headed "progress" policies from both parties of politics, we now had a Government with at least a timid claim to caring about the environment. But did anyone believe green policies would win when the going got politically hard? Politics is merciless, and idealism often loses out. Wran had not yet had a tough green issue to solve.

Those of us in the New South Wales area willed ourselves to believe being green might be getting a little easier. Now indeed was the right time to push for the green advantage.

In two days, we produced a bumper newsletter and mailed it in record time. Theme: *Terania Rainforest.*

———

Ollie travelled with Jo and me to Terania. The five-issue newsletter term was still bugging him, and he was considering whether he might continue it onwards if I stopped after the five.

We decided to make it a single day journey, and headed out before dawn. While they both slept, I drove, through Sydney. We pulled over in the Hunter wine district at a road-side spot to prepare a very late breakfast. We had brought camping facilities and stove and food for several days. By now, hours along the road, we were hungry, so we raided what we carried.

I don't understand why we didn't settle for cereal and milk, or even toast and jam. Instead I asked, "Anyone for eggs and bacon?"

Our hunger devil made us do a cooked breakfast on the gas stove, toast and hot tea included. The morning was crisp, and just tea and anything quick should have been a sufficient fix.

So it was late in the day when we approached Nimbin from the south, past the landmark knife-edge cliff hundreds of feet high to our left. The *Nimbin News* office was closed.

The pub was open. "No, not directly from here. If you came from Lismore, you have come the wrong way. Take the road out from here right down to The Channon, and from there you need the Terania Creek Road back north. And expect gravel."

I don't think they wished us much good luck.

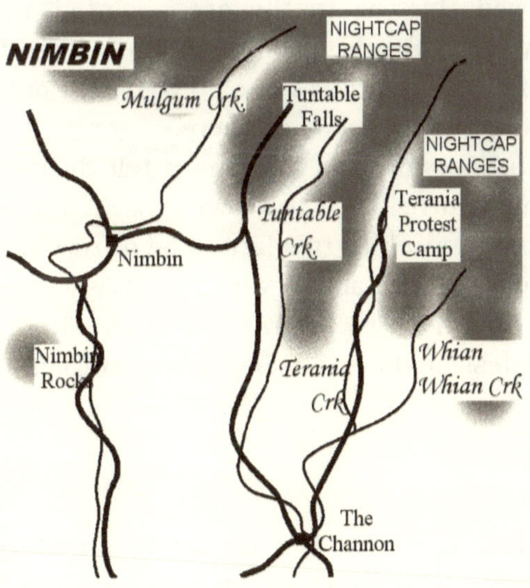

The slow Terania Creek Road had considerable back traffic as we got closer. Was there some event on up ahead? But there was little ahead, only Terania Creek itself.

At dusk we reached the property of Nell and Hugo Jamieson. This was the base camp for the ragged green army of the Terania Creek battle. It was Nell, drawn and looking exhausted, who spotted the new car arriving, and who came to introduce herself and welcome us to her home place and to the camp. A few Down to Earth groups had been turning up in the past couple of days. There were rumours that more contingents of support were coming from all over the country, and now it was happening. Would we please arrange our camping down below the community kitchen and fire area, and join in as we were ready. She was offering to speak with all newcomers tomorrow to bring us up-to-date. The local protesters had been here for weeks and even months, and there had been many heated and violent hostilities inside and with the loggers. Many were sorely battle wearied.

I moved the car to the area pointed, and we were greeted by old friends, including Lee's friend Lily from Queanbeyan, and Jenny's large crew from South Australia. Peter and the Sydney folk were here.

By an hour into the morning it felt difficult to avoid a few unhappy truths. We, the growing band of Down to Earth arrivals, were a week or two late to be of use in the protests. For now, at least, the action was over. We were not going to contribute much to the rainforest cause. In this camp of protest professionals, we were naive tourists in the sub-camp.

—

Nell and Dudley called us together mid-morning. The Down to Earth squad had grown to more than fifty. We sat on the dusty grass in a circle.

"You've seen us around, but let us properly welcome you here to Terania Creek. A lot has happened recently, and we can do with the support and the publicity. I'll let Dudley give you an action roundup, but I'll start with the background.

"Hugo and I moved to this delightful old dairy farm a year ago from further south, near Canberra. It's at the end of a quiet road here, and it adjoins the rainforest park. We wanted to grow our own food, live with the environment.

"Our other dream was to develop a rainforest nursery to promote and preserve the native species. Many are not even catalogued yet, but they are under threat of extinction before we know they exist."

She held up two seedlings. "These have no name yet. We found them.

"This land is one of the few remaining pockets of Australian native forest not clear-felled, although they harvested some trees out of here forty years back.

"Six months ago we found by chance that the rainforest next to us was indeed slated for logging. Our first reaction was to sell out again, but all our neighbours and friends were horrified at the prospect of the logging, and we decided to stay and fight. We have determined to draw a line on the ground here.

"We tried negotiating with all the authorities, tried lodging objections. They bluffed and stonewalled us, and then the bulldozers arrived to have their way. Now what began as our own local struggle has grown to a pivotal confrontation for overall rainforest preservation.

"This is our home. Welcome. Join us, add to the three hundred fighters we have here. Many are from Tuntable Falls Cooperative in the next valley, but we have many equally passionate protesters from across the Rainbow Region. Support us and help spread the story of what we are doing.

"In the physical action on the site here, Dudley Leighton from Dharmananda, which is a Buddhist style farm community here in the Terania Valley, has in many ways been our mentor and our speaker. He is the leader we say we don't have. It has been a dramatic and testing role.

"Dudley ..."

"Thanks, Nell.

"We got a part concession many months ago from the Minister of Conservation that Terania would not be clear-felled, and that the loggers would only selectively harvest the Brushbox and Blackbutt trees.

"But that wasn't acceptable to us either. The new settlers formed ourselves into the Terania Native Forests Action Group, and we demanded nothing should be logged without an Environmental Impact Statement, and we began intensive letter-writing and lobbying in the media. That's when you may have seen our TV coverage start appearing. We went professional with photographers and press people, and city folk saw our message in their homes, in their papers, on their radio.

"We set up a protest camp here, and commune people and ferals and every sort of new settler poured in. We built our numbers up to a thousand at one point. The police established an opposition camp along the road, and the press milled everywhere to get exciting copy. We knew the loggers were coming. We were determined they shouldn't come. Police arrested the protesters, dragged them to jail, and we filmed it all. We staged it as a viewable drama, and we did it well—the old generation around here and the loggers and the authorities were wrong-footed.

"How do we support a group like we are? We created our own Rainbow Army Corps to physically run the show, supply water and sanitation, keep us fed. The Army is from among our own, and their discipline and morale are inspiring. When they're not on the front line, they are aware that they're still part of the protester machine.

"I try to be a peaceful man, to make love and not war. Resist by passive blockading.

"But many of our protesters fight harder than this. Some believe violence must be met with the same. A bulldozer has been damaged with gravel in its gearbox, equipment was smeared with shit, vehicles had the electrics cut, trees had lethal steel spikes driven in. We have much tension and anger in this dispute. Hippies versus hippies. Hippies versus loggers. The police have not been on our side, they cordon us off to protect the logging.

"Most mornings we meet in a circle group right where we are now. We try to share our thoughts, air our grievances, plan our tactics, clarify our motives. It's hard to reconcile the Gandhi approach with the angry reactive method. As Nell said, I facilitate our circle groups. In this warfare, our credibility out there depends on us staying courteous and nonviolent. I'm finding it difficult.

"Two weeks ago the dozers forced their way through and felled the first trees. We pulled chainsaws from the loggers, we climbed the marked trees, but some Brushbox were still cut and carted. That was when the press were here in force taking shots of 'drag away the ferals', and you would have seen it all across the country, I hope. We wanted a total barrage of copy out there.

"We made it hard and very slow for the logging company, Standards of Lismore. Three days back, Standards pulled out their logging crews for a rest.

"Yesterday we had an open day here, and two thousand locals came—and you know the long difficult track that leads here—and they listened to Aboriginal Burnam Burnam speak of the spiritual significance of these lands. We are winning some hearts.

"But the logging supporters are rallying too and it's worrying us. They have a deputation in Sydney today to get Neville Wran to send more police effort to remove us and guarantee safety for the logging work.

"We don't quite know where Wran stands. This is a recession. He may feel he has to support the struggling logger families.

"That's where we are up to. Lull in the storm."

We had listened carefully. This was why we were here, to learn and to help if we could.

"So we are not out of the woods at all?" I asked. "We thought the battles of the past week or two might be now over."

"Not at all, these are deceptive days. But choose your metaphor carefully. Words like woods carry a lot of meaning around here." Laughs.

"I know you will all be here for some days, and perhaps these may be the best days for that. Give cheer to those of us who are on this job for the long haul. Take our message across the country. We appreciate your contribution."

Still the tourists. But that is what we have to be. We should do it well.

"Today's a rest day for us," said Dudley. "Bring food, join the Army kitchen, talk with us, walk into the forest. Most importantly, take pictures. We are resting and preparing for whatever is the next round.

"Tomorrow, I suggest we should arrange a guided walk through the rainforest. We can show you the trees we are protecting, and felled ones still lying on the rainforest floor. Thank you." Gandhi, leader of the ungovernable.

We did go into the forest. We were city folk. The forest just looked like forest.

The moon was bright and high at dusk, and a public fire was burning near the kitchen. Drums came out and it became a subdued drumming evening with a hundred or more sitting, dancing and smoking. More feral than a ConFest night, but not so very different.

Before next morning's circle had finished, a phone call to the house delivered the bombshell. Premier Wran had this morning decreed that all Terania Creek logging will stop, pending a cabinet meeting next week. His reason was that widespread community support across the State was now moving towards rainforest protection.

The Terania media campaign was working.

—

I helped my daughter Jo lace her boots. I still felt mauled inside, powerless, from last week's arguments with Lee.

Nell had set out an hour earlier into the forest with thirty of the Down to Earth horde. Now there were thirty more of us ready, and that included Chas's sister Vaney from Adelaide, whom I had shared fireside thoughts with last night. Iris was our assigned guide, heading into the forest now, late morning. Iris was a resident of the Tuntable Falls Cooperative across the ridge directly between here and Nimbin, and she had been camping with the protesters for the past three weeks.

"This morning I'm going to show you our rainforest, and why we are so desperate to preserve it," she started. "Interrupt me anytime, ask questions, take any photos you want. We want to spread our message as far as we can. However, it will be dark inside, and good pictures will be difficult." Dave and several of us carried cameras.

Carolyn said, "Well, I want to try to capture any sound as well. We can play some effects on the Down to Earth Radio Show in Melbourne."

Iris looked us all over. Trying to establish an emotional bond? I saw her staring at our white-haired Lily, but Lily kept her silence.

"Why do we want to preserve the forest? Because we used to have huge estates once, and most of Australia's rainforest is already logged and now lost to other uses. Because rainforests are the biggest biological resource of diversity on earth, and we are losing it rapidly, before we understand what it is we have lost."

Dave interrupted, "If they clear-felled and left it to lie, wouldn't the rainforest grow back? It's the natural ground-cover for the area."

"No, it wouldn't grow back as it was. If only a tiny pocket gets cleared, and is surrounded by otherwise undisturbed forest, it can sometimes seed itself back to be a little like the original. It did happen to a little area called Corn Patch not far from here that was cleared forty years ago. Some rainforest has come back in from all the surrounding forest, but it's not what it was, and never will be. Our rainforest is the end product of millions of years' history. It is not replicable."

We had passed from the cleared land of the protest camp and were scampering down a foot track into the forest, and we came to a further cleared out area that bore plenty of evidence of recent mechanical and vehicle activity. "This is the log dump. It had been used in the earlier felling forty years ago, and the loggers reopened the back road up to here last month."

Two fresh trunks lay to the side. "These were Brushbox, three-hundred-years-old. Standards got three truckloads out in a week, before they pulled out for a break. They would have liked to haul several trucks every day. We got in their way so hard that three trucks is all they have won so far." Dave was taking photographs.

Iris led us further in, upwards, and the trails were poor, the undergrowth tugged at us. "Watch out for these broad leaves—they sting like a nettle." And I understood why we were all wearing substantial footwear: I dislodged a leech from Jo's left boot, leaving her to gasp in horror.

Sunlight appeared again as we gathered around Iris. A bright giant gash shone in the overgrowth, the swathe cut as a mighty Brushbox had crashed to the forest floor, wrecking the lesser trees and Bangalow palms. The debris of the kill was still here, branches and whole trees scattered and tumbled, and skid marks of the machines that had dragged away the prized carcass.

"This was the first tree to fall," explained Iris. She spoke carefully, as though pausing to compose her words first. "We didn't know when they might start cutting, but we patrolled the forest every day. When the chainsaw first started, Peter from our camp got here, and discovered the cutter starting, the cops and the press ringed around. He managed to run up behind the logger and grab the running chainsaw, trying to pull it from him. He was arrested, thrown in the wagon, and carted off to Lismore. But the press got it all." A chainsaw-tackle action arrest was better copy than the mere blockade arrests of the past few weeks.

"We all arrived, and the police kept us at a distance. When the tree came down, we cried and yelled. It stirred such spiritual feelings inside me I didn't know existed. We felt so frustrated and defeated. The press caught that as well. The papers cried '*Logger Victory*', but in the end we knew that publicity even like that could only help us."

"Dad," said Jo, back at camp, "can I be a rainforest ranger when I grow up?"

"You and me both, when we grow up, sweetie. There are some things we need to do. A world to change."

———

Two afternoons later, a truck, Iris driving, arrived with a load of logs and branches. She threw them on a wood pile beside the all-day fire below the Rainbow Army kitchen, the kitchen that stubbornly supplied endless vegetarian burgers, hot teas and oven bread to all the outposts. The camp atmosphere was lighter than it had been. We were upbeat by now. Tonight was party night. Tonight was special.

"Lily, penny for those thoughts," I said, coming upon her along a short track. She was sitting alone on a fallen branch. Two downturned cards were beside her.

"Worried about rain. A lot of rain."

It won't happen. What sky we could see through the canopy was sunny, cloudless.

Lee and Charlie had arrived yesterday, and I was enjoying that, too. I forgot the arguments. Lioness Leonie was a handful, fiery, but we could always find solutions. Negotiation school. I was Halleys Comet always swinging close to her small stormy planet? I understood her, I think.

I had started coaching her in mature-age entry exams for study at the Canberra College of Advanced Education, and she hoped her activist passions might one day carry more measured backing.

She had suggested last week that somewhere buried down, I still loved Rose. Not true, I said, and it became an obsession. She yelled. I yelled. She stopped pursuing it.

She parked her car.

"Brian, guess this. I just gave a ride from Queanbeyan to Lismore to a woman named Jann. Works at Honeysuckle Creek. Said she knows you. Jann Cassin. Big frizzy hair."

"Oh, yes, we've met. It was at Bredbo ConFest, so a year or two ago. Thought the planets were sending us radio messages that her antennas could read. No, not fair. She was very interesting."

"Well, this week she's in a desperate hurry to get to Tuntable Falls and find Donny German. The prophet man."

"Yes, Don talks aliens at times. What was her panic?"

"She was blabbing on about her probe diving under rings, but it made no sense."

"Newspaper news a few days ago. I saw it. A Pioneer space rocket whizzed past Saturn and sent back close-up pictures. It would have to be that."

"Brian, this Jann is paranoid. She kept telling me we were being tailed on the highway. I left her in Lismore to catch the bus or hitchhike to Nimbin. I was exhausted."

That Jann has seen too many alien messages.

———

Down to Earth

Yesterday's festival coordinator meeting here had been short, in the circumstances. The Rainbow communities were well under way with doing a ConFest their way—more a workshop format than earlier gatherings. That was approved all round.

Tonight, Paul Joseph had been strumming away, Joseph the survivor from Hair the Musical. He was singing a selection of the protest songs that we had been sharing for a few days. Some were his own work, some were adopted from elsewhere, given new lyrics to suit the occasion. "*All we are saying, Is give trees a chance.*" John Lennon would have stamped his imprimatur.

Joseph began one of his own. We knew it: "*Let's all go down to the forest,*" he sang.

Gaze in wonder. Bask in a million years of peace.

Jo and I walked up to the fireside where a group had gathered, and we sat to listen. Lee, Lily and Summer followed us up, and Charlie, and more of our mob. But it was impossible to merely listen. We clapped along until we were picking up the chorus lines, and we added our voices. Dave went back to his car, returning with his bodhran drum. *Hands off our greenery.* He fitted his rhythm to the guitar music, and by now there were three guitarists.

Another drum came out, a real one. *Take your machinery.* The night of defiant euphoria wasn't going to let up for many hours.

It was full moon night, but we were in a valley, and we had to wait for the moon to appear over the range. The drumming built up. It eased again. It evolved from rhythm to rhythm. Tribal drumming will sometimes stop, pause while one of the players teases out a fresh rhythm to restart the others. But tonight the energy ran higher than that. It surged and fell, as a surf can surge and slow, but it never quite stopped, the next rolling wave coming inevitably in. I had never seen or heard a stronger group of drums.

The moon came over, and the hysteria grew. *Drive those bulldozers away.* Some danced deliriously. Away from the fire, the night was cool, but still two naked bodies writhed in the moonlight. Lee pranced out to the dusty arena.

The children tired nonetheless. I put Jo and Charlie to bed. The seats of my Mazda could lie back low, and the kids chose to set up bed in the car together instead of in the tent. That way they could be in bed and they could watch as well, or watch until they slept. I returned to the deafening drum performance.

Then it started. We knew it would. The first corner of the moon's circle darkened. The crowd roared, and the roar did not let up. Progressively, the bite out of the moon became bigger. The drumming grew more frantic. Voices were getting hoarse. The eclipse swallowed every last part of the moon, and the forest valley camp fell to darkness, a thunderous, hysterical black.

A frantic tap on my arm pulled me from my ecstasy. Your kids are crying, they need you.

Stumbling through the dark, I ran to the car, and both were trembling and sobbing. "Dad, we are so scared. What's happening? Why is the moon switched off? It's so dark in the forest, and everyone is screaming." Jo spoke for both, as she was wont. Young Charles, competent and smart, lived that vulnerable life of someone who had never ever spoken. Jo sobbed and shook in my arms, and I held Charlie, too.

I stayed holding for thirty minutes or so, as the moon slowly returned to its bright full circle. The drumming was still rolling on, but the climax had passed. A saxophone had joined. The night resumed to being a normal night of music, for hippies. I lay with Jo and Charlie, and I was sad, sad for letting them down. The eclipse and the forest music were a unique and overpowering event. I had the privilege, the good fortune, to share in it, and I had failed to guide my daughter, not six yet, safely through the intensity of it all. I was lost in my own experience, and had not been wise enough to support the kids, both of them. We should have been together.

The drumming didn't die away until dawn. I slept awkwardly in the car with the two kids. The night was long and fitful, until Lee found us at dawn.

The protest village was buzzing when we staggered out. Voices, shouts, people arriving and leaving. Someone had torched the Standards Timber Mill in Lismore in the dead of the night, and the reports had just arrived here. No-one was sure who had done the deed. With most still breakfasting, an urgent circle group meeting was called to consider the scraps of information available, to check if anyone knew any of the details, to plan for a first response. Was it one of our own? Was it a cynical company ploy? No answer was forthcoming.

"Have a great dance night?" I asked Lee at breakfast. A pause. A slow expressionless gaze. And then, in slow motion, I knew. We both resumed as though no question had been put.

Finally, Lee wandered away. Jo and Charlie had joined a hula hoop circle. I slumped on a log.

And logging at Terania or at any of the New South Wales rainforest was never to resume.

Leonie – Summer Storm

Early Summer

Yes, Dave is Brian's friend, but he's edgy. With me, at least. Is it my bluntness? It's the women friends I keep? Do I really want to go with Brian out to Sandford?

Brian had decided to drive out to Sandford to see Dave, on Dave's day off. Summer, too, if she were home. He had called in to see Leonie at Queanbeyan on the way through.

"But he's more your friend," she had said. "You know we don't get on much."

The morning was pleasant. She was persuaded to go anyway. She'd see Summer.

OK.

The radio was playing and Lee sang along. "*You're a Heartbreaker, Dream Maker, Love Taker.*" They turned and laughed. "Ah, Pat Benatar," she said.

They turned into the Captains Flat Road.

She wondered if Brian had any feelings still bubbling over Summer. He had never said so. It wasn't jealousy, though. She was content, very comfortable, in her deal with him. Both Martians. But her feminist friends never got it.

"Sandford is such a trendy rural estate now."

"I hate most of those houses there," agreed Lee. "I could never live in those expensive brick mansions."

"But you could handle Dave's place?"

"Oh yes, I think the old tin shack is fabulous. It has this ramshackle character I like. I have only been there once, though."

"Did I ever tell you I nearly part-owned it?"

"No, you did not. When was this?"

They were cresting the top of the long hill down to the Sandford drive. Brian slipped a hand under her thigh. She liked that. It said so much in no words.

"Many years ago," he said, "when Rose and I moved to Canberra, we were trying to buy a house, either in town or out of town. Through some common friends, we met Miriam and then Dave, and we got on well together. Rose and Miri, especially. The two skinny sisters, I called them. You wouldn't have recognised Rose then."

Lee knew the Rose of today, Jo's Mum. She let the reference pass. "Miri was the girl who died?"

"Yes, Dave's wife. She was a good woman, and so happy. They crashed their car along this road one night going home. Dave took it very hard."

She knew Dave had lost his woman, but she had never heard any detail.

Brian turned uphill on the Sandford Estate road. "This sealed road wasn't here then, no houses except the old house Dave and Miri were renting. Both of us couples were struggling to find and afford a place, and we had a few talks on pooling our money and buying the house together. We reckoned we could manage the finance part, but Rose and I were not sure we could do the household sharing bit with them. Well, with Dave more particularly. When the discussions got personal, he would close up. Sometimes it felt like he had an emotional fence around Miri, or was it just around himself? We pulled out, and they found a way to buy it themselves."

"What were you looking for? Shared household or shared relationships?"

"We never got that far. We withdrew and looked else-where."

Enough.

At the top of the rise was a T-intersection, and they turned left. The car almost struck a running woman, holding a shoe high, and waving in panic.

"That's Summer," screamed Lee. Summer on the road had also realised it was Brian driving. She was crying hyster-ically, and Lee opened her door, changed her mind, twisted backwards, opened the rear door, and pulled Summer by a sleeve into the back seat.

"Take me away," she sobbed. Lee clambered over the seat and joined her in the back. Summer buried her face and clung. Brian reversed up to turn at the intersection, and without speaking he drove down, back to the road, back into Queanbeyan.

They were all in Lee's lounge room with coffee before Summer was ready to let anything out. Lee was staying with her charge, until she was ready.

"He had a gun." Summer was shaking and still sobbing. "He wanted me out, and he kept pointing it at me. I was so frightened. We'd been in bed, and I had to throw some clothes on and get out fast. I don't know where he got it, he just came back in with it and yelled at me to get out."

Bloody men, why do you do it?

"Do you want to tell me?" she asked quietly. "Only if you want."

"I've been going in each Tuesday to The Foundry in town." The Foundry was a craft centre, low cost, creative, covering various arts and styles.

"I stayed in town this Tuesday night with my friend Sally who teaches pottery. We slept the night together. Not a lot happened. We kissed a little, that's all." Summer closed her teary eyes, struggling with the memories of it. "Dave was pestering me wanting to know what I had been doing Tuesday night, so I told him about Sally. I should have kept my mouth shut." Her face twisted and she dissolved into more tears.

———

Seven days later, Lee drove Summer out to Sandford. No-one had heard from Dave for the week, but they were hoping he would be at home. For four running weeknights each fortnight, Dave's daughter Sunday had been in the habit of staying with her Grandma Suzanne, who took her to school in O'Connor. Lee wondered if Sunday would be back with Dave this week, for driving to O'Connor twice each day sometimes kept Dave in town for the day.

Brian had kept out of Dave's contact also, but he had agreed to drive out to Sandford today if Lee hadn't phoned by late afternoon.

Summer stepped out slowly to open the farm-style gate at the cul-de-sac ending the sealed modern road. Lee watched her lift the key-plate with its heavy chain off the retainer post, bent metal, a phallus that kept things retained, restrained.

No, Leonie, stop it. Hold an open mind.

Dave's car was home. An old blue bus sat to the side, half-buried in long grass.

They knocked on the corrugated iron door. Dave allowed them in, grudging, no eye contact, no words. He hadn't shaved for a few days. He wore a long black skivvy, nothing else.

"We need to talk," said Summer.

Silence. Summer glanced at Lee. Big Dave waved feebly towards some chairs. They sat.

"I'm sorry," he said. He was looking away and down into a far corner. "I'm sorry," he repeated.

"Dave, I'm sorry too, but sorry is not enough. I thought you were going to kill me. I thought I loved you. You were so angry. I was terrified I would die. Don't you understand that?"

"I didn't want to lose you."

"You didn't want to lose me?" Summer's voice was rising. "Lose me? Dave, I was in bed with you, curled in your body. Was that lost? You weren't losing me. I was there. My soul was there, my heart was there. Your spunk was warm and juicy in my belly. Man, what were you thinking?"

"I just snapped. It was Sally ..."

"I know it was Sally. I should never have told you."

"I couldn't bear the thought. My head exploded."

"Dave, you have grabbed at a butterfly because it looked beautiful to you, and now you are crushing it."

"But with Sally?" pleaded Dave.

Oh, thought Lee, it's the *woman to woman* issue, not just the *my woman is elsewhere*.

"Dave, nothing happened."

"Of course it did. Summer, I don't want to lose you."

No, correction, it's the *keep my woman home*.

"I said, you were not losing me." Her voice was sad.

He didn't hear. "I can't afford to lose you. Losing is too hard. It's too hard." He was fighting tears.

No-one answered. Lee was struggling to absorb it all. Finally, she said softly, "What is it, Dave?"

"I don't want to lose her." The flood started. "I loved Miriam, and I lost her. I killed her. I could never undo it. I can't let it happen again."

Lee went to search for tissues, looking back, trying not to break the contact.

"Christ, I'm so lonely, I'm so screwed up. I lose everyone in my fucking life." He was yelling, crying, walking across the room.

"I'm sorry about Miriam," said Summer. "I'm not Miriam. And I was here."

"Accidents happen in life," said Lee. "You didn't plan Miriam's death. You can't punish yourself for all your life. Eventually, we must all go onwards, trust, love."

"I lose every time." Bitter. He stopped.

"Every time?"

"I lost my father. I drove him away."

"When?"

"When I was four. I was naughty and we fought. He smacked me. He never came back."

"You were four?" said Lee. "No four-year-old is responsible for his father. Dave, that's crazy."

"He never came back." He paused. "Barrie never came back."

"Barrie?"

"My brother. He died in Vietnam."

"Well, you can't possibly say you caused that."

"Mum always used it against me. I wasn't worthy of being Barrie's brother. I still lost him."

Hmm, maybe it isn't always the men.

Dave lay crumpled in a large chair, crying, bereft of dignity, eyes closed.

"Summer, I'm sorry."

"Me too, Dave. I'm sorry too."

Dave remained in his own depths for some while. Lee boiled a cup of tea.

"I guess I've blown it?"

Tears filled Summer's eyes. She nodded. "Yeah, I think we have. Sorry." She cried.

He had lost her.

"Dave, what's Suzanne's phone number. I'm going to ask her over."

Where's the phone in this house?

"Oh shit, no. NO." He closed his eyes. "Yeah, you should." She could see the humiliation making him smaller.

I'm calling Brian, too.

Brian – ConTest: French Island

Mid-Summer

I sat on the jetty at Stony Point awaiting the ferry, which was still a few hundred metres away. The crowd of more than a hundred started stirring, checking  their packs, and I recognised no-one. It was ConFest time again, and a new generation was plunging in, ready to be enthralled, confronted, shocked, or, more likely, just entertained.

No cars could get to French Island, or not for the ConFest crowd anyway. The advice had been, don't even bring cars to Stony Point, come by train, and most had. We loaded aboard and motored off for Tankerton wharf. I had my pack and some papers.

A month ago, Jim Cairns had announced "ConFest 1980, French Island". Every grouping of Down to Earth was dismayed. "But we agreed on a new format for this year, the workshops in the Rainbow Region. We have been planning it for most of a year." Jim had rarely joined us any longer.

Jim was adamant he could call a ConFest as he chose, he had created ConFests after all, he had called together what was now Down to Earth. Anyone could announce a ConFest, he said, if they could summon the interest and organisation. The new society recognises freedom to do, not right to suppress.

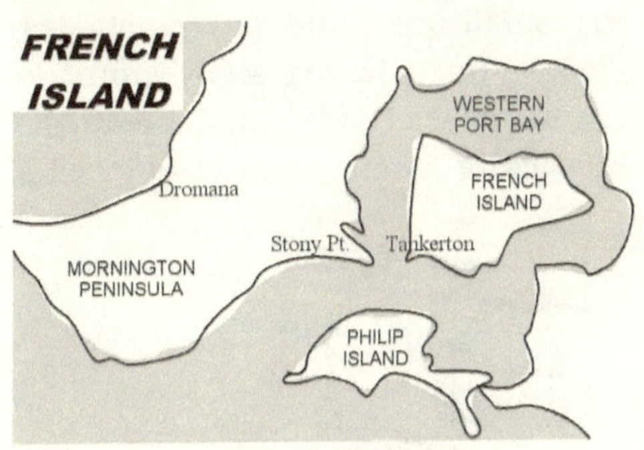

Here is how it came about. DTE in Victoria, well-organised by now, and incorporated even, were still looking for a site to hold another State festival. They were offered the use of a property on French Island by Cairns and the property owner/estate agent George Santaro. Negotiations between the Victorian group and Jim and George broke down a month ago on financial matters and Santaro's veto powers. Jim wrote to DTE Victoria that "it is impossible for us to agree about the conduct of the ConFest at French Island." He went ahead with the festival alone, billing it as "The Down to Earth ConFest" for the year. Most of the DTE network across the country took exception to the implied broad allegiance behind that title, and we sent Jim a letter of unhappiness, signed by every State group. The daily press smelled Cairns scandal once more, and the issue went public in the Melbourne papers. Jim played through the press, he was a politician, and we for once followed.

In Canberra, we also published an emergency edition of our newsletter last week, relating the story as we knew it, and we sent it as far afield as we knew. We had always intended our one-year newsletter to be a facts disseminator, and the unashamed little four-pager, unscheduled, was the hardest and bluntest edition yet.

Caesar: Et tu, Brute? Then fall Caesar.
Cinna: Liberty! Freedom! Tyranny is dead.
Brutus: People and senators, be not affrighted.

A bus shuttle service was running from the wharf to the ConFest site, which was in the middle of the Island. ConFest was a sea of very small tents and canvas shades, and at the centre was a dome, one I hadn't seen before. So the country looked almost familiar. I just didn't know the language spoken here. But lack of language never stopped a tourist getting around.

I stayed three of the four days. Was it a "real" ConFest? Sure. It had work-shops, massage tables in the sunshine, kitchen stalls (all commercial), colour, fire twirling, drum and dance. Two thou-  sand people had no trouble enjoying their experience, for most of them their first. Donny German from Tuntable spoke on the 'New City-State Economy'. A sauna room, freestanding this time, used a firebox looking quite the same as the Berri one.

I met Peter and Cheryl from the Sydney DTE mob. Peter had told me he would be here, but there were not many of the other familiar faces. We sat in the market on the first evening, trying to make sense of the whole story.

"In Sydney, we have been worrying about it so much. There have been so many strange sides to the Down to Earth saga. Some of us have suggested that you should be the one to write it into a book," said Peter.

Down to Earth

"I've never written a book," I said. "Why me?"

"You are the one among us with the words. Words when they are needed," explained Cheryl, Cheryl the six-foot redhead girlfriend, Cheryl the blunt talker. "Many things need to be said. A complete inside story of Down to Earth, the real one, not the public one."

"You don't understand me. I am not a politician, I'm not the forefront person. I'm not sure you have the right person."

"Brother, you see through issues, and you speak clearly when you are ready," said Peter. "Think it over."

Peter had a small shop in Sydney, and in his spare time, as "Peter Rabbit", he ran clowning workshops. Was he joking with me now?

The clown. The timelord. The alchemist. The riddle of joy and sorrow.

Jim held a talk late on the second day, 'A Turning Point'. By then I had come across Leon from Pialligo commune, who hadn't commonly been a ConFest goer. We sat together for Jim's speech.

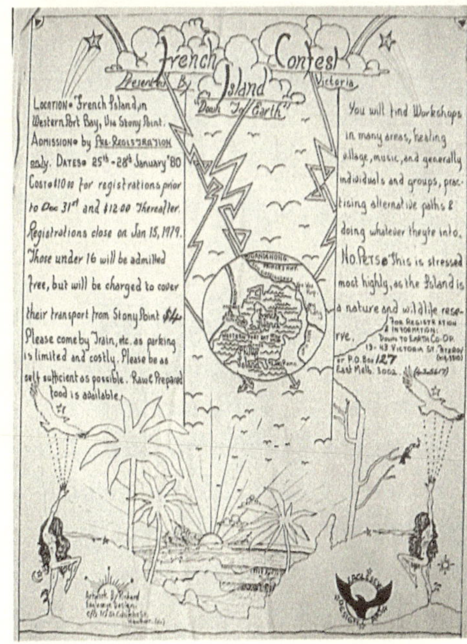

"We have reached a turning point in Down to Earth activities," said Jim. "Should DTE be controlled by a central body of coordinators? Should there be power to ban what individuals may do? Where is self-determination and autonomy?

"This issue is now public, and a group of so-called

national coordinators have laid it down I should not use the words Down to Earth for this ConFest. The only 'national' gathering is to be in the Rainbow Region this year. For me, DTE stands for liberation from sensory repressions, and for self-determination. Only once before in twenty-five years of alienated capitalist politics have I been told to submit in that way. This matter has even been taken to the capitalist press. I have always opposed State bans, on meetings, leaflets, marches, and I didn't expect bans from DTE. Your national coordinators are centralising power and authority, and Down to Earth should instead be based on spontaneity. Patriarchy still holds sway. DTE must change."

"What do you think," I asked Leon.

"Well, he has a strong point," said Leon. He tugged his small beard. "He won't accept democracy, and he won't accept consensus. He accepts only total autonomy. You play different games. I'll think about it."

"At your Pialligo commune, do you each operate claiming total autonomy?"

"Sometimes we wish. But no."

I had my answer. In my tent were copies of an "open letter" paper I had penned at home after talking with the others. Whether I would present the letter I hadn't decided, until now.

Jim,

I am sad and angry. Sad because we, you and us, believe our aims are the same, personal integrity, freedom. I am angry with us because we have felt tensions with you for a long time, and we have not tabled and solved the conflicts that are there. I am angry with you over one key anomaly over what you do and say: your belief in structurelessness as a solution to personal oppression, and your great use of personal power in the absence of structure.

                                               Down to Earth

Jim, no group runs without structure and power. If they are not admitted, they exist anyway, in secret and unaccountable. Autonomy and freedom (for you, for me, for DTE groups, for anyone) can only exist when the structure and power are explicit, and are voluntarily and wisely chosen and controlled by the people involved. You have alienated wave after wave of good people by enforcing your own decisions, while trying to keep the rest of DTE as amorphous as "the fifty thousand people who have attended ConFests".

We must resolve our approaches to structure, autonomy and tyranny. Or there seems no future between you and DTE."

Brian

Next morning I saw Jim and Junie standing talking near the dome. I hurried back, fetched my letter, and offered one first to Jim. I told him it was an open letter, and he was polite to thank me. I continued handing around copies.

On the afternoon ferry, I left the island. Was Peter Rabbit right?

It was later I found Leon staged a last day forum on 'Power, Politics and Anarchy'. It was subtitled as 'Jim Cairns versus DTE'. I understand Jim was not present.

———

Early Autumn

Dave reported in for the March newsletter work. Suzanne had stayed with him at Sandford for the couple of months after he lost Summer to Sally, helping him through the worst of it. She found a counsellor that Dave had used to hunt down some of his demons.

He didn't turn up subdued, either; he had some fire back in his belly. "Brian, I have a document here I think should go in. It's *The Tyranny of Structurelessness*. We discussed it at our national coordinators' meeting two years ago at EarthHaven, remember?"

I hadn't gone down to that meeting, but I did know the treatise. My last meeting with Jim came into focus.

"Oh, no, you weren't there. It was the meeting where we set up the Council of twelve elders across the country to be a think tank, our philosophical foundation. Hmm, that seems to have slipped away too. Well, we thrashed around this paper the women's liberation movement had been using. They'd been finding power problems rather like we were finding."

I flicked through it again. In any group, when there is no structure, there is much noise and little action. Without some planned organisation, some people will assume a role of spokesperson or organiser anyway, and being unelected they cannot easily be controlled. "You don't think, with all the French Island story, this is labouring the point?"

It went in.

So did a quantity of information on the Wytaliba People's Project. Wytaliba property was thirty-five hundred acres between Grafton and Glen Innis in the New England Tablelands. It had State Forest adjoining, a good river through, and pleasant climate. Two

Down to Earth

hundred folk had put up their $500 to join the cooperative, a hamlet project like Tuntable Falls and others similar further north. For four years they had been trying to get that critical mass of subscribers to complete the purchase. It was approaching give-up time. They were begging Down to Earth for publicity to help get them across the line.

Perhaps we were suckers. After Mount Oak, I think we were. We decided to run with it.

The issue hit the streets. The heavy politics stuff, while recording the facts—our truth, was there another version?—wasn't news most readers wanted to spend effort over. But various families of the Down to Earth network picked up the Wytaliba promotion, and Wytaliba quickly added new takers to its subscription book.

———

One good turn deserves another.

We all gathered one warm weekend at Wytaliba property, a crowd of the Wytaliba community, and seventy or more of the Down to Earth folk from all over. The Rainbow Workshops were almost upon us, and still there were many hankering for a conventional ConFest big gathering. DTE revellers come to each ConFest from all over Australia, or from this half of the country anyway. By comparison, the distance from the Rainbow Region proper (Lismore, Nimbin, Byron) to the Wytaliba property (uphill from Grafton), wasn't far, merely two hundred kilometres. Why, even the alternates around Bellingen near Coffs Harbour could identify themselves as Rainbow if it suited.

The exercise was to spend time with the Wytaliba people, and to examine whether we could stage a ConFest at Wytaliba following the Rainbow Workshops. Could we keep our cake and also eat it? We could be staging the combination Rainbow Workshops and ConFest. Had no-one told us the name Wytaliba meant "Where the fires went out"?

Dave and I took the train from Canberra to Sydney, and on to Grafton. We planned to hitch-hike up the Glen Innis Road, but hitching was not happening, so we trudged back into town and hired a Mini Moke.

"Dave, it's worrying me."

"Worrying you? Driving up the mountains?"

"No," I said, "it's the ConFest possibility. We were not having one, and now we might be, Wytaliba. A few months ago we were also not having one and we did, French Island."

"Hey, we didn't have French Island."

"No, you're wrong. We had a Down to Earth ConFest at French Island. That's what the public knows. Could we allow the ConFest theme to lie quiet for a time, allow some dust to settle? For our own peace as well as public perception."

"I can't agree," Dave insisted. He hadn't been at the Island, hadn't seen the pain, the damage, first-hand. "We have a fine opportunity to have a ConFest here," he continued. "The venue has fallen into our laps, both parties would love the event, the drama, the exposure, the mutual advantage. The location of a start-up commune settlement fits well with all the Rainbow Region has stood for. I'm going to propose all the workshops should record their work on video, and we could have showings at the ConFest, to tie together the two halves even more closely."

I didn't know how to press further my misgivings. We were climbing high up the Gibraltar Range, not far from the Washpool rainforests, which were currently under focus and protest. We were two-thirds towards Glen Innis on the table-lands when we turned into the property. Wytaliba is six square miles of timbered rolling hills, one-fifth of it cleared, and it has a four-kilometre frontage to the Mann River. That river flows in even the driest of seasons, and this was one of those dry seasons. The Yellow Jacket Range stood within the property, with two dams, and the river edge areas were black soil river flat. It was a place of beauty, even in these drought times, and it could well offer a comfortable communal life.

Beth Barry was a director of the Wytaliba Trust still based in Sydney, and she met us when we arrived at the old homestead building surrounded by acacias and silky oaks.

"Thanks," I said. "You have a magnificent property here."

"We are pleased with our purchase," she replied. Contract settlement was a week away now. "We're happy with our community, too."

"But you don't live here yet." Maybe not, but she looked quite at home: she had come from inside, and she wore only sandals and a pair of shorts.

"We do have a few staying here already," Beth said. "But we've welded ourselves into a community. There were so many hassles to raising the funds and meeting the contract terms. Our first contract lapsed, so we're on another one that we have now managed to meet. Our meetings, our clashes, our communication have forged some hard-won understandings over the several years, and some left, some who couldn't handle the boiling down process. We know each other well, even though we have yet to be here together."

Positive sentiments and "can do" attitudes surrounded me, and I felt compelled to forget my doubts, allow in the spirit of promise and light.

The Wytaliba ConFest was adopted enthusiastically. "Festivals are larger meetings that are born in smaller meetings," we told ourselves. We took photos, we made sketches of the grounds, marked up the market arena, a workshop avenue, camping estates, an amphitheatre on the rock cliff. Bill Mollison was there, preparing a Permaculture masterplan. After two days of mini-ConFest itself, we departed to our corners of the country to promote the new big event, make posters, gather work parties, for reconvening after the May workshops. Dave even wanted to craft the Wytaliba setup week as a workshop in its own right.

Rose approached me later that week. Could we start again? I hadn't had that choice before.

No, I said.

I hadn't had that answer before.

Dave – NonFest: RainBow

Late Autumn

May arrived. The drought broke.

A week of rain might be OK, thought Dave, and certainly the Bureau was forecasting it wasn't going to stop in one or two days. A week would soak out that dry dusty landscape. Allow another week to spend on-site to build the structures of a ConFest, and by mid-month, as the workshops were winding up, the Wytaliba property would be as ready and primed for the hordes as it could ever be.

Vaney was in Canberra, and Dave had been enjoying her company: they planned to be at the Wytaliba festival together.

By one week, the rains kept rolling across the north of the State. Dave delayed leaving Canberra. "Don't come yet," were the calls. "We're getting very wet in many areas. We'll call when it clears."

Dave was to be coordinating the site-works. Calls started arriving from Sydney and Melbourne, and from Brisbane, too, which itself was getting a lot of water. "What do we tell our people? We've spent a month promoting the ConFest heavily. Is everything going to be OK? What about all the workshops? They are about due to start."

Damn, he thought, the workshops are going to be more of a problem than the Wytaliba part. No central office coordinated the workshops. Each of the programmed twenty-eight workshops was autonomous; they each had their own phone or postal contact.

Throwing clothes and sleep gear into his car, Dave set off alone on a dash to the Northern Rivers. He went inland, the natural way for a Canberra start. Going the coast highway would be risky in any case, as the highway at Grafton was notorious for flooding. Heavy rain made travelling slow. From Glen Innis, he tried to phone into the Wytaliba homestead, and the phone rang out. He headed on towards Nimbin.

Driving was difficult and dangerous. The rain was relentless, and the scratchy wipers were struggling. Visibility was short. The roads, twisted and steep, were unstable as the dark was settling in.

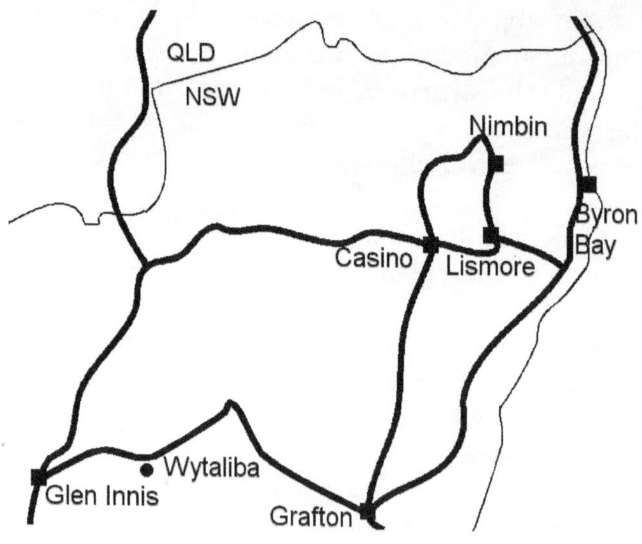

RAINBOW

Down to Earth

Filling petrol at Casino, he learned that the Richmond River was flooding at Lismore. Possibly the Kyogle route could still get through. Maybe not. Dave pulled to the edge in the main street, hoped the car would not be swept along in the broadening gutter waters in the dark, and he tried to prepare for a long and surreal night marooned in the car.

The phantoms played among the swirling storm squalls. *Damn Jim Cairns. This is not how it is supposed to happen. And where the fuck is Brian?* He had vanished a couple of weeks ago.

The chemo-ravaged face of Mum's friend Lily, her weird sister, grinned through the fogged windscreen. *And why did I leave Vaney behind?* Sleep came late and very troubled.

Chaos and bewilderment was the only response when he struggled into the *Nimbin News* shopfront by noon. The rain was still sheeting. There had been no general workshop announcements, because, as feared, all workshops were independent. Dave arranged for a stack of coin, and settled in for a long session at the Post Office phone. He got through to Wytaliba. He started on his DTE contacts. All DTE regional groups should use whatever access they had through their networks, and the local press and radio. Please blitz the media.

Please don't come. No Down to Earth Workshops. No Down to Earth ConFest. All is rained out.

The rains continued another ten days. Some foolhardy punters had managed to drive into the region, rains notwithstanding, press warnings notwithstanding, and all told of adventures pushing through flooded roads, skirting closures, of waiting on surging waters. "Big River" country was in full flood. Most workshops didn't happen. There were no customers. The 'Alternative Press — Publishing your Own' school in Bellingen to the south did manage to start very late after four students, including our Ollie, still managed to cross the flooded Bellinger River. Ollie was planning he might take over the Canberra newsletter and continue publishing. Wytaliba stayed closed. It was a quagmire.

Brian – Winter Snow

Late Winter

The days were brief, the nights were cold and long. The Gunningbar shearers' house was a joined pair of two transported construction team huts from the Snowys Hydro-Electric Scheme of the '50s. It had been home for two months, and every day was little different from the previous. Except Thursdays. Today.

Dreams troubled me, old unsettling ones. Stuff that had not been in my life for years. Security of my monastic days, the dedication to that communal life, the rituals, the certainty of belief. In my dream I contemplated re-applying, if they would have me. I should be back there. My soul ached. As I woke, I was confused and disgusted. That life was so long ago, lost in the mists. It hadn't worked.

I staggered out from the sleeping bag piled around with woolskins, and lit my little camp stove for a coffee. Damn, I had no water inside. Pulling on a jacket and a pair of boots, I took the saucepan outside and around to the rainwater tank at the side. To take out the whole twenty-litre jerrycan was too hard; I'd do that later when I wasn't so chilled.

At the door, I changed back out of the boots, because the wet and muddy ground outside made boots unfit to bring in, even onto this old floor. I had a pair of old slippers for indoors.

Relighting the stove, I sat and waited. Last month's paper was still on the floor: "*10,000 at Franklin Dam Rally*". It was too hard.

Brian, Brian. What now? Were we really all going to change the world?

Rose knew where I was, and Lee. They were both occupied with life: Rose trying to understand what went so hurtfully awry—once again—with Georgia, Lee starting at her college studies.

And Mike knew. Mike came some weekends, but he stayed in the main farmhouse, which was up over the hill. He'd call to see me, but otherwise he kept to his own house. At this time of year, he did only a little farm work, checked things, did some maintenance, mended fences, took a look over his mob, moved them to a different paddock. Perhaps he reminisced in his own space.

Mike bogged the old Ferguson tractor one week. He left it, and it was two weeks later, when the ground was a bit drier, that he called and asked me to help pull it out.

Red George wasn't here. For our winter, George had taken a few months to return to his native America. Old business? Family? I never knew. Had he told me, would I have believed him?

I was the only person around.

But today was Thursday. Goulburn day. It was late morning.

The kerosene fridge was the one luxury here, and I could keep some milk and vegetables. Yet it was so cold most of the time that food should keep itself fresh without a fridge. I sipped steaming coffee and tried compiling a list for Goulburn. It should feed me for a week.

The old Mazda had been my brother's. Last year it had gained a bold and clumsy hand-sprayed rainbow down one side. Driving up to Mike's house was slithery, and I needed to dodge groups of sheep that were in the home area this week. Keep moving, Brian. Stop and we might bog.

Down to Earth

"Good morning. Is Mike Shepherd in the office, please?" The one phone on the property was in the farmhouse. "Hey Mike, Brian. Anything for today?"

Four sacks of chook pellets, to refill the big pellet feeder. Otherwise, nothing this week. Mike would bring his own food this week, as he had time to shop. Many Fridays he left straight from work in Canberra, and if I shopped his weekend food order on Thursday, that gave him a precious hour here before dark. But not this week.

A gas-fired heater serviced the shower-head over the old bath in the farmhouse, and I took the opportunity. The warmth was good for these bones.

Goulburn was twenty-five minutes away. I locked the gate.

Why had I jettisoned the computer to come here? It was a Tandy model, the first accessible home microcomputer. I had rewired the boards and hacked apart the operating system and supplied software, and redesigned them both with improved functions. I would work until dawn. Sometimes I forgot to eat. I had a friend Peter running a young maverick computer business back in Canberra, and he had onsold some of my versions for his clients. I hadn't been making any useful money from the computer.

The first stop in Goulburn was lunch at the central cafe of town, the Paragon. My one decent meal for the week.

I wanted to solve the chicken pellets next, so I drove to the produce supplier in the back street. I ordered and quoted Mike's account. They took some time to trolley the sacks out, and as I went to sign, I was asked to relay to Mister Shepherd that payment of the account was overdue. There would be no further supply until the account was paid. On the previous pickup I made here, I was being eyed warily. Why was I copping someone else's problems?

But the town clown was doing me a far bigger favour that was more important. The shearers' hut was my bunker, my safe place, and I was paying nothing but a few small tasks in return.

I loaded the sacks into the boot and went to find the craft shop. In the main street near the park, Mike had said. It was Mike's Mum who staffed the little shop on some days. She lived in town, in a little bungalow on the high side of the Melbourne road out. Kids move on in life, oldies get left.

Not as left out as my family. They had seen little of me since I left Melbourne, and hadn't known even how to contact me for a few years. Neither they nor I ever knew why it had to be like that. Why I needed to untangle life my own way.

So was it Mrs Shepherd who was in the craft shop today? Maybe. She looked like she might be a Mrs Shepherd. I didn't ask. I bought some leather dyes and a box of decorative leatherwork rivets. Why more leather stuff? I wasn't believing in the life of the productive famous craftsman much anymore either. But no replacement belief was in sight yet.

Some old kid's toys sat on a shelf. I picked up a little cast cannon, recognising immediately it was the same as one I had owned as a boy, carried it in my pocket. It could fire a matchstick or a similar "dart" using a spring loading. A crowded West Melbourne schoolyard came into focus. I had fired several sewing pins into the calf muscles of bare-legged schoolmates, boys who didn't remember my name but simply called me The Professor. I had just wanted to see what happened. "Brian, you can't do that." I forfeited that first cannon. I put this cannon back on its shelf.

The Franklins supermarket was the last call. The paper headline was "*Ayers Rock Dingo Takes Baby*". It had another article further on that page. "*Space Expert's Body Finally Found Near Lismore*". I didn't buy it. I had enough for one Thursday trip.

More faded memories plagued me driving back. Those years in the order? Why could I ever go back? Silently crying

myself to sleep most nights the first year there. The utterly
untellable shame on my first crush—over poor Brendan, who
ran a mile. The paralysing depressions that made study so
hard. The disillusionment over that life that pleaded holi-
ness. The loneliness. The sheer inability to go on. And the
prison of that self-referential belief framework that banned
all doubting. I'd never told anyone this version.

No, the monastic days were now well gone. Funny, I'd
since been invited in by a collection of other cults, by Opus
Dei at University, by permaculture enthusiasts to join their
Tagari commune in Tasmania, by a young GreenPeace to join
their activist/investing elite. I imagined that I'd stayed
fiercely freelance. What did that mean? What did it achieve?
What sort of illusion was it?

If you see another guru on your road, kill him.

I hadn't lit the wood burner before I left for Goulburn.
That would be senseless, as it would have burned down by
when I returned, and any warmth would have vanished. It
would have been a waste of wood. I rarely left it loaded up
when I went to bed at night, either. It would never burn
through until morning, no matter how I set its damper. I lit it
now, then carried my supplies in from the car. I brought in
some cut wood before I closed up the door for the day.

No, I couldn't completely close up for the day. A
minimal-use toilet was in the hut, and I dared not look into
how or if its plumbing was anywhere half acceptable. But for
a pee, I would put boots on and wander outdoors.

Back to the wood. Mike had hauled several large logs
to a woodpile behind the hut. Fallen trees littered the back
paddocks. A warrant was pinned in the kitchen of the main
house ordering the fallen trees be cleared from the farm,
because they provided a haven for rabbits.

I knew a contract rabbit catcher had been on the property in the last month, so I presumed Mike must have
arranged that. But as for the tree removal, the only action

taken so far was carrying or dragging a few back as firewood to the farmhouse, or here to the hut, or, earlier, to the yurts.

Mike had a chainsaw somewhere that he used for cutting up. I had no access, and no experience with chainsaws, and I didn't seek to start now.

There was only the axe. The axe was moderately sharp, and the wood was seriously hard. The weather outside, week after week, was miserably cold. I didn't cut much wood these days. I would rug up inside rather than venture too often out to wield the axe. It was all too hard. Hands don't work well in the cold.

I had bought kerosene in town. The fridge used some, but for now I filled both the hurricane lamps, trimmed the wicks and cleaned the soot from the glass. Doing that after the dark catches you first is an irritable, resentful job. The hut had no electric supply. The light of the two lamps was all I had at night, and I tried to believe they offered a tiny warmth, too.

Another cup of hot tea, and I went to the bench I used for the leather. Several patterns were getting crumpled at one side, and near those was an assortment of knives, punches, steel rules, a riveter, brushes, and some needles and several small bottles. I still had most of four good hides left, including a suede one I hadn't worked out how to use, but there were some good handbag designs I still wanted to try. The whole corner smelled of leather. I was getting used to it now. I sat down to browse again through the new designs book.

At midnight I still hunched over the bench, gluing and burnishing. Two completed new works were waiting to be rubbed and softened. This was how I spent most nights, often until three or four am. The hurricane lamps were poor light, sure, but I made do.

Those lamps smoked a bit, even when I tried to adjust them. I coughed and cleared my throat a lot these weeks. Was it the kero lamps? The wood heater?

I pulled on my boots to go outside. I needed some wood, and I needed a pee. The moon was high and a moderate dusting of fresh snow covered the ground. The car had snow. The trees were snowed. All was still fairyland, except for the occasional crispy crackle sound carrying across the paddock. It was the sheep. They would shuffle along every few minutes, and sounds of their feet, usually not noticed, were tinkling tonight, and travelling. So it was not only me awake.

For half an hour I stood and looked. And listened. And wondered. My whole body became wracked with the cold. My eyes were stinging and damp at the corners, but it could not have been real tears, because real tears would be ice.

———

The days passed.

The snow went.

Leave the gate how you found it—farm rule anywhere.

I walked out to the road and kicked stones away, heading away from town. I hadn't been this direction before. To say I was taking in all the delights of a country stroll would be wishful thinking, because more was processing behind my eyes than was shining in at the front. But perhaps the human mind could handle all at once. Maybe the real world, the grass smells, the pink of early wildflowers, the dusty boots, and that half-world of memories and failures, of dreams and howls, maybe they helped each other. Did they make eventual sense only when tangled together?

It was lunchtime when I returned to the shearers' hut. But before going inside to down-dress and to rustle up a cuppa, I strode straight to the car, and rummaged deep in the boot for my tin box of personal stuff. I took out a very old exercise book. Glancing down a couple of the pages, I closed it again. For a year very, very long ago, several lives back, I had tried to articulate fragments of what plunged around inside, on the premise that on later days I might read some pieces, and recognise and admit to them. It had always been too hard to read. And those days now were too far back.

I found Rose's letter too, left it folded up, and took it inside. Only once ever had I read the letter, and that was more than two years back.

I could hear the baying of hounds, distant firecrackers, thunder across the hills, but all that made no sense, as a quiet farm-side breeze was the only sound.

Out in the thin sunshine I sat, and glanced across the green of rolling hills. Taking a sip of the tea, I unfolded the letter. That impossibly articulate letter. That fiery word-storm, neither withstood nor understood.

Brian.

You have written notes to me, and we have done much talking. Now I want to write a few things down. We are going in circles. I want action! Resolution! I want proof you are doing what you are saying: changing, facing you. You could call this a demand, a condition.

I am sick of seeing your tears. You are bitter and angry to me —well, get it out and stop talking.

I admit I broke the relationship up. I withdrew emotionally, but if you think I destroyed your trust, please remember I withdrew after you destroyed my trust by your actions. They proved to me you are one hundred per cent selfish. I felt you never considered my needs. Way back, you wanted to move us back to Melbourne after I lost our first baby. It was so insensitive. I withdrew, why shouldn't I, it was hell for me, I was desperate.

I set off in search of something else. It was the only way I could go. Probably I didn't do it in the most expert way, the proper way, in a caring way.

When I set off, there were many things to assess, to rethink my values, my lifestyle, to question, to find answers, to learn, search for more knowledge, to learn effective skills in communicating and relating. New ideas about life in general, about me, to come to terms with the many problems in me. I had to do this first. How, to what extent, where it would end I did not know. But I wanted to take all the risks and get there. It was exciting. It was growing. It had its difficulties, moments of insight, dark passages. All was a learning experience, extending me.

As I felt more me, I wanted to talk with you, share with you. But by then you were in a different world—we were talking about different things in different ways. We don't understand one another now. I felt secure enough about me and my ideas to share with you, to work things out to a new plane, forever growing and changing. Exploring, growing. There was a lot to do, to explain, to set up a new type of relationship with everything more open, new values, new ways of behaving and caring from newly developed skills.

But I think it was time: you had to change. This to me was the next most important step in our evolution. You must confront your feelings. The rejections. They stand in the way of our relating. You call out to me to stop the hurting—I bloody well can't—you have to face them—and I know they hurt. Face the anger. You are angry with me. Look towards your parents and others. I don't want to cop it all.

I withdrew, hoping but not knowing if eventually we could build something out of the ruins.

But you then withdrew physically—you left. That affected me a lot. I am sad and hurt about that. My feelings closed up in me towards you. You blame me, you act so hurt. Well, I am not impressed any more. Face those feelings and I will be prepared to talk. Not before. They don't tear me to pieces any more, they don't evoke my pity and protection. I am not hurting you, you are hurting you.

Be strong and brave and face them. That is the only condition under which we can renegotiate. Those areas are deep. You must go there alone. It's lonely and scary. Until one day your stuff doesn't hurt you.

I'm still in the deep, too. I hurt.

Rose

It's not what I remember.

It's not the same story.

Rose. Catch-22. Letting go of the crippling need for her. Healing that and more. Because that was the only way to win her back?

No, that wasn't quite right. Giving up that need more honestly, changing yourself without requiring her back.

Just let go of her. Keep repairing yourself. For you. Period. I have been there alone. Yes, it is lonely and scary. But it's not for going back. There is no "back". My choice now.

Always finding myself holding the guilts of both. If life around me was too unworkable for Rose, I had to live with that and go forward—somehow. She needed me different; I hadn't known how. I'll learn, but it will be too late for her.

Lee's instincts understood owning her share of the deepest themes. I had learned some of the answers already. But learning to love is a mystery that still needs lots more solving.

Brian, the precarious and seductive edge of sanity is just three feet sideways, but that way is not the right way.

Tomorrow I should go back to Canberra. Funny, Rose and I had wanted the same things. Why had we been so fatally out of sync? I thought I had tried so hard for her

                    Down to Earth

when she struggled, but there was so little patience when I needed the time. Her version of where we had travelled was so painfully *Annie Hall* different from all I recalled.

Rose, my love, I'm sorry.

The Catherine Wheel in my head sputtered to a stop. I folded the letter. It was time to pack and go.

What had happened to my new edition of the meaning of life? It promised way more dream, so much more truth.

But dreams subvert, no matter the passion. I did not know how to make it all work. The belief remained, but the energy was over-spent.

Brian – Commune: Rainbow

Autumn

"Thanks for picking us up, Iris. We could've caught the bus service. And hello again, Anna."

"You're my guests, silly. There's only one small bus north into Nimbin each day, and that left an hour ago. It doesn't wait for the Sydney train. It leaves after work and school knock-off. Then the Nimbin bus stop is nowhere close to home."

"I know, I know. I suppose I feel a little guilty getting you right down to Lismore."

"Leave it. Come and enjoy Tuntable Falls. I have been at your place several times, and this is the first time you have come into my space. I am thrilled to have you. And Jo, how are you, sweetie? How was the trip?"

She was right. I was being a twit. Go with the flow. Enjoy the experience. I'm not just the visitor, today I'm the lover. This woman is one of life's beautiful souls. So why the awkwardness?

My Sydney housemate was a dear friend of Iris's also. It was funny, that, because the original circumstances behind that were another story. We sometimes negotiated who Iris was down visiting on any time. No, not right. She would visit us both, and we three would knock around

Sydney together, but who she was sleeping with was sometimes decided at the last minute, and we made it work. Iris at home on Tuntable? We didn't ask.

I knew that the public society has apoplexy over loving more than one. Its own version, monogamy with regular cheating, forever but with trade-ins, proves its own dishonesty, its disconnect from the human within us.

So why had I started edgy? True, Iris was a quirky one. She would hesitate sometimes over an answer, eyeing me angle-wise before replying. She was a bit gangly moving. Something was endearing and vulnerable. Self-assembled. Split into colours and re-merged. Yet I knew she still had a clear enough feel for who she was, even if she had two-second freeze-frames. Was she double-checking herself?

Start again.

So we started again—and it worked. We drove past the Nimbin Rocks.

———

"Welcome to my home." She beamed. We had walked up several hundred yards from the communal car parking yard, past a few buildings, carrying the old backpacks.

"This place?" I was wide-eyed, and Jo had stopped walking.

"My place."

It was a large A-frame timber home. This was no hippie shack. It wasn't any suburban home either. It was crude organic. A two-storey crude organic solidly built comfortable home. "How did you ...? Did you ...?"

"I built it."

"Shit." I could not have built such a place. I was seeing another side of Iris. How come the expectations you don't have can embarrass you so?

"Gavin and I started it four years ago. It was our big project. When he split soon after, I stayed. I bloody well threw my weight around until I finished it. You like?"

"Like it? I am impressed. Congratulations, Madam Builder."

"They got to calling me Sarge then. It was so funny. Me?" Her eyes gleamed. "The blokes would still try to take over for me. We said we left chauvinism behind, but it comes back to bite."

"So show me around before it's too dark."

Jo was long out of sight, upstairs with young Anna.

—

"Brian, come back to bed. I haven't seen you for a month." Standing, not a stitch on. That head angled again. The simplicity of living with nothing to hide.

"I was trying to make you a cup of tea. I've found the tea. Now I need to light your spirit stove." I'd seen the stove used to effect last night.

"Are you going to stay with this little stove?" It had the look of replaceable.

"Come to bed. Anna is well trained on the morning tea routine in our house. If she wakes, that is, after that ruckus with those two for half the night."

I knew Iris's "hither".

"One day I might install gas cylinders. I have an ideological objection to burning any fuel, but then all food would be raw. And some people on Tuntable do cook nothing.

"What I can't do is use electricity for cooking. Tuntable Cooperative school down below is on the grid, but all the houses here are not. Most of us use solar power for lighting and even for a fridge. But cooking takes both too many instant amps and too much total power for a solar system."

Don't mess with a born-again scientist. Then I remembered. "You *are* solar power, aren't you?"

She snuggled in tight. "Sure, I'm Rainbow Solar. We have set up most houses at Tuntable with solar panels and batteries. We started as a simple fair stall at The Channon market, but now we operate out of a shopfront in Nimbin, and we're getting sales from all across the country."

"We?"

"Gavin and I set it up it with David the 'sparkie' in town, and Peter Pedals. Gavin's gone, but we bought him out. Rainbow Solar is growing and it's earning well."

Solar panels and cuddles! What's wrong with this scenario? I thought. I rolled her away, out of the clasp, and lay looking for a while. The move created a silence for us, a fresh start. I touched my finger lightly to her lip, which quivered as if to cry. She closed her eyes. I painted with my finger a slow unbroken line down her chin and under, and her head fell back so the neck could arch to my finger. Between her breasts I followed down, and laid a soft palm on her belly. Her knees and pelvis rose slowly to betray the lust that was seeping through her. We were both betrayed.

"Brian, again. Slowly." She opened her eyes and gazed simply upwards. Nothing to hide. I could hear the girls making breakfast.

———

I showered in the semi-outdoor washroom. The shower water was piping hot. That didn't take much guessing—solar. This woman had taken control of this house-building effort. So why did she still present some vulnerability. What was the story behind the story?

The four of us started up the track behind the house. Up into the National Park. It got more overgrown the higher we went.

"There's money up here in the park," said Iris.

"Green weed money?"

"Of course. You won't find it even if you look. They hide it well. As many crops are up here as houses in the Co-op."

"What about you?"

"Aww, I've dabbled. Not at the moment, I'm too busy. But I have made a few idle dollars, I confess. You want some? It's not a problem."

"I'm not taking a train trip with a stash."

"But would you use it?"

"Sure. But I'm a wimp. Not on the train."

"Is Jo OK around the dope?" The girls were up ahead.

"Huh. When we were out visiting at *The Willows* a year ago, Jo and two of her mates managed to nick a small pinch out of Wombat's stash. Summer sprung them behind the pump-house trying to light up. Kids. They weren't old enough to know how. They had to apologise to Wombat."

"Well, you can't say she's dangerously innocent."

"No, dangerously knowledgeable."

Iris paused. "Have you heard about the super-dope?"

"No."

"Much of the crop here is super-dope now. It gets you high further and faster, by a long way. It packs a punch. The power of selected breeding."

"So I suppose that's what everyone'll want to smoke from now on."

"Yes, but there've been reports of folk around here smoking it and being carted off to hospital in a psychotic mess. Some of the older settlers want to stick to the gentle dope they know. They feel it's safer."

We'd walked up one forest track and then back down another, and we were exiting to the semi-cleared land where several of the houses were. "How many people are on Tunt-able?"

"We had five hundred commune shares, and they were all sold. Some are being resold now. But we never had all five hundred families settling here. Some shareholders live in Sydney or Brisbane still. They have rights as shareholders on the Co-op, but they don't get a say in affairs that residents worry about."

"You know Brendan Smothy from Artarmon in Sydney? He's a filmmaker I ran into at a workshop, and he told me long ago he was a Tuntable foundation shareholder. I don't think he ever lived here."

"Yes, sure, I know Brendan. He came up for a month last year and did a documentary of our life here. He's a great fellow."

"What about Tom Warrior ...?"

"Tom, yes. Tom is precious to us. He paid a foundation membership on principle, I heard. We spent such a lot of time talking with Tom in our early days here."

"Were you and Gavin here at the start?"

"No, we bought in after a year or so. We were one of the last of the five hundred shares. There were few separate houses then, and we lived communally for a while in the original farm buildings, sleeping in one of the converted pig-sties. We were here for the big Tuntable Bust of '76, though. Dawn raids, shotguns in faces, forty-three arrested. Thrown out of court, it was, invalid warrant." She grinned.

"But back to Tom, he's a church minister."

"Yes, I know Tom well. From The Buttery rehab centre at Bangalow on the coast. We had one of the DTE planning meetings at The Buttery. Tom is one fine man. He's been a tower of strength among us Down to Earth crowd."

"Tom founded The Buttery clinic," she said. "He saw what was happening after so many lost and dreaming people stayed around Nimbin and Rainbow Region after the Aquarius Festival. Alcohol and marihuana initially, and that was bad enough. Now we have had the heroin pushers move in for their cut. There's an awful drug problem along every creek and track around here. Tom decided to make some solutions."

Iris continued. "The Buttery's been a huge success in the region. It's a truly difficult problem. But he isn't at The Buttery now, not since a month back. He's moved down to a mission chapel in the middle of Kings Cross in Sydney."

"Pan to fire?"

"Yes, but Tom's that sort of minister. Captain Tom, we sometimes called him."

We walked down along near the Tuntable Creek. "Can you see those two houses across the other side? Can you see it, Jo?"

"Just—it's well camouflaged, eh? How do they get to it? That looks to be partly up a cliff."

"That's the point. It is hard to get to it. Jeannie and Josef and Rosalie live there, and they come out only on occasion. They have no normal access, no bridge. A few rocks in the creek, is all, once they get off the cliff. Their one concession is the flying fox device you might be able to spot across there—that's for construction materials or food boxes and stuff like that. We get all sorts, from hermits to ravers."

"I do know one of your ravers. Donny German."

"Oh, we learned to ignore our long-bearded Donny. He still writes great apocalyptic preachings on broadsheets that he posts in the hall. Everything's assessed against his 'New Age paradigm'. We treat him as part of the environment."

"Too many tabs of LSD? We had to cope with Donny at several of the Down to Earth meetings, too, and the ConFests."

"And this is the cooperative school building."

"Your own school. Anna, do you go here?"

She did.

"It took us a lot of lobbying to get our school approved. We fought through one heap of bureaucratic stonewalling.

They weren't going to have a bunch of—" She paused. "—immoral addled hippies in charge of a real school. Come in, and we'll have a look around. I have a key, I'm a cleaner."

"So do the teachers live on Tuntable, too?"

"Two of our teachers are shareholders living here. The others are from outside. As we're a cooperative school, the parents do a lot of class watching, playground duty and auxiliary teacher help."

After dinner, the school came up again. "Our school put a deal of work into the Rainbow Workshops."

"You mean last year's Down to Earth festival fiasco?"

"We were holding one of the 'secret' workshops for the festival. It was on 'Running a Cooperative School'. Obvious really. Like all the other workshops, limited details came out before the start of the festival. Then the festival collapsed in the deluge and floods. You know that part."

"Yes, I know that part."

Pausc.

"Why was Jim so afraid to come here?"

"His vision needed compliance, naivety, adulation. Rainbow people have a self-drive, a renewal, a structure already forming. Transforming your society."

"Our own revolution?"

"Yes. It wasn't his model. Not the Cairns revolution."

The morning was Sunday. The girls painted flowers on their faces. After a lazy start, Iris took us into Nimbin. Not much was open. We sat outside the Rainbow Cafe, centre of town, opposite the hotel. All our side of the street bore old murals. They were in crazy hippie-art, and I expected they were once far brighter. A small and faded signature was on one: Benny Zable. We had to sit at the correct table: it had a picture of a flattened earth, figures tumbling off the edge.

We found ourselves a non-caffeinated drink, something grain-based. That was as close to real coffee as was available. Nature's Cuppa, or a name like that. Even the girls had some.

A stray and friendly dog lapped water from a bowl at our feet. Iris was wearing a cute anklet of many colours that her daughter had woven an hour ago. I sat, looking at Iris. In the morning sunshine her long hair glistened, and I loved her. "So why is everything 'Rainbow'?"

"I'm not sure I can answer that. I wasn't up here for the year or two after the Aquarius Festival, and the name was in widespread use when I came. Perhaps it means infinite psychedelic possibilities. Or maybe it refers to what fortune sits at the end of the rainbow. I don't know. All I know is that all this area uses that term, provided you are referencing in a new settler or hippie way. You don't use it if you are of the original landholder mind, or for official electoral stuff."

We just sat.

"Brian, this s-street was such an amazing scene b-back in '73. I was so young then. What could I do with an event like that if we held it now?"

"Can't use that way of thinking," I said.

But what if we could? What if we invented some machine that took us back through time. Could we play it all again, have another chance?

I think she was crying.

Winter

I called my family in Melbourne. Yes, I was still alive. "I was OK." They needed that.

Down to Earth

Spring

I had brought us a picnic lunch. Iris and I sat on the grass in Weston Park, a delightful parkland peninsula on the south-west of Lake Burley Griffin. Canberrans come to Weston Park for a barbecue, a family cricket game, or to watch the small yachts that play on the lake.

I was staying the weekend at Dave's at Sandford. We had chewed the fat last night, going over old times, looking at old photos. I tried leaning on him to come up to Tanelorn Festival at Stroud next month. Sunbury corp inviting the hippies to their world. Dave sported a ponytail now—the crew cut was gone. No black. The bloke looked positively normal. I also knew he now rarely went out, just to work each day, still at the Gallery in town. Then back home alone to his tin shack. What had happened with Vaney? I had asked. That had seemed a stable relationship. Do we ever know our friends? Dave had dumped her when he found her shooting up one afternoon. He prefered his own company; I think he was happy.

I had really driven from Sydney to see my daughter, my Jo. I ached over her; I was guilty over her. But to Rose she was Rose's girl. I tried to spend time when I could, and sometimes she came by bus to Sydney for the weekend. The highlight by far had been a week's expedition together across the Northern Territory last June.

For now, I was with Iris. Iris was down from Nimbin visiting her widowed Dad. She needed to see him. For both of us, we had coordinated our family visit to meet today. Two children hurried past us, fighting happily for a ball. The sun shone. Spring had sprung.

"I'd like to be simply your friend, I like being your friend," she said. "Please, I don't want to make any exclusive claims on you."

It wasn't that Iris was proposing never again meeting, never staying, never being lovers sometimes. No, it was the commitment layer or the *I need you* layer that sat behind the relationship that she was claiming to forego. I was hedging.

I had opened the little feast, olives, pull bread, some Edam cheese, tomato slices. "Tea?" I had a flask.

"Iris, I have been enjoying our relationship. But I keep feeling a need you have for me, a panic if I should not be part of your life. You tell me you're not asking for any obligation, and yet it's your need for commitment that I feel. It's as though your words and the vibe of being with you are in conflict."

"Is the struggle not in you?"

"I don't know. I don't know what I want at the moment."

We had met at a Barry Janes rebirthing workshop at Stanwell Tops down from Sydney. I hadn't even recognised her there. She had, immediately. From Terania days.

"Brian, that workshop was great for me. And I found you. Challenging. Always some new ideas struggling out. You are good company, and we enjoy our times together." Two halves?

I looked at her. I was sad.

"Before we met, I was doing many rebirthing and Reichian sessions, chasing them from city to city. You caught me halfway through all that. Reconstructing."

We paused to watch two youths paddle past in an inflatable canoe.

"I met Paddy at another Janes session in the Paddington church hall. I moved to Sydney, and lived in Paddy's place. That became an entree into a support group in Sydney." The Paddy who was now Iris's lover as well.

I offered the watermelon. She waited.

"Now, it's time to stop the workshops, the untangling, the learning how to live."

It was time to go back to living a life. A new one.

I'd burned the ancient diary. Need a new diary, too.

"I've broken off my work-life I had in Canberra, the friends I had, my lovers. I've walked away from my own daughter, God help me. I moved out of Paddy's now, too. I need to start afresh, clean slate."

Border crossing.

"Iris, I'm sorry, but I don't have what you need from me."

"But I don't have any needs from you," she said. "C-can't you understand that?"

I couldn't.

Brian – Another City

Many, Many Winters Later

Damn woman. Robyn. She doesn't walk away, bolt, grow tired. She just accepts my company and enjoys us together. "Different. I can work with that."

For two years now, I've promised her nothing. She really doesn't understand where I've come from. How could it work?

But she leave? Not a sign of it.

Scenario: So if we now drifted and drifted with no further plan, and then it became me who wandered away …

… well, dammit again, then I'd wonder all my days onwards why I'd stayed so blind.

— Intermission —

They all were his mates. All with their stories.

There was no .303 rifle, he admits, and the car crash death of "Miri" was an unabashed fiction.

Jann Cassin was also embroidery. Gian Cassini belongs to a different story.

Nor was there any suspicion as described of "Lee's" involvement in the (unsolved) Lismore timber mill fire.

He does want you to know (but doubtless you guessed) that the house-bus was his own, not "Dave's".

"Sammy's" Goulburn cheque of February '78? That was a very real $31,279.

Mix around a date or three, and that's it. The narrative, shaky but there. Our hippie still insists this is how it happened, how it all came down to earth.

Evolution

From the tropics, it had been a relentless two-day drive. Locust bodies from the Hay Plains plastered the front of the Falcon.

"Well, finally I should find your mud tribes and do my Yoga under the gum trees," quipped Robyn, my mate of more than two decades, years she termed gripping the tiger's tail. She was driving. We had the tent aboard, and food and water. "Show me how it all worked."

I laughed. But what really was here for me? The charismatic rituals of another old religion? Safer schoolyard? Dionysian carnival of the diaspora? The surviving revelry after the philosophy was lost? More happenings on the holodeck? Ageing windmills that ignored all tilts? Or just a fossil ancestor of a Woodford festival?

"I've met only a couple of your festival crowd," she said. "The yurt bloke at a trade fair in Wollongong, remember? ... and I knew Peter Rabbit in my Sydney social club years ago." Those wizards of joy and sorrow?

"Not true. You've met Dave out past Queanbeyan, the eccentric hippie grandfather; and I introduced you to Leonie, the personal counsellor in Canberra. Iris is well-known now as a greens activist—you've seen her often enough on television." And Robyn knew Rose well, but Rose had died a few years ago.

"Ok. But I never did get to the bottom of all that Jim Cairns and Junie Morosi story."

"It wasn't about Cairns. Still isn't." So many pages back.

A tepee served as the 2009 ConFest gate, and we stepped out. The gatekeepers, cheery and welcoming, were an old man, naked except for the earrings, and a faery's child, a thin young woman wearing long, long gold-blonde hippie hair, ponytailed to be clear of her fresh happy-clown face. I paid our seventy dollars each, and returned to find a bright flower painted on Robyn's forehead.

I swapped into the driver's seat. Yes please. I headed towards the river, the mighty Murray, along the bush track. The entrance flew a long colourful banner: "There are no strangers here, only old friends you have to meet."

My old mates ...

... that we could meet.

The Clowns

And to the clowns in my story, a special *Thank You.*

Clowns have a different knowing.

B.

The Non-Fiction

- *Anti-Vietnam War Moratorium March, VIC, 8 May 1970*
- *Second Sunbury Music Festival, Diggers Rest, VIC, 26–28 Jan 1973*
- *Aquarius Festival of the Arts (2nd), Nimbin, NSW, 10–23 May 1973*
- *Cotter ConFest, ACT, 10–14 Dec 1976*
- *Bredbo ConFest, NSW, 24 Dec 1977–2 Jan 1978*
- *Berri ConFest, Martins Bend, SA, 12–16 Apr 1979*
- *Terania Creek Protests, NSW, Aug 1979. Mill Fire & Eclipse 6 Sep*
- *Purchase of Mount Oak, Bredbo, NSW, Dec 1978–Dec 1980*
- *French Island ConFest, VIC, 25–28 Jan 1980*
- *Rainbow Workshops (abandoned), NSW, 9–15 May 1980*
- *Wytaliba ConFest (abandoned), NSW, 16–19 May 1980.*
- *Learning Exchange (newsletter) ISSN 0312-2425, 0312-6544 (1974–78)*
- *Alternative Canberra (journal) ISSN 0312-7052 (1975–77)*
- *Down to Earth Canberra (newsletter) ISSN 0158-0000 (1979–80)*
- *The Tyranny of Structurelessness (speech), Jo Freeman, USA, 1970*
- *"Down to Earth ConFests" (special collection) – Mitchell Library NSW*
- *Posters and photos. (But time and life have taken their toll! Surviving quality is low. Sorry.)*

- *Dr Jim Cairns – Federal Minister, even Deputy PM, 1972–1975*

Clues on Strine

Strine — short form of 'Strayan, a dialect
FOE — Friends of the Earth
CSIRO — Commonwealth Scientific and Industrial Research Organisation
ANU — Australian National University
MCG — Melbourne Cricket Ground
RSL — Returned Services League
DTE — Down To Earth — also name of famous historic book
WEL — Women's Electoral Lobby
LP — vinyl disks before mp3 or spotify
78 — heavy bakelite music disks, long before LP
LEX — Learning Exchange
MP — Member of Parliament
PM — Prime Minister
Joh — Joh Bjelke-Petersen, QLD premier
Fuck — the ins and outs
Labor — worker/socialist party
Liberal — conservative illiberal party
Country — party for city people with mining shares
Wagga Wagga — 1. not a town like Alice   2. refer to 1
Gunna — one day
Organophosphate — chemical, real good for sheep dips
VIC NSW QLD SA TAS WA NT ACT — states & territories
Football (VIC) — Aussie Rules
Football (NSW, QLD) — Rugby League
Football (foreign) — soccer
Rainbow Region — hippie top corner of NSW
Bloke — Aussie(/Brit) for guy, but strictly male
Mulesing — a ball game for rams
Nosh — food for thought
Dunny — lavatory outhouse
Chook — hen, chicken, person

Cuppa — never coffee, probably just ocker tea
Ocker — typical, rough Aussie
Trothal — not Strine! — check ancient Greece?
Goanna — between Darwin's iguana and a komodo dragon
Skerrick — the tiniest amount
NASA — not Strine — check USA
Fair dinkum — genuine, truthful
Fag — cigarette
Eureka Stockade — 1854 gold-miner rebellion
Didgeridoo — world's longest, oldest wooden flute
Woodford — folk fest, tame Aquarius/Woodstock cross
Sydney Push — libertarian radicals of Sydney pub scene

For my daughter Rachel ("Jo"),
the survivor,
an amazing woman,
who didn't have any choice on joining the wild ride,

And for Robyn,
my partner,
she of the tiger's tail,
who did.

*(If I can show you how the world works,
will you show me how to live in it?)*

The Author

Brian Lavery was born in Sydney, a few hours before that first atomic bomb. That's what he blames, anyway.

He's been a monk, a teacher, a hippie, a nomad, a rebel, a corporate geek, a trainer, a world traveller, and now an idler.

He tried surviving Melbourne, Canberra and Darwin, but he settled in Queensland with Robyn, and he wonders where the years went.

Also by Brian Lavery:
Cassini's Vision

Published by Brian Lavery:
White Dawn
by John J Lee

Contact Us

Visit the web page of this book:
https://downtoearth-thebook.blavery.com

Or email us at:
downtoearth-thebook@blavery.com

Contact Us

Visit the web page of this book:
https://downtoearth-thebook.blavery.com

Or email us at:
downtoearth-thebook@blavery.com